WOMEN
IN COMBAT

*Civic Duty or
Military Liability?*

Controversies in Public Policy
edited by Rita Simon

Previous titles in this series

> *The Privatization of Policing: Two Views*
>
> *Does Family Preservation Serve a Child's Best Interests?*

WOMEN IN COMBAT

Civic Duty or Military Liability?

Lorry M. Fenner
Marie E. deYoung

GEORGETOWN UNIVERSITY PRESS / WASHINGTON, D.C.

Georgetown University Press, Washington, D.C.
©2001 by Georgetown University Press. All rights reserved.
Printed in the United States of America

10 9 8 7 6 5 4 3 2 1   2001

This volume is printed on acid-free offset book paper.

Library of Congress Cataloging-in-Publication Data

Fenner, Lorry.
    Women in combat : civic duty or military liability? /
Lorry Fenner, Marie E. deYoung.
        p. cm. — (Controversies in public policy series)
    ISBN 0-87840-862-2 (cloth : alk. paper) —
ISBN 0-87840-863-0 (pbk. : alk. paper)
    1. Women in combat—United States. I. DeYoung, Marie.
II. Title. III. Controversies in public policy.

UB418.W65 F458 2001
355'.082'0973—dc21   2001023269

Contents

Authors' Biographies

Colonel (select) Lorry M. Fenner, USAF, is the Vice Wing Commander for the more than 4000 women and men of the Air Force's 70th Intelligence Wing with missions and personnel at locations around the world. She is a qualified senior intelligence officer and a master space operations officer. In addition, she earned master's and doctorate degrees in history from the University of Michigan and a master's degree in National Security Strategy from the National Defense University, where she also completed National War College. She is a member of the editorial board for the journal *War in History* and serves on the executive board of the Alliance for National Defense. She has served as a staff officer in Major Command Headquarters and at Air Force Headquarters (Air Staff); as a strategic planner for the Joint Chiefs of Staff; and as a Satellite Systems Flight Commander for the 6920th Electronic Security Group, Misawa Air Base, Japan; and as a Squadron Commander of the 91st Intelligence Squadron at Fort Meade, Maryland. She has taught undergraduate and graduate students at the U.S. Air Force Academy and the National War College; her courses have included military, world, women's, American, and European history, as well as historiography, the history of Christianity, military strategy and operations, the Balkans, and the Holocaust. She has won numerous scholarships and fellowships in these areas of study. Her military decorations include the Defense Meritorious Service Medal, four Air Force Meritorious Service Medals, the Joint Services Commendation Medal, two Air Force

Commendation Medals, and the National Defense Medal. She also is an expert military marksman.

Marie E. deYoung is the director of the Newman Catholic Center at Northwest Missouri State University and a captain in the U.S. Army Reserves. She previously directed the Center for Women in the Church and Society at Our Lady of the Lake University in San Antonio, Texas, where she also founded and directed the Smart Friends Abstinence Education Program, a mentoring program for at-risk middle and high school children. Ms. deYoung graduated from the University of Missouri-Kansas City Conservatory of Music in 1981. She graduated from Officer Candidate School in 1984, and she served as Chief of the Services Branch at Oakland Army Base and as a detachment commander of the base. She then completed her Masters of Divinity degree and completed clinical pastoral education at Stanford University Hospital and the hospital of the University of Pennsylvania. When she returned to active duty in the Army in 1993, she served as the first woman chaplain to the 2nd Armored Cavalry Regiment, as well as the first woman deputy command chaplain for the 19th Theater Army Area Command (TAACOM) (South Korea), and the 44th Combat Engineer Battalion in the 2nd Infantry Division. She was an Engineer Brigade chaplain for the 4th Infantry Division and the Corps Support chaplain for the 363rd Corps Support Group in the 90th Reserve Command. Ms. deYoung has returned to the Catholic faith community, and is a lay campus minister and parish volunteer. She is currently also a doctoral candidate in the Education program at the University of Missouri-Columbia.

Preface

Women in Combat is the third volume in the "Controversies in Public Policy" series published by Georgetown University Press. Lorry Fenner and Marie deYoung write from extensive experience in the U.S. military. Lorry Fenner was recently selected for promotion to Colonel in the U.S. Air Force and is the Deputy Group Commander for the 2,800 women and men of the 694th Intelligence Group. Marie deYoung served in the U.S. Army for eight years. She is the author of *This Woman's Army: The Dynamics of Sex and Violence in the Military* and numerous articles about gender issues in the military.

Both authors also draw on a broad range of empirical data and are deeply committed to their respective positions. For Lorry Fenner, it is unequivocally clear that women should be fully integrated into the military and should serve in whatever capacity for which they are qualified, including combat units. Marie deYoung believes just as strongly that serving in combat would be a personal and social disaster for women.

Lorry Fenner argues that the nation-state is based on the government's ability to protect its sovereignty and the lives and prosperity of its people. The armed forces are a core institution, and combat in this institution is a defining feature. The U.S. military should reflect the democratic society it serves—and such reflection involves women in the military serving in any position for which they are qualified. If women are to be considered on par with men, they must have the right to serve in the military wherever they are qualified.

Women should not be forced to sit on the sidelines. They must accept and engage in their civic responsibility. People who oppose women in the military damage morale and create division. They do not support national security, enhance military effectiveness, or contribute to cohesiveness.

Fenner takes issue with deYoung on the matter of standards of physical fitness to carry out the tasks to be done in combat. Whereas deYoung focuses on fitness standards, Fenner emphasizes job standards and claims that women have proved that they are physically capable of doing the tasks to which they have been assigned. She further claims that "gender norming" of physical standards is not evidence of lower standards. Job standards, Fenner insists, do not change to accommodate gender, age, or the physical condition of a service member.

With regard to women's ability to cope with the stresses of military life and war, Fenner cites historical evidence and concludes that women have the emotional courage to withstand the brutality of war—including imprisonment as prisoners of war, such as was the case in the Pacific theater during World War II.

Marie deYoung rests her argument against combat duty for women on the following major grounds. First, the standards of physical fitness are lower for women than they are for men. Although deYoung agrees that in noncombat jobs, women can work around or improvise against lower performance standards by using various types of equipment, in combat such improvisations are not possible. Women's failure to meet the same standards of fitness as men results in lower morale and training failure. She quotes studies that show women's failure to meet the physical requirements that combat would require.

Second, in no way does the failure of women to serve in combat units deny them their full right as citizens. Women's full rights as American citizens are contingent on their birth as Americans, not upon their service in the military. deYoung refers to the argument about a universal obligation of citizens to bear arms as an outdated appeal to emotion. Universal military service for the United States would be necessary only if we were engaged in a world war. She points out that even during World War II, only 10 percent of our population served in the armed forces.

Third, deYoung agrees with Fenner that women's failure to engage in combat limits their opportunities for promotion; unlike Fenner—who views this practice as discriminatory—deYoung argues that the practice is no different than that of men who because of physical or mental disabilities are not eligible for service in certain units (e.g., Intelligence Corps). For both men and women, deYoung argues, service in the military in whatever capacity and rank is a valuable contribution to our nation's defense.

deYoung takes issue with Fenner for equating women who oppose having women serve in the military in any capacity with women who oppose women serving in combat as anti-feminist for doing so. deYoung charges Fenner with political correctness and with a failure to recognize the important differences in the two positions. Like Fenner, deYoung reviews the evidence in the debate on male sexual appetites, sexual harassment, social bonding between men and women, and their impact on military efficiency and cohesiveness, but deYoung arrives at different conclusions.

For readers who want an exhaustive treatment of the history of the performance of women in the U.S. military, the debate about their role in combat, or the challenges that have developed as a result of their roles in combat, this book is a must-read. Few persons are more qualified to take on the positions that Fenner and deYoung have assumed and to articulate them as well as these authors have succeeded in doing. For those who want more, each author has provided an excellent bibliography.

—Rita J. Simon

PART ONE

Lorry M. Fenner[1]
Moving Targets: Women's Roles in the U.S. Military in the 21st Century

☐ INTRODUCTION

This debate purportedly is about whether women should be further integrated into the military services—that is, whether they should serve in even more "nontraditional" roles than they currently do. Several other issues also are subsumed in this discussion, however. For example, despite many years of successfully integrated basic training in all of the Services (except the Marine Corps, which has continued segregation), recent sexual harassment and misconduct allegations at follow-on occupational specialty schools have revived arguments over whether gender-integrated basic training should continue. The most vehement arguments, however, still center on women's fitness for and access to "combat" positions and the societal implications of the draft. These arguments usually have focused on two areas. The first issue is a combination of a set of shifting objections that are based on the supposed visceral and wholly negative responses of military men, the American public, allies, and even adversaries to women as combatants, combat casualties, and prisoners of war. The second is a presumption that the integration of women into "nontraditional" roles has hurt, and will continue to damage, military readiness and effectiveness—and thereby our national security in the 21st century.

I would add to these two arguments a third. When we get beyond mischaracterizations of the past performance of, and experience with, the integrated military; beyond the myths surrounding current public attitudes; and beyond imaginings of the future about which one person's educated predictions are as good as another's, this debate really is a struggle over our democratic political philosophy—what it means to be a full, first-class citizen of this nation, with all the rights, privileges, and obligations that pertain to that status. We will see that these three arguments overlap, making the issue as complex as any that confronts us today.

Most of the jobs that remain closed to women are in specialties that the Services consider likely to engage enemy forces in direct combat (or that serve in close proximity to those that do) and those in which members run a higher risk of capture. These restricted occupations include infantry, armor, field artillery, special operations forces, and special operations aircraft. In addition, several other specialty areas are closed because of other considerations; for instance, the submariner community alleges that privacy issues and the cost to refit vessels for separate berthing demand the exclusion of women.[2]

Submariner objections notwithstanding, most of the arguments presume that not only American women but American society will be harmed by exposing women to danger in combat (as combatants). Yet the integration of women into the armed forces to date has not only been of benefit to women but has been essential to military effectiveness and our nation's defense. Continuing their integration by eliminating the barriers to service that remain will keep faith with our security needs, our democratic heritage, and our political philosophy. We put our young men at risk, even in times of ostensible peace, and we have regarded their participation in the draft registry as an obligation of citizenship. We put our young women at risk as well in support positions that are "noncombat" on paper but are well within the range of even the crudest military or quasi-military weapons. We thereby limit our options, while sustaining the myth that military women are not in "harm's way" and denying them the opportunity to contribute to their fullest capability. Opening remaining military positions to all qualified individuals (determined by relevant tests, not sex) and requiring young women to register for the draft if we require young men to do so are simply the next logical, practical, and necessary steps in our military's and our nation's evolution toward our ideal of civic responsibility and equality.

This evolution is appropriate for three reasons. First, arguments against women's greater inclusion are based not on historical reality but on visceral responses to ideas that threaten an outmoded and no longer useful cultural ideology. These constantly shifting, visceral reactions fail to account for changes in national and global political, social, and economic realities. Yet these same national and global changes are rapidly altering the contexts of and conditions for national security and military effectiveness.

Second, we need to plan force structures and recruiting campaigns for the future, not the past—and future conflict appears increasingly likely to be small-scale, high-technology, "remote control" warfare. As a recent example, more enemy aircraft were destroyed on the ground through careful surveillance and "stand-off" bombing than were destroyed in air-to-air combat in the 1999 effort to stop Slobodan Milosevic's ethnic cleansing efforts in Kosovo. Although I do not believe that the infantry has lost its usefulness or that warfare is no longer brutal, our ground soldiers never saw combat during this most recent "war."[3]

Finally, the rights, responsibilities, and privileges of democratic citizenship politically, socially, and culturally demand this further integration. All citizens who enjoy the benefits of a free society should have equal obligations to protect that society, and all persons in a democracy should participate in that protection according to their ability rather than their membership in a particular group—especially as defined biologically. The complete integration of our society and the military that defends it is nothing less than essential if we are to be consistent with our democratic political philosophy.

I maintain that for opponents of women's integration the real debate is not about further widening of women's military participation but about reversing the gains already achieved by women, the military, and the nation. In fact, the logical extension of arguments opposing broadened opportunities for women—and for the Services to capitalize on women's valuable contributions even further—would be exclusion of women from military service altogether.

Though opponents of women's further progress in service to their country no doubt would protest that I mischaracterize their position,[4] I believe they would be most satisfied by policies that would decrease women's participation through attrition, while accepting no new female servicemembers, until the forces reached their new downsized levels and take their future shape. Although they may claim that they have no objections to the Services "using" women in "traditional" roles—primarily in medical, administrative, and support positions—such limited "uses" are illogical in terms of force employment and inconsistent with military needs, security requirements, historical trends, and our political philosophy.

Even if one were to accept the premise of using military women only in traditional roles on its face, knowing where to draw the line would be difficult. Other specialty areas beyond nursing and clerking, in the military and civilian spheres, have been "feminized" so that it would be difficult to attract young men to these fields, even if there were enough young men to recruit or draft (the shortage of which, in the all-volunteer force, prompted the greater inclusion of women in the first place).

Clearly identifying "combat" positions or designating the "front lines" also is increasingly difficult. Indeed, as has been the case for decades, many medical and administrative personnel are expected to serve well forward in the "battle space." Finally, in modern warfare, support functions such as communications and supply are heavily targeted in a conflict. It is much easier for an enemy to destroy one command or radio post than all subordinate or connected units or to shoot down one tanker aircraft rather than all the fighter aircraft it has to refuel.

These examples reflect the history of military operations and women's integration. As women proved themselves more capable and civilian society became more accepting of "nontraditional" roles, justifying barriers that were based on gender or the older realities of warfare became more difficult. Even as broader recognition of women's work outside the domestic sphere, evolving technology, and changing military recruiting and strategy goals developed, however, the barriers to women's full participation did not fall easily. They came down in fits and starts, one at a time and in bunches, as Congress, presidents, the courts, or military leaders themselves saw the folly of unsupportable and unequal restrictions on women's service.[5]

My arguments here are not necessarily new (as substantiated in the bibliography and in my other work).[6] I hope to accomplish two things by repeating them here, however. I want to synthesize them in a more comprehensive way and, through repetition, steer the public debate away from the visceral toward the practical and pragmatic. I hope thereby to do justice to our past, honor our present, and add value to our future.

❏ MYTHS AND ASSUMPTIONS: STEREOTYPES AND EMOTIONAL ARGUMENTS

One of the most common condemnations of a military action is the accusation that the aggressor is killing women and children. Women seem to make "moving" victims in war: Rape, brutality, and death are routinely the fate of civilian women in any war zone, and their plight often is used to continue, exaggerate, or even start hostilities.[7] On the other hand, female military casualties have barely warranted mention in our history books. Far from abhorring the death of women in war, we apparently require it to justify war. The idea that American society will not tolerate—and American fighting men cannot endure—harm to women is simply inconsistent with the realities of most wars; enemy and even allied civilian women are routinely killed or harmed. The inclusion of female military casualties in our reckoning, however, dilutes the effectiveness of the "killing women and children" propaganda. It brings all too close to the surface the possibility that we do not object to killing women in war but to women killing. In other words, rationalizing war as the necessary defense of women and children (the requirement to protect them) is more difficult if women themselves are doing some of the fighting. These and other inconsistencies in our view of women and war have made arguments on the subject of servicewomen's participation in war "moving targets" as opponents try to disguise essentially emotional arguments in terms of military effectiveness.

The constant effort to camouflage emotionalism as pragmatism makes focused discussion nearly impossible. For instance, as women have repeatedly demonstrated their competence in ever-wider military spheres, arguments against their further inclusion have devolved from assertions that women do not have the physical strength for most military specialties to assertions that they do not have the emotional strength to endure crises, that they do not have the intellect to overcome challenges in battle, and that their sexuality and vulnerability would destroy men's essential battlefield bonds. Any or all of these factors then undermine mission effectiveness by diverting men's attention from accomplishing the mission to helping and protecting their female peers.[8]

It is important to note here that some of these same arguments were used to keep minority men out of the military and then to keep them out of combat and leadership positions. Opponents of racial integration first claimed that minority soldiers were lazy or stupid or lacking in courage; integration opponents then worked to ensure these men did not have an opportunity to demonstrate otherwise until military necessity forced the issue. Despite all evidence, opponents were convinced that integration was not a matter of necessity but a political attempt at social engineering. Nevertheless, given appropriate training and a fair opportunity, minority men proved that they measured up to their Caucasian counterparts in every category.[9]

Women, too, have shown by their performance that they generally are strong enough for most jobs; emotionally stable enough to cope with wartime stresses; more than smart enough for military work; accepted as credible leaders; and not only do not damage unit cohesion but often improve morale.[10] Opponents similarly have denied that women have been integrated because of military necessity and label women's induction as social experimentation or the result of feminist triumphs in political arenas. History shows a much different picture.

Women have proven that they are physically capable enough to do the tasks to which they have been assigned. Some individuals have shown that they are capable of more. Example after example can be found of women exceeding the expectations of their physical capabilities, finding work-arounds for heavy tasks, or teaming with their co-workers to complete their assignments to best effect. Furthermore, historical evidence shows that physical "requirements" for most military specialties are not based on any real measure of the specific strengths required to do a particular job and that the military has repeatedly changed standards for a whole variety of reasons, the least of which are political. In fact, when opponents cite "gender norming" of physical standards as evidence of lowering standards, they most often are referring to physical fitness or health standards rather than job standards; even young men may be given waivers excluding them from combat—or even worldwide duty—because of conditions that arise after they are accepted for service. In contrast, specific job standards do not change to accommodate gender, age, or the physical condition of a service-member.[11] This fact, of course, does not mean we have not had inaccurate perceptions about what those requirements should be.[12]

In the 1970s, the Navy staff began a program to determine physical strength requirements for particular jobs. In an attempt to start with something easy, they first decided to define a standard for postal workers. They set up an experiment using typical forty-pound bags of mail. The bags were set on the mailroom floor, and postal clerks were told to weigh them. When the first clerk entered the room, he lifted each bag onto the scales on the counter. When the next clerk entered the room, she took one look at the bags and the scales, then moved the scales to the floor and proceeded to weigh the bags. The requirement, after all, was to weigh the bags, not to lift the bags to counter height. The researchers discovered that they would have to take creativity and initiative into account in setting physical job standards.[13]

In another case, volunteer firefighters were required to be six feet tall, but no one really thought much about why. When some women and shorter men challenged this standard, the department told them that the ladders were placed on the fire trucks at such a height that lifting them off required a tall person. Managers discovered that there was no operational requirement for the ladders to be hung that high, so the brackets were lowered, and the standard was changed—which, in turn, enabled more women and men to volunteer.[14]

Sometimes form won over function in setting physical standards. As women started having to complete a wide variety of basic obstacle courses in military training, they encountered barriers that required upper body strength. These courses were not attached to any specific job requirement; they were intended to measure general fitness. In other words, having to scale a wall is not a test of whether one can figure out how to get over it but a test of whether one can do a pull-up. Most women approaching a wall would have to jump to grab the top, and many could not pull themselves up and over with their arms and upper body. Though some women could surmount this obstacle and some men could not, people pointed at women's failure with the wall as a sign of general incapacity or weakness. Appropriate physical training helped men and women get over the wall while improving their self-esteem and acceptance by the group. Such tests often reflect a lack of physical conditioning and training more than an inherent incapacity. In any case, the problem with this kind of standard became obvious when at least one woman—not knowing that she was supposed to fail or refuse this obstacle—jumped up, grabbed the top of the wall, used her legs to walk up the wall, and threw herself over. The male instructors, shocked at this audacity, shouted that she had failed to complete the obstacle because she had not done it "the right way."

Similar examples abound, including many cases in which men have been willing to help their weaker or smaller male counterparts on physical tests but were not only unwilling to provide similar assistance to women but unable or unwilling even to recognize that the two cases were the same—that assisting one's teammates is part of "teamsmanship," not a way of voting for who should be allowed on the team. According to Linda Francke, male students at West Point who thought of themselves as progressive and not prejudiced against women still could not appropriately compare men's and women's abilities. These earnest young men insisted that women as a group were unqualified for combat arms, because they could all think of at least one example of a woman who needed assistance carrying her load on a long march. They did not claim that all the women needed help, or that none of the men—including themselves—had ever needed help.[15] Their concept of "team" also obviously was formulated by socialization that prepared them to recognize an individual woman's need for assistance as a particular instance of women's general weakness but did not allow them to draw a similar conclusion with regard to individual men whose comrades (including, sometimes, women) helped them carry a load when they otherwise would have fallen behind.

One final example shows that work-arounds and team concepts prevail in the military among pragmatists and people who are more interested in getting the job done than in finding and focusing on divisive issues. When the Air Force started to place women in nontraditional jobs such as aircraft engine maintenance (mechanics) in the 1970s, the women often went from their technical training to jobs in which they were the first or only woman. Their new units automatically assigned many of these women to desk jobs. Highly (and expensively) trained female aircraft mechanics were relegated full-time to processing the unit's paperwork, and male mechanics acted as if they had been given secretaries. Not only were these women obviously lacking when the time came for them to test their job skills for promotion, the male mechanics also criticized them for not pulling their weight on snowy or baking runways and in cold or boiling hangars.

In one such case, a young female airman arrived at her first duty assignment as a B-52 mechanic. Her male counterparts had been leery of the move to train female mechanics and specifically about her impending arrival. When they saw her they were even more convinced of the folly of this "social experiment": She was four feet, eleven inches tall—the service minimum. The men decided that they would demonstrate this folly by not helping her carry her fifty-pound toolbox out to the runway—but she did not request help and carried it herself. The men found that she would not ask for favors, nor would she be content to work in the office. They also eventually realized, however, that although she was not as strong or as big as they were, she had other desirable mechanical skills—including an ability to get into all the small spaces of the airframes and engines that they had to disassemble to reach or injure their hands and arms trying to get at, which saved the whole group considerable time and effort. In a short time, they accepted her as part of the team and built her a trolley for her toolbox.[16]

Obviously, not all women are strong enough for all jobs—just as not all men are. We could continue to trade anecdotes of successful women and women who failed. Still, women have proven, in this country and elsewhere, that they can do far more than many people thought they could.[17] The historical evidence shows that appropriate physical standards should be used to measure the ability of all servicemembers—regardless of age, gender, race, or other characterizations—to meet specific, relevant job requirements. The Services cannot match individuals to appropriate jobs by relying on some imagined or generalized group stereotype; they must allow each person the opportunity to measure herself or himself against appropriate standards to field the most physically effective military force.

We also want the Services to have the most effective force emotionally. How can we measure a person's ability to cope with the stresses of military life and war?[18] Instead of arguing opinions or using models and tests, we can examine the historical evidence for women's success and failure under combat conditions, serving in harm's way, experiencing death and destruction. When we study history, we find that women have coped with every aspect of war.[19] Women have demonstrated the emotional courage to withstand the brutality of war, including during lengthy imprisonment as POWs under very harsh conditions in the Pacific and in European work and death camps; in very dangerous and stressful resistance fighting; in the face of rape and mutilation; and at the moments of their deaths.[20] Labeling women as a group incapable of emotionally coping with the stress of training or combat is a supreme insult given that women through the ages have demonstrated exactly that strength. We need only look to history to find numerous and, sometimes, most unlikely examples of courage and emotional stamina from individuals large and small, old and young, of many races and of any gender.

Intellect also is not bounded by physical attributes. We all recognize that some occupations demand more intelligence or education than others, and the first step for the armed forces is to decide how much intelligence a person needs and how to measure it accurately. The Services measure intellect and aptitude with standardized tests. A qualifying test and the Armed Services Vocational Aptitude Battery (ASVAB) are used for enlisted personnel; the Armed Forces Officer Qualification Test (AFOQT) is used for officers.[21] The Services combine test scores with other academic criteria—possession of a high school diploma (or GED) for enlisted members and (usually) a bachelor's degree for officers—based on statistics showing that individuals who can meet these standards usually complete their first enlistment, have fewer discipline problems, and even have a higher potential to survive in combat.[22]

Opponents of women's integration often claim that the Services have lowered standards to accommodate women, but their main argument rests on the aforementioned flawed and inconsistent physical tests, rather than the aggregate criteria the Services actually use. Intellectually, for example, women traditionally have had to score higher on military entrance exams.[23] The Services have been able to limit female members to those who were most intelligent because they have always accessed a much smaller percentage of women (especially during the draft) relative to the number of female applicants. Women's representation has always been strictly regulated (capped), with authorized percentages ranging from 2.5 percent (until 1967) to today's ceiling of nearly 20 percent. With women making up a greater percent of applicants than accessions, the Services have never had to take women who score in the lowest intelligence category (Category IV). The Army, in particular, often has resorted to taking men in the lowest intellectual categories when it could not meet its recruiting goals for men and was unwilling to take more smarter women.[24] Thus, the military has been able to use women to raise the general level of intelligence and education in the forces, and historical evidence indicates that although we might be better off without genius soldiers, smarter individuals generally are more successful in the Services (as in civilian life) and make a more effective combat force.[25]

Still, some occupations do require more intellectual capability than others, and most military thinkers predict that tomorrow's technology and operations will demand even more intelligent warriors. Just as with physical standards, rather than setting a fixed standard for induction we should try to set realistic and appropriate job standards, including intellectual ones, to select the best person for a particular job.[26]

Although all of the Services insist that officers meet higher educational requirements than enlisted personnel, their real intent is to recruit for leadership potential—another category in which women historically have been considered lacking. The arguments used since the 1940s against women as leaders are similar to those used against racial minorities. The

Services felt that they could distinguish members who possessed leadership potential and could effectively exercise it, based on race and gender. From our most senior military leaders to our lowest enlisted ranks, white men insisted that minority men lacked the biological capacity and the moral fortitude to lead other minority men, much less white men.[27] Today, we are completely offended by such a notion, so we tend to forget that not so long ago, not only were we completely convinced of this immutable "truth," senior military leaders passed this belief off as their considered and *experienced* "professional judgement"—in spite of the fact that they had never served with minorities in leadership capacities. Similarly, women were not put in command of military men until after 1967.[28] As a group, women have proven to be effective leaders in every job. As individuals, they have sometimes succeeded and sometimes failed—just as men have.

When assertions of a "natural" lack of leadership ability among women and minority men began to fall flat, opponents of integration tried to blame cultural programming. For instance, opponents claimed that Caucasians would not follow black officers and that male soldiers would not follow female officers. We hear today that heterosexual servicemembers will not follow officers they know to be homosexual. We have learned in the cases of women and minority men that these claims generally are not true; moreover, arguments that are based on cultural conditioning fail to recognize that the military has its own culture to a significant degree. The military constantly compels its members to do things that run counter to civilian social mores; servicemembers must obey lawful orders or be discharged or imprisoned under criminal charges. Usually, this threat has not been required to gain compliance.

In late 1999, a flurry of articles and editorials claimed that women could not be senior leaders if they have minor children. This argument hearkens back to the 1940s through the 1970s, when military women were not allowed to be natural or adoptive parents. This argument is just another form of glass ceiling: A woman might be successful in the rank and file, but only men—who can ignore family responsibilities—can really concentrate their efforts to be successful senior leaders. One might think, therefore, that childless women, or those whose husbands are the primary child caregivers, might be successful as senior leaders, but these women and their family situations often are considered socially aberrant and, therefore, still culturally unacceptable.[29]

Despite women's success as leaders in politics, business, sports, schools, religion, and other traditionally male-dominated arenas, including the military, emotional arguments against their full participation continue at the most basic level—biology. These arguments can be categorized as those pertaining to bodily functions, sexuality (both predatory and vulnerable), and women's effects on the bonds between men—all of which have been used as rationales for prohibiting women from contributing in positions for which they are otherwise qualified.

The old canards that women will be temporarily dysfunctional during menstruation and permanently during and after menopause were everywhere in the public debate in the 1940s. Occasionally, the specter that certain types of nontraditional work might harm women's childbearing potential or cause other serious gender-related problems arose as well.[30] In spite of medical and scientific advances, these red herrings reappear from time to time. Hard data usually dissuade opponents from using these arguments today—notwithstanding Newt Gingrich's bizarre contention that women who are barred from more civilized hygiene facilities develop debilitating infections in the field.

Now, we more often hear the assertion that pregnancy causes women to be nondeployable in such large numbers that they harm readiness and military effectiveness. This position usually is supported with anecdotal evidence or questionable statistics and studies. Most women are not permanently disabled by pregnancy; none are pregnant all the time, and many military women are never pregnant.

If there really were reliable data and evidence, military and political leaders who are opposed to women's military service—of which there are many—would use it to bar women from deployable positions and perhaps from the military altogether. The evidence simply is not there. More important, focusing on women as nondeployable during pregnancy focuses on the wrong issue. The issue for readiness is not who is pregnant but who is nondeployable, how often, for how long, and for what reasons. When we conscientiously define the problem and tally *all* nondeployable personnel, we find that men are proportionally (and numerically, of course) more often nondeployable than women, for elective and nonelective reasons.[31] We should focus our readiness efforts on identifying the real challenges for deployments and then rely on our leaders to work on those.

When arguments relating to menstruation and pregnancy fail to win the day, the sexual victim and predator arguments are used against military women. The former I address elsewhere in this essay. For now, suffice to say that women also are at risk of sexual victimization in the civilian world. Adult women recognize that their chances of being sexually assaulted increase from an appalling 25 percent in peacetime America to a much greater probability in wartime and to near-certainty if captured by the enemy. Air Force lawyer Wayne Dillingham has written cogent legal and philosophical arguments maintaining that women should be treated as adults with inherent free will, able to decide for themselves if they want to volunteer or be subjected to such potential harm. According to Dillingham, the government has not proven that it has a compelling state interest justifying denying women this choice.[32] Not only do we not deny men the opportunity to choose risk, we compel their vulnerability, even though men also are sexual victims—particularly in situations intended to torture or demoralize. Men probably are vulnerable to a much greater extent than we have evidence of or than they have admitted. Furthermore, arguably, American women may be culturally better equipped to cope with the trauma of sexual victimization than men, for whom sexual violation is not merely terrifying, painful, and deeply humiliating but emasculating as well.

With regard to the issue of probable sexual activity between consenting servicemembers, I dismiss this argument as emotional and generally much ado about nothing. To paraphrase a popular expression, "sex happens." Preventing unit cohesion- and mission-damaging relationships of any kind is a leadership issue—and we should prepare, expect, and allow our leaders to deal with it. Most human beings have sexual relations during their lives, and our young military members probably are at their most sexually active age. The presence of military women obviously does not cause men to have sex. Men have sex with civilian women or each other (as heterosexuals) when military women are not present. At times this behavior can be just as or more damaging to military effectiveness and readiness than relations between unit members, yet it is accepted as a normal part of men's lives, and leaders deal with these challenges without much uproar.

Civilian leaders and managers also deal with inappropriate relations between their employees every day. This issue is just one more among many difficult challenges—and far from the most significant—our military leaders must face. The answer is not to remove all women, or military women, or to quarantine men.[33] The answer is to deal with reality as responsible adults and to give our young people training and education to enable them to make wiser, healthier, and more professional decisions about their personal lives.

This argument also pertains to the debates about good order and discipline and about sexual harassment. Most often, in cases in which good order and discipline have been compromised, we find that senior military men have had relations with more junior women, whether coerced or consenting. Recent cases (1999) involving two Army generals, who were found to have violated their positions of trust and leadership by having relations with subordinates' spouses, did not even relate much to military women at all—except insofar as they decreased the overall trust and esteem in which the women, as military professionals, held their leaders.[34] No one suggested that married men be barred from military service so that their wives would not tempt these officers' superiors. Just as military women cannot be blamed in these cases, neither could their presence be blamed for the Tailhook '91 case, in which civilian women were assaulted (as they had been in previous years). The only difference in 1991 was that civilian and military women reported the crimes. We have the means to deal with these transgressions under military law, though we often appear to enforce our standards inconsistently.

People who decry women's demoralizing impact on men and organizations not only ignore the preponderance of senior male misconduct; they also ignore the fact that military fraternization rules were written to prevent inappropriate relations between superiors and subordinates of the same sex—men. We have been so caught up in the sexual implications of fraternization in a mixed-gender force that we often miss the damage done to unit cohesiveness by superiors who develop friendships with one of their male subordinates, which gives others reason to believe that person receives preferential treatment. We also often punish least severely the people who are supposed to be most responsible for their actions and who most affect morale and unit effectiveness with their indiscretions—senior leaders.

Opposition to women in the military that is based on the presumption that men cannot control their sexual appetites also is not only insulting to men but irrational in terms of the implied solution: quarantining men or excluding women. In addition, consensual "sex in the foxholes" occurs a lot more frequently in fiction than in real life: Other concerns—such as temperature, filth, exhaustion, shrapnel, or chemicals; an utter lack of privacy; and the possibility of imminent death—tend to take precedence. Historical evidence and recent interviews indicate that people in crisis situations are less interested in sex than in security and comradeship. In fact, testimony from members of mixed-gender resistance units in World War II shows that, even when two people were interested in each other to the extent that after the war they married, they did not have sex under fire. On the contrary, most testimony reveals that people in mixed-gender units feel like brothers and sisters, just as most men under fire commonly regard each other as brothers.[35]

In her previous work, Marie deYoung has suggested that, regardless of actual conduct, putting men and women in close proximity allows occasions for improper perceptions and false accusations and costs the government too much money. Again, this is a leadership issue. Rumors and innuendo can be damaging to people and units whether military women and sexual activity are present or not. False accusations of favoritism also happen when military women and sexual activity are not involved. False accusations happen much less often than deYoung implies, in any case. We expect leaders to ensure rumor control when the subject is not sex; suggesting that we cannot do so when it defies logic.[36] As a military woman, deYoung also must be aware than even when women do nothing to warrant the slightest suspicion of improper activity, rumors may still be spread about them. In fact, these rumors function as a control mechanism— women are falsely accused of being lesbians if they are not sexually available or promiscuous if they are. Either way, the rumor enforces boundaries or imperatives on their activities.[37]

My conclusion regarding sexual relations among military members is that we should first set realistic and fair standards that are based on less invasion of privacy rather than more. We should identify the real problem with each issue of damage to good order and discipline in setting those standards. Then we should enforce the standards fairly and consistently. With education and a firm, equitably enforced set of policies that really do aim at good order and discipline, real leaders can effectively manage relations with and between their subordinates in single- and mixed-gender units as appropriate.

The final biological argument against integrating women into the military further is their alleged deleterious effect on unit bonding—that women cannot bond with men in the same way that men bond with each other; that women inhibit bonding between men by their mere presence; and that women create jealousy between men when they have relations with any of the men in the unit. Women thereby negatively impact the bonds that presumably existed or would have existed in their absence and therefore detract from mission accomplishment.

Again, strikingly, these same arguments were made with regard to black men when the Services racially integrated. Military sociologist Charles Moskos found in his fieldwork during the Vietnam War, however, that although members of mixed-race units might not bond socially on the home front, these men task-bonded in the field. Furthermore, the degree to which they bonded increased according to the danger they faced: Battlefield units exhibited much stronger interracial bonding than relatively safe units in rear areas.[38]

From another perspective, political scientist Elizabeth Kier sheds doubt on how seriously the military actually tries to create unit cohesion. She argues convincingly that the military does not promote bonding with its personnel policies and that, in fact, social bonding is counterproductive to mission accomplishment, whereas task bonding enhances it. Available evidence shows that individuals of different races and genders (among other categories of difference) task-bond just as well as homogeneous male units.[39]

Fundamentally, when we refer to *bonding* we are referring to the concept of the team. People who have played team sports intuitively understand the argument I make here, although they may not have thought to apply it to women in the military.[40] Some people believe that in a perfect world all our soldiers would be the androids or robots of science fiction. They would all be the "right" size and have the "right" strength, speed, and stamina. They would all have the "right" intellect and character for war, and they would have just the "right" amount of aggression, which we could switch off in peacetime—or we would quarantine them away from civilians when not in use.

Although we might never build this futuristic soldier corps, if we could agree on the "right" criteria we might attain a similar result by assembling a small force of mercenaries. We have decided as a polity, however, that this ideal is not what we want. Even within our all-volunteer force, we have retained the concept of the citizen-soldier—not only with our reserve component but within the hearts and minds of our active-duty force. Our professional soldiers do not view themselves as mercenaries. They consider themselves full citizens and members of their communities. Although we discuss Samuel Huntington's thesis on the professional officer *ad nauseum*, we actually subscribe to the principle that militaries should and will reflect their parent societies. When we begin to move away from this principle, we cause great societal consternation—as several recent studies have shown.[41]

Beyond our commitment to keeping our soldiers a part of our social and political community, even though it may result in a less "perfect" force, we have another dynamic. Historian Linda Kerber describes our larger historical national struggles between paternalism and liberty and between individualism and community. Our impulse is to value the individual above all else, but we implicitly understand that our military must be a team. Although we highly value members who can act independently in crises where they may lack direction, the team ethic is the real foundation of our forces. We preach it every day.[42]

A team is made up of individuals. To be successful, the sum of their efforts must be greater than their individual efforts. Team members should not all be the same size and have the same skills if the team is to be successful.

From the small and quick to the smart and fast to the big and strong, we maximize the team's abilities by constructing the most diverse group we can within our game plan. (I discuss that "game plan" and the inherent strength of diversity in the next part of this essay.) We have all seen the synthesis of diversity applied in team sports. The fact that we often use sport analogies to describe armed forces and warfare or that we use military analogies to describe athletic contests is no coincidence. From captains and quarterbacks to coaches, we call these leaders field generals.

We call them generals because we know that leadership and other intangibles are keys to a team's success. Even teams with lesser physical skills and abilities may prevail with superior leadership. Our most distinguished military philosophers have always recognized that numbers and skill and equipment or arms were not always the keys to success.[43] Other immeasurables—in sports or war—include home field advantage, quality practice of game situations together, the will to win and a winning tradition, superior intellect and intelligence, and, significantly, the bond between team members.

Some opponents of women's integration argue that women disrupt this bonding because they do not have the experience of team sports and competition that men do. Although that characterization may be true of past generations, it no longer is. Since Title IX was passed in the 1970s, ensuring increased opportunities for women, more girls and women have been participating in team sports. There is no reason to think we will see a decline in the future. In fact, more and more younger children are playing coed team sports, from little league baseball to soccer and even football and hockey. These teams do not seem to have a general problem with mixed-gender bonding. Well-led, successful, adult coed athletic teams do not seem to have a problem, either. Although some opponents suggest that women are not suited to team play, one need only interview coaches who have coached men and women to find that women generally are less selfish team players, whereas men are more individualistic, less cooperative, and more competitive. Although we have not determined that a competitive attitude is not essential to success, we can say with authority that too much competitiveness within an organization can destroy any unit, and strong leadership must prevail to get all-stars to play as a team. Moreover, even all-star teams must practice together to win.[44]

To continue this discussion, I return from sports teams to work teams in dangerous occupations. Wide experience with firefighters and police officers suggests that gender bonding, given strong leadership, is not as problematic as people once feared. Predictable issues have arisen—from leaders' lack of commitment to diversity to dealing with the closeness that develops between partners and among squads—but bonding itself has not been a general problem.[45] Ignoring this evidence from similar, previously all-male occupations, some opponents to women in the service propose that men and women cannot bond because male bonding is essentially sexual—that it entails establishing a sexual polarity between men and women.[46] Although this type of bonding may be one model, it definitely is not the only kind; nor—as we have seen in the social bonding versus task bonding discussion—is it the most constructive for military effectiveness.[47]

Finally, there is no lack of evidence for intergender bonding in the military itself. I cannot in this essay explore the stories of the thousands of men and women from the coeducational military services in our own country and others, throughout history and today, who could recite millions of stories of male and female bonding. Those stories are available for the asking, however. The work of Elizabeth Kier—specifically on cohesion and bonding in the military—is very instructive in this regard,[48] and studies conducted at the U.S. Air Force Academy reveal that men and women with training and strong leadership do bond in military settings. In fact, the more stressful the situation, the better the bonding. These studies show that as young men and women enter the Academy and experience their doolie (freshman) summer and year, they bond with the members of their coed squad. These young men and women bond so strongly, in fact, that their leaders know it will be problematic if they cannot transfer primary loyalty to the larger institution and the military mission in general to uphold the Constitution. Still, not until after this most stressful year is some of this bonding destroyed. According to studies by the Academy's behavioral science department, considerable (perhaps unintentional) efforts by older male cadets and recent male graduates on faculty and staff are required to again polarize the genders. The researchers insist that informed and committed leadership is required to prevent that polarization.[49]

The story of human history is a story of our attempt to control our instincts and biology in order to come together to form societies and polities. Our laws specifically attempt to mediate between our biological impulses and the common good. With regard to the military specifically, we require that all military personnel know and adhere to a complex and rigorous Law of Armed Conflict, which we fully expect will mediate our warfighters' actions in the heat of combat to minimize loss of civilian life, inhumane treatment, or other violations of the Hague and Geneva Conventions. The laws are not perfect, but they do work. Suggesting that all soldiers, sailors, marines, and airmen can control their most basic biological instinct—self-preservation—under the most adrenaline-charged circumstances in favor of the laws of war but that under those same circumstances, or those less stressful, they cannot get past their sex drive is profoundly insulting.

Although the foregoing arguments against the inclusion of women in the military pretend to focus on practical issues that militate against further gender integration in the armed forces, a cursory review shows that there are few, if any, pragmatic objections to this expansion. In fact, these ever-shifting claims of one imagined female shortcoming after another show that this part of the debate is not really about anything fixed or easily measurable at all. The intangible nature of this frenetic opposition forms a "moving target" that is difficult to counter with logic and historical evidence. In fact, for more than 50 years the doomsayers' emotional arguments have lost in the court of public opinion and policy as they have successively trotted out anecdotal, illogical, and ahistorical evidence (if any) for support. Their last resort—after futile attempts to resurrect old canards we thought had long ago been put to rest—is to move to the purely visceral level.[50]

This appeal is the most emotional of all—the portrayal of female soldiers as victims of war. Although people who use this argument rarely address female civilian casualties, they fervently maintain that they are repelled—and that military men and the public also are repelled—by the idea that if women are allowed to serve in combat positions, many more will be "brought home in body bags." These opponents of expanded roles for military women argue that men would be unable to accomplish their missions under such circumstances: They would be too overcome with shock at the sight or, alternatively, would neglect their missions in favor of trying to protect their female comrades (the same comrades with whom, supposedly, they cannot bond). The proponents of this view assert that the American people would reject this prospect, as well as the prospect of women being brutalized as POWs, with such fervor that the public would exert pressure on the government and thereby scuttle military missions and, ultimately, precipitate the withdrawal of American forces from any conflict.

The logic of this argument fails in every point, and again the historical evidence does not support these emotional assertions. First, men do not try to protect women in wartime to the detriment of the mission any more than they ruin missions while protecting male comrades. Clearly, civilian women in combat zones generally have not benefited from this mythical male imperative; they often are left behind to fend for themselves because men in the community think they themselves are the enemy's targets. In fact, adversaries intentionally target women and other civilians. For some aggressors, their very strategy is to terrorize the population, demoralize enemy forces, and demonstrate control of conquered territory. Resistance fighters in World War II showed no hesitancy to send women into harm's way on some of their most dangerous missions of infiltration. In our more recent history, female military officers in Vietnam experienced just the opposite of male overprotectiveness: During routine rocket, mortar, and small arms attacks, as well as during the Tet Offensive, women were pushed out of the way or left behind as men scrambled for cover.[51]

With the integration of female aircrew members (aviators are most likely to be captured in modern war because they fly over enemy territory), trainers for the Air Force's survival, escape, resistance, and evasion (SERE) course postulated that many men would have an impulse to try to protect their female counterparts. The trainers and the men learned what the women already had figured out: If men give in to their captors when their female colleagues are brutalized, the women will be brutalized every time the captors require further capitulation from the men. Yet what SERE trainers found most surprising is that young men in training actually were no more likely to give in to the enemy's predations on the women than they were when their male friends were abused.[52]

To further debunk this myth that men are more likely to try to protect women they serve with in combat than they are to protect other men, to the detriment of the mission, we can look at everyday circumstances for more evidence. Men as a group do not protect women in peacetime—not even women they know. Not only do men assault women daily in large numbers in our cities and towns on public streets, but the highest incidence of sexual assault is between people who know each other. Other studies show that male college students would harm women if they knew they would not get caught.[53]

This finding holds true for the military as well. During the Tailhook gauntlet incident, no men intervened to protect women civilians or military members.[54] During the incident in which Naval Academy midshipmen chained a female classmate to a urinal in the men's room and subjected her to numerous indignities, no men intervened to protect her. In fact, men learn in these situations that if they come to a woman's rescue they will be derided—and completely ostracized if they give evidence against other men. During the Gulf War, more American women were assaulted by their comrades in arms than by enemy soldiers. Even when "friendly" assaults and enemy abuse (on prisoners of war Rhonda Cornum and Melissa Rathbun-Nealy) were made public, we have little evidence that men came to their rescue or defense or that men sacrificed missions to save the women. In Cornum's case, although two male noncommissioned officers (NCOs) were upset by the enemy abuse, she quickly got them to realize that they would not be helping her by reacting.[55]

Although there surely are some men who would be protective of women, these same individuals also would most likely attempt to protect their male counterparts. This assertion is neither uncommon nor inconsistent with military culture. We need only look at the recent case of American involvement in Somalia to see an example of the military mantra, "Never leave a man behind." In one instance in which we might have lost only two soldiers, the other Rangers were killed because they did not want to leave their comrades, living or dead.[56]

Another myth regarding female casualties is that the American public, always risk- and casualty-averse—sometimes to the point of sacrificing national objectives—will not countenance the possibility of "our women coming home in body bags." Air Force lawyer Charles Dunlap, Jr., among others, has suggested futuristic scenarios in which ersatz-Middle Eastern, religion-crazed aggressors will specifically target this alleged democratic weakness by brutalizing our soldiers—especially our female combat sol-diers.[57] These scenarios are presented as explicitly and brutally as possible, apparently with the intention of once again eliciting emotional recoil rather than realistic assessment.

The whole argument of risk aversion is misplaced, however, when it focuses only on women. There is much evidence for this aversion in the post-Lebanon, post-Somalia, post–Khobar Towers military. Since the Khobar Towers incident, in particular—following which an Air Force general was disciplined for negligence in the terrorist bombing of a barracks—and notwithstanding the attack on the U.S.S. Cole, force protection has become the U.S. military's first mission. We saw this imperative with our forces in Kosovo in 1999: Efforts to ensure that no Americans were harmed con-strained mission planners primarily to high-altitude bombing and did not allow ground troops. The stringent protection measures for the current U.S. peacekeeping forces provide additional evidence. This aversion to risk, however, is attributable to military leaders rather than the public at large and focuses not on women but on combat units (almost exclusively male). Alleged casualty aversion among the American public is not supported by any evidence. In fact, a 1999 study by the Triangle Institute for Security Studies (TISS) suggests just the opposite—that the public is much more sanguine than military leaders about military losses.[58]

Historical evidence shows that if the mission is explained clearly and the war itself has broad public support, the public regards it a soldiers' duty to put themselves at risk for the common good. This attitude is especially true for our all-volunteer force (AVF). In today's American military, people not only volunteer to serve, they even have some choice regarding the occupation in which they will serve.[59] The public seems to feel the same way about female servicemembers generally: If they volunteer for the military—and volunteer for hazardous duty—then they are responsible to do the job; casualties are an occupational hazard.[60] This attitude also is true for other high-risk professions such as policing and firefighting. Though women's deaths or serious injuries certainly are cause for emotion and grief, so is the loss of one of their brethren.[61]

Even though the public's presumed casualty aversion is not substantiated, it remains a very powerful myth, especially in the context of peacekeeping missions. It seems, in fact, to grow stronger with the retelling. As the TISS survey and my own experience as a National War College faculty member validate, this inaccurate perception permeates discussions at senior Professional Military Education (PME) schools. It has become dogma, and the numerous, intelligent counter arguments are but whispers in a storm.

Just as we tend to accept this myth of the public's casualty aversion, we also tend to accept the argument that the public will react even more vehemently if those casualties are women. During the 1991 Gulf War, when the public learned about women's deaths, injuries, or assault—by enemy or ally—there was no outcry criticizing the men, favoring the women, or calling for an immediate end to the conflict. In fact, there was no public outcry at all. There was appropriate grief for those who died in the Scud missile attack, and there was short-lived interest in the female POWs. The media-created sensation around "mommies going to war" (which ignored the historical reality of women's participation in war) raised the profile of military mothers *and* fathers and highlighted the difficulties they face in finding suitable childcare. In fact, despite columnist Fred Reed's contention that the armed forces have become "homes for unwed mothers," there are more married couples in the Services than ever before (as well as more military personnel who are married to civilians who also have demanding careers)—and there are more single military fathers than mothers. Notably, Reed does not mention children who have been fathered by military men who abrogate any responsibility for them (leaving that to the mothers or the taxpayers).[62] Overall, among the larger public, the focus on potential casualties among military mothers and fathers did not last much longer than a media nanosecond.

More recently, the death of Navy pilot Kara Hultgren elicited barely any public reaction at all. This particular casualty got much more attention after the fact from people who are opposed to women in the military because of the alleged "politically correct" promotion of unqualified women in carrier aviation. In 1999, the female aircraft commander who died in a crash in the forests of Colombia received barely a nod from the press or public, even though our involvement there might have had serious political repercussions. Instead, public attention focused on the crash that killed John F. Kennedy, Jr.[63] In 2000, the death and wounding of female sailors aboard the U.S.S. Cole was barely mentioned in the media.

Instead of recognizing the prevalence of violence against civilian women, and in the face of claims that men are socialized to protect women in war, we get Jesse Ventura's interview with *Playboy* in September 1999. A popular state governor and potential candidate for the Reform Party's presidential nomination, Ventura's criticism of members of organized religion as weak-kneed and misguided garnered a great deal of follow-up coverage and was the subject of a lot of ink in editorials, op-ed pieces, and letters to the editor.[64] A second comment, referring to the 1991 Tailhook incident, barely made it through the first day of coverage—though it was tantamount to endorsing assault. Ventura suggested that it was understandable—and, by extension, permissible or even expected—for "men who live on the edge" (in this case, military professionals) to assault women ("to grab their buttocks or breasts"). There was no additional coverage of this statement in the national media. There certainly was no hue and cry in support of women, military or civilian.

Women in dangerous professions make the news, to be sure—especially when their service is relatively (or perceived to be) new—but our memory is not very long. Although the public may remember that there were female military casualties during the Gulf War, they probably do not remember the military women killed in World War II; even then the public had a short attention span, a short grieving period, and a short memory.[65] Certainly the public did not feel that it owed any special debt to the Women's Air Service Pilots (WASPs) who died on duty. These women received little, if any, news coverage and no benefits from "a grateful nation" until after a legislative fight that lasted more than 30 years. The female POWs in World War II received no combat medals or devices for valor, although they nursed male soldiers under fire and through illness, wounds, and deprivation—and they risked their own lives to provide that care. Some military women even rejected opportunities for rescue so they could continue their work.[66] Female soldiers and airmen in Panama and women flying in action against Libya did not receive combat awards; yet men who served in the Grenada invasion had been given time waivers so they could receive the coveted Combat Infantry Badge, and male aircrew members traditionally had received such medals for similar missions.[67] Beyond the first couple of frenzied weeks, these women in danger received very little media or public attention. Much less was there a significant movement for their return to home and hearth.

Actually, we should not be surprised that the American public pays so little attention to the deaths of female service members given that it sees such a large number of women in proverbial body bags everyday on the "home front" without exhibiting much concern. There is no hue and cry demanding measures to protect women better or to prosecute their tormenters, harassers, and killers with more energy. On the contrary, obtaining and enforcing restraining orders or even enforcing our scanty gun control measures (background checks, waiting periods, and prohibitions on gun ownership by persons already convicted of violent crimes) remain difficult. Instead, we seem content to watch over and over the too-common story of released abusers, already subject to restraining orders and gun prohibitions, killing their estranged or former wives or girlfriends. Perhaps opponents of women in the military should exercise their considerable efforts to protect women from the epidemic of peacetime male violence, rather than prohibit women from exercising their civil liberties and civic obligations in defense of their nation and its ideals.

Putting military women in harm's way seems to be significant to a distracted public—as with civilian casualties—only when these casualties hit close to home. Even opponents of women in the military or combat would not try to tell a father and mother that the loss of their neighbor's daughter was more important than that of their own son.

We do not make policy in deference to parents' grief. And just as our grief is the same, so should women's obligations be. The public intuitively agrees when faced with the reality of this juxtaposition. For example, when I gave a talk at The Citadel in 1999 on the obligations of citizenship and called for all of our citizens to be allowed to contribute equitably, I expected disagreement from mothers of daughters. Instead, I received support from mothers of sons, who told me that they too felt that the government (and, by extension, all of us) should not ask their sons to register for the draft if their neighbor's daughters, born on the same day, are not compelled to do so.[68] There were no politics or ideology behind these mothers' words—only emotion and an intuitive feeling of fairness and equality of potential sacrifice. That evening, we did not discuss who would have to serve in combat if eventually drafted in a conflict. We did not discuss whether the son in question might be a small, artistic, nonviolent pacifist or whether the neighbor's daughter was a tall, strong, athletic, and aggressive risktaker. We did not discuss physical, intellectual, or emotional qualifications for military service or war. We simply discussed the equal obligation of citizens to serve.

Few people want their children, male or female, to be subjected to brutality and death, at home or abroad, for a good cause or questionable policy. There is no different measure of grief for conscripts or volunteers, sons or daughters. Although the larger public may regard these young sacrifices as a shame, most have not participated in campaigns to stop registration for the draft, nor the draft itself. Nor have we mounted campaigns to stop volunteers from serving in war—or to stop wars more generally. Even at the height of the Vietnam War protests, only a minority of Americans was vocal or active in opposition. We generally remember that we sacrificed approximately 50,000 American lives in that war. Yet there was no public outcry at the number of those victims who were military women, either in Vietnam or in any of our conflicts. When we are ready to spend lives, men and women alike appear to be suitable sacrifices.[69]

Government and military leaders throughout history, when faced with war, expediently turned to women—not as fictional heroines but to augment "manpower" in their armed forces. These efforts were not social experiments. For instance, Josephus Daniels knew the value of including women in the Navy in World War I, and Black Jack Pershing remarked that his female signal corps recruits from Alaska were so tough he wished he could use them in combat. During World War II, the more desperate a nation's plight—on either side—the more likely they were to recognize women's talents as warriors: Poland, the Soviet Union, France, China, Japan, and even Germany, in the end, used women. Since World War II, we have seen garrison states and revolutionary movements, as well as adversaries in civil wars, use their female fighting power.[70] The evidence does not support the contention that adversaries will fight harder rather than surrender to a force that includes women. Evidence from the Gulf War indicates that some adversaries (allegedly some of the most fanatical and misogynist) were even willing to surrender to news crews.[71]

Only in peacetime do we have the luxury of ignoring military "manpower" that comes in a different color or gender. Only in peacetime do we have the luxury of debating emotions and personal feelings. It was in peacetime that Air Force Chief of Staff and fighter pilot Merrill McPeak made the emotional and very personal argument to Congress that he opposed putting women in combat aircraft not because they were incapable of flying and fighting but because he would not want his daughter or his wife to do so.

Because opponents like to cite the Israeli case in support of their argument, we should note that only in peacetime have the Israelis debated whether religious women should be conscripted with the others. Opponents of the integration of women in the American military constantly point out that once modern states "have arrived," they would not think of using women in combat. Yet in the year 2000, Israel again began to use women in combat positions.[72]

Pragmatic and effective political and military leaders in conflict know—whatever they say in peacetime—that they need the best and smartest fighter or flier of whatever physical description, rather than an ineffective soldier of a particular size, race, religion, gender, or even sexual orientation.[73] In fact, we have witnessed numerous conversions of our senior military leaders throughout our history. Men who in peacetime railed against the integration of women and then in wartime saw them in action—on our side or the other—were convinced that the government did not mobilize enough women, fast enough, or in nearly enough capacities, and even suggested that American women were derelict as citizens for not volunteering in even larger numbers.[74]

Those conversions also show that attitudes and behavior can change. We have evidence that society at large, not to mention our hierarchical military, can change—in crisis or through committed leadership—not only behavior but attitudes. Laws and rules, particularly in the armed forces under the Uniform Code of Military Justice (UCMJ), have dictated behavior pertaining to race relations, and attitudes toward race have changed—not completely, but extensively and obviously. In civilian society and the military, we have decided we would restrict smoking behavior. We need only travel to Europe to realize how extensively we have changed attitudes toward this habit. We have changed and will continue to change not only behavior but attitudes toward relations between men and women in professional settings.[75]

Leadership and practicality, rather than emotion, should be key in this debate. Women certainly do make "moving targets" in fiction, as well as when they are portrayed in the press as the real victims of war. Restricting them to the role of victims, whether to elicit sympathy or ostensibly to preserve military culture and masculine bonding, has not affected the nation's ability to make decisions on national security and involvement in conflict. Although visceral reactions may sell newspapers and heat up stale arguments, they are not useful. As we have seen, however, these emotional appeals are the most consistent means by which opponents of the expansion of women's military roles obscure any logical and practical debate. Although countering deeply held faith or felt emotions with logic is impossible, we can reveal and counter strategies that deflect debate from the most important issues.

From shifting arguments[76] that women lack physical strength, to their imagined intellectual or emotional shortcomings, to rampant sexual activity in foxholes, to interfering with essential male bonding, opposition to women's roles in the Services constantly has seen emotionalism fall to logic and military necessity. These emotional arguments have not been the only "moving target" we must address, however. Another hard-to-pin-down aspect of this debate is military effectiveness—essentially, what future war will be like and what forces we will need to prevail in 21st-century conflict.

We do not have a winning record in evaluating our past wars. Our historical memories are seldom accurate: We continually learn the wrong "lessons," and we have not been prescient in predicting the future. Nevertheless, our political and military leaders must construct a force and design a strategy that we hope will be successful over the entire spectrum of conflict and military operations. The question really becomes: In which direction do we want to hedge our bets? Because we really do not know what we will face, maximum flexibility that capitalizes on the efficient use of the greatest amount of resources our civilian economy can spare would seem to be the best approach for national security. Historically, the only thing we can say for certain is that the keys to success appear to have been appropriate combinations of leadership, luck, and resources.[77] What does this conclusion tell us of the future, and how can we determine women's appropriate participation in that future?

Focusing our sights on fiction and momentary public and personal reactions—if any—sidetracks a real and necessary debate on the requirements of 21st century military effectiveness and first-class citizenship. We can take this debate out of the realm of the emotional and visceral and elevate it to a more logical plane. In this historical, logical, practical sphere lies the real support for women's roles in civic life in general and in national security and military effectiveness specifically.

❏ IMAGINING FUTURES: WOMEN WARRIORS AND 21ST-CENTURY WAR

Every noted military theorist over the past 10 years has noted that the post-Cold War world demands new kinds of armed forces. Strategists and planners contributing to the National Military Strategy, the 1997 Quadrennial Defense Review, and the National Defense Panel Reports agree that our forces in the future must and will integrate more "smart" information technology to reduce our physical "footprint" and increase our agility and that our servicemembers must be smarter and more flexible. Our forces and people must be able to shift from Smaller-Scale Contingencies (SSCs) to Major Theater Wars (MTWs), from combat to peacekeeping to humanitarian relief. Our military must be smaller and more mobile, and it will try to minimize military and civilian casualties by incorporating new weapons and new tactics, techniques, and procedures (TTPs). Some of our most noted military thinkers also insist that our forces must be better integrated politically, economically, socially, and culturally—that the armed forces must more accurately reflect the civilian society that employs them in order to successfully complete future missions, from defending the homeland to fighting terrorists abroad and preventing humanitarian disasters.[78]

Exactly what our future will look like remains uncertain, however. There are almost as many visions of future war and the forces we will need to prosecute it as there are military theorists. Certainty constantly eludes us. That difficulty makes trying to discuss possible roles for women in our future force the second "moving target" in our debate.

Some thinkers propose a future in which wars are never actually fought in the sense that we use that term today. Conflicts would be resolved by compelling an adversary to accede to our demands through information operations. At the other end of the spectrum is the prediction that future war will be bloodier as ethnic conflict and religious wars increasingly become the order of the day. Some theorists see more continuity with the past; others anticipate radical breaks in the way nation-states resolve their differences.

As we engage in these very serious efforts to understand and predict post–Cold War international structures and issues, we also must try to understand and predict what forces we need and what they will have to do. Trying to situate a debate about integrating women further into the forces is extremely difficult in this context. Nevertheless, to inform our debate with as much clarity, objectivity, and pragmatism as possible, discussion of the nature of war, changes we have seen in the recent past in the character and conduct of war, the dynamics of national security today, and current trends that might point toward possible futures is worthwhile.

Military planners constantly confront these questions and hope not to be too far off the mark. They try to inject enough flexibility into our strategies and force structure to enable us to change course rapidly—at not too high a cost—to react to unanticipated challenges in the future. One thing is certain: We will face the unanticipated. We must be able to cover the range of possibilities, and we must achieve this flexibility within the resource constraints that are a constant reality.

Despite our growing experience in military operations at many levels, historically we have guessed wrong with discouraging consistency when we have tried to envision future war. Specifically, in the context of this debate, we have never been able to objectively and reliably define the standards our military personnel should meet for successful performance in war. We have constantly changed service standards for strength, intellect, education, and character, as well as for age, race, and gender. We have changed these standards for a variety of reasons: We needed more people during wartime; we needed people with certain skill sets; we experimented with force composition; our society and culture changed; we learned more about human physiology, psychology, and behavior; we learned more about war. The fact that we constantly have changed these standards and requirements is evidence that they are not immutable—that they are culturally and socially based.

Women's roles in our society and culture also have changed over time. People who have resisted women's increased opportunities often have claimed that they could not meet standards or do the job—only to resort to emotional pleas (as we have seen) when women proved that they could. Even where women have succeeded in entering new occupations in greater numbers, resistance has been such that their organizational advancement has been stymied by a glass ceiling. They have not been accepted into formal and informal organizational hierarchies beyond token numbers. In the military, this dynamic has played out in the struggle over whether women, regardless of individual capability, should be allowed to compete for positions in the core, or defining, functions of each of the Services. The time has come to stop allowing this delaying tactic; we do not have the resources to squander valuable servicemember talents for the sake of holding onto an obsolete power structure that is based on arbitrary biological distinctions. In the interest of national security, we should refine standards and performance measurements to recruit and retain the highest-quality people we can, from whatever demographic, to create the best possible military for our future.

Military thinkers have been trying to foretell what militaries of the future would need as long as armies have fought each other.[79] We still study the most famous Western military thinker—Carl von Clausewitz, the Prussian officer who witnessed and examined the Napoleonic Wars. To his own experience and contemporary accounts he added a thorough study of military history. Most political and military theorists believe that he best captured the essence of war not as separate from but as a part of political interaction. Rather than write a "how to" manual that would have been rapidly outdated, in the best tradition of German Realism and the Hegelian dialectic Clausewitz sought to gain and provide insight into war's nature. Unfortunately, he did not live to see his project completed. Through careful extrapolation and faithfulness to his method, however, we can gain insights into the history and the future of war.[80]

Clausewitz characterized war as a violent human phenomenon that takes place in an arena of uncertainty. A cursory reading might lead one to believe that he meant to prescribe to military and political leaders that they should seek to apply maximum violence or force,[81] backed by the committed will of a passionate public and by a capable commander who can control much of the "fog and friction" of the battle or campaign. The first thing on which serious scholars of this subject will agree, however, is that Clausewitz did not seek to prescribe anything. He sought understanding and encouraged others to study and seek understanding. We can examine each of the components of war's nature separately and then together before we apply our understanding to the debate on military women.

Although a key component of warfare up to and through Clausewitz's era had been violence (in every sense—physical, psychological, economic, etc.), Clausewitz claimed that this violence would always be limited, to a greater or lesser extent, by many factors. Historically, wars were limited by the sizes of armies; by the level of commitment of their soldiers; by the intellect of officers; by the numbers, range, lethality, and accuracy of weapons; and even by geography, the weather, and the season of the year. Many of these limitations have been overcome over time, but at least two things that limit wars have not changed: Human beings have limited capacities, and wars are fought for political reasons.

A second element in the nature of war, according to Clausewitz, is that it is a human phenomenon. Human beings get tired, cold, afraid, and hungry, and sometimes they are not very smart. Human beings also can be courageous, creative, and brilliant, however, and they can ask their bodies to do amazing things. In the end, however, war will be limited because the human beings who fight wars are limited. Even if they were not biologically limited, people have had enough good judgment and intellect to understand that wars are fought for a reason and that no political reason has called for self-annihilation. Clausewitz knew of religious and revolutionary wars that had called forth the most passionate and extreme warfare of earlier eras and his own. Yet even in the nuclear age we have not yet married an ideology with a weapon that would destroy an enemy completely. If this combination eventually comes to pass, the nature of war will have truly changed, and the type of forces we have in the field will not matter—rendering our current debate moot. To date, however, wars have moved back and forth along a spectrum of more or less violent, more limited or more total. Consequently, our discussion of optimal force structure remains relevant.

Humans have been able, more or less, to limit war as they assess the value of their political goals. This practice is imperfect—at best an art. It cannot be a science, as Clausewitz's contemporary Antoine Jomini tried to make it, because of the essential element of chance. This aspect of war allows for the creativity of military leaders in the field as they act in the service of a political purpose—a national interest. This aspect of war may be changing as more nonstate actors take part in conflicts or threaten our interests; for the foreseeable future, however, most theorists posit the continuation of the nation-state amidst the countervailing trend of globalization.[82] We can examine the implications of both trends in international relations and national security.

In the military revolutions since Clausewitz's day, only the character and conduct of war have changed; its essence has not. Clausewitz would only shake his head at people who think they can plan out the friction, the chance, the human element, even the violence of war. If the most extreme of the information warriors are correct, war's nature will indeed change in this next century. We can examine what that might mean for forces and missions and military women later. First, however, we will examine changes in the character and conduct of war through several military revolutions since the mid-18th century and look at other possible trends for the future.

Military historian Walter Millis has characterized changes in the nature and conduct of war as several revolutions—Democratic, Managerial, Industrial, and Scientific. Later we will add discussion of the current information technology-based Revolution in Military Affairs (RMA) to which I have alluded. For each of these earlier revolutions, Millis examines changes in the combatants and arms used. We can use a matrix to trace the developments. On one axis we use military categories of weapons, tactics, armies, and aims. On the other axis we look at the political, economic, social, cultural, and technological context of the period. Each of Millis's revolutions entailed a comprehensive change in the character and/or conduct of war but not a change in war's nature; it remained violent and filled with uncertainty. Although the aims or purposes may have changed, they were always essentially political. We do not see a linear progression over time in the scale of wars' violence; instead, we could describe the trend as the swinging of a pendulum: Limited wars became more total and then, as societies reacted against the toll, became more limited in their cost and effects, until they once again escaped tight control.[83]

As we consider these four revolutions and the dynamics of change in warfare and militaries, we must remember that men did not often predict the future of conflict accurately—that they were often caught unprepared even when they were very smart and very sure of themselves—and that the contours of change become only marginally clearer with hindsight. Historians, as much as contemporaries, often are confined by their frames of reference.

Only the most prescient could have predicted how the 18th-century democratic revolutions would change warfare. Before the seventeenth century, European monarchs traded land and privilege to their aristocrats for service as officers. These officers led relatively small armies that were recruited or impressed from the lower classes and nonproductive parts of society. Most soldiers were male, but armies in the field were followed by an extensive array of camp followers, and some women disguised themselves as men so they could fight.[84] Although some mercenaries fought for profit, the bulk of the soldier class fought at the monarch's pleasure in return for food to eat and a place to live. With the strengthening of the nation-state, some rulers developed more disciplined, long-term, professional forces; not until the advent of the people's armies of the American and French Revolutions, however, did militaries' size and passions for the fight grow.[85]

Because these revolutionary armies were fighting for a political cause or ideology they believed in, coercion was less necessary, and soldiers fought harder. Corporal punishment was less necessary and less often tolerated in these new armies. These armies were raised hurriedly and were not well trained; they could not fight in linear formations against traditional armies. Their advantage was that they fought with passion for their principles. Because they shared a goal, these soldiers could fight in open formations and irregularly, without close supervision—which, in turn, allowed them to use their initiative. Moreover, although these people's armies used essentially the same weapons as their opponents, they could put many more people in the field. Although we have evidence that women fought in even earlier conflicts, these armies saw more women march to the colors as revolutionary ideologies called for all persons to participate in the fight for political liberty and soldiering required less training and experience. I do not argue that these armies intentionally put large numbers of women in uniform or combat; we can see, however, that when the fight was desperate and the cause popular, women would fight, and men accepted them as comrades in arms. This revolutionary spirit is part of our military heritage.

The 18th-century ideological revolutions unleashed the power of the citizen-soldier and updated the idea of obligation to the democratic state. I discuss the implications of this development in the next section of this essay; what is important here is that there was no going back. Later wars would find "nations in arms" enlisting whole peoples in *levées en masse* to support the fighting—war socialism. As entire nations and economies were enlisted to support the fight, civilians and industry became targets of opposing forces. Despite the reality that some fighters were female, "civilians" would become synonymous with "women" as all able-bodied (male) citizens were called to arms to fight for their community. Yet although the evidence shows that more women supported the war effort, especially as nurses, it also shows that many more than we have recognized participated in combat.[86]

Our Civil War also was an ideological war, and in it we again saw the mobilization of more people, with more passion, employing more unconventional ways and means. Despite this clear trend toward democratic warfare in our own culture, we still fail to account for the phenomenon when we consider wars against other countries. We predict the future incorrectly, neglecting to apply historical lessons in so many cases they are hard to count: Vietnam, Somalia, Kosovo. One thing we can know for certain is that this genie will never go back in the bottle. We should expect that we will see passionate civilians mobilized against us in war. By the same token, sometime in the future, we also may call for the mobilization of our entire nation to fight for our values.

Back to the future in the past, contemporary military analysts were slow to realize Millis's second revolution, even as today we are slow to change our industrial war paradigms. At the very beginning of the Industrial Revolution, this nation called its sons to fight against each other for deeply held principles. In our Civil War they fought for those causes passionately. The Industrial Age gave soldiers newer and more lethal means of combating each other at greater ranges and with more accuracy. Soldiers killed each other faster with repeating rifles, rifled artillery, and Gatling guns, and we got more soldiers to battlefields quicker with railroads and steam engines. We strategically controlled those forces better by means of the telegraph.[87] The evidence was before us: This first industrial war showed that war between mobilized citizenries with industrial-age weapons would be long and bloody.

That was not the lesson that European and Asian colonial powers, despite their advancing industrialization, learned from their late 19th-century military operations, however, because most of their conflicts entailed victories over indigenous peoples in veritable slaughters. They virtually ignored the American Civil War. They also ignored the destructiveness and ferocity of the Russo-Japanese War, in which two industrializing nations faced off.

With their success still fresh, European and Japanese military thinkers and leaders downplayed the impact of their material advantages and decided instead that their supposedly superior moral positions and greater "will" were the power behind their victories.

Military thinkers at the turn of the 20th century chose to focus on the war that highlighted what Millis calls the managerial revolution. The well-schooled and well-disciplined Prussian armies defeated Denmark, Austria, and France in short wars, and the master of *Realpolitik*, Otto von Bismarck, unified the German states. Millis shows how, in these wars, the Prussian General Staff system and *Kriegsakademie* brought their forces to victory, and he traces how other powers tried to adapt or adopt a more advanced managerial scheme to more efficiently organize their larger and more heavily equipped forces for future war. At the same time, they sought to improve and increase their forces through eugenic policies and mobilization plans for the industrialized nation-in-arms. In the United States, the military's managerial revolution was reflected in Elihu Root's reforms and Emory Upton's organizational proposals. Americans, like the others, saw the usefulness of centralized management, better force organization and planning, and improvements in training. Industrialists and military leaders also saw the advantage of interchangeable weapons' parts and mass production of those weapons. In this democracy, however, we were not ready to adopt Germany's bureaucratic and militaristic measures wholesale.

Ultimately, Germany's methods worked against it, and the country lost the next war as the officer corps became more and more separated from society and civilian political control. We should not forget these lessons in our own age. States can become militarized, and political leaders and citizens can abdicate to the professional judgment of soldiers, even as their militaries cease to reflect their parent societies. Military leaders, too, are trapped in their age and their professional milieu. Only a few have been able to transcend their paradigms to see the future a little more clearly and act accordingly.

Unfortunately, none of these clear thinkers were in evidence on the eve of World War I. Well-meaning military leaders and intelligent futurists all guessed wrong. Almost to a man, each believed in his force's moral superiority or *elan*; they focused on colonial wars and misread Clausewitz.[88] Because forces and strategies had become more technical and complex, political leaders acquiesced to military technocrats and managers with overly rigid strategic plans. The forcing mechanisms of military mobilization plans, railroad lines, and geography pushed them to throw their industrial might into a war that would prove that human physical abilities and spirit were no match for a "no man's land" filled with mud, barbed wire, and machine fire.

Only the Polish civilian industrialist Ivan Bloch predicted that war between industrialized powers would be long and brutal beyond imagination, rather than swift and relatively clean like the 1871 Franco-Prussian War. What we had to learn was that throwing more brave men's bodies into the meat grinder would not bring victory in wars of attrition. Instead, governments would have to mobilize their whole nation—population, industry, and passion—to support a war effort in which victory might not mean complete destruction of the enemy but would bring almost complete control of the opposing nation. In addition, we learned that material strength might be worth nothing unless the newest technologies could not only be developed wholesale but also properly integrated into tactics and campaigns to break deadlocks on the ground. To break through the stalemate of the tactical defensive in the trenches, we would have to integrate more media into the fight—making use of the air, sea, and electronic spectrum.[89] We also would be forced to demand the resources of whole populations, including the politically, socially, and economically disadvantaged—with the result that eventually we would have to include and empower these citizens. In our case, this trend meant new rights for women, racial minorities, and workers as their responsibilities in defense of the nation grew.

Individual women did not find much of a place in this historical review, as in most military and political histories. In more holistic histories that recognize that social and cultural contexts are equally important in telling an accurate story of the past, however, one finds a coincident evolution—a fairly steady trend of American women's increasing political, economic, industrial, and military participation. When we admitted that minority men did not have all the rights, privileges, and obligations of first-class citizenship during this period, we also increasingly recognized that women were similarly dispossessed. The stories of the Civil Rights movement and the women's suffrage and women's rights movements are much too long and complex to delve into here; we should not ignore these stories, however, in a discussion of changes in warfare and militaries.

Our Millis matrix shows how political, social, economic, and cultural contexts affect and are affected by war.[90] In the American case, the public debate about the rights of citizenship almost always has included a discussion of military obligation. This debate swirled around whether rights or participation should come first,[91] but some women—like some black men—did not wait for the debate to be resolved (or for equal political and social consideration) before making the ultimate commitment of serving with or in the military. Before military medical entry exams were instituted, women disguised as men served in our wars. As those medical exams became more routine and warfare more industrialized, professionalized, and bureaucratized, fewer women could pass as men, and more women served the military as nurses.

Medicine in general and military medicine more specifically advanced quickly from the mid-19th century. With larger armies and more lethal weaponry, casualties increased—as did calls for improvements in battlefield medicine. At first, women simply served the military in larger numbers as volunteer nurses. Before long, however, the military and the women realized that their participation would have to be institutionalized and better managed to be most effective, and through the Civil War and Spanish–American War the Army and Navy nurse corps were regularized.[92]

By World War I, numerous other civilian occupations were becoming feminized—specifically those in the service industries (e.g., administration and communication). With increased efficiency and improvements in medical services as their example and the needs of larger and more bureaucratized armed forces as their imperative, military leaders called for the induction of women into the regular forces—or at least as reserves or civilian auxiliaries.[93] After their service in and with the military in our first major 20th-century war, along with other economic and social imperatives, women finally were given the right to vote. As with minority men, the privileges of first-class citizenship accrued only with the catalyst of wartime military service.[94]

The interwar years also saw women's rights and roles expanding, from flying records to athletic records to every other field of endeavor. Social and cultural boundaries, even if they were only semantic or imagined, steadily gave way. Although the trajectory was temporarily reversed by conservative and economic backlash during the depression of the 1930s and again after World War II, the outlines of women's increasing participation in the public world, and in every sphere, was obvious. Another global war would further erode the anti-feminists' tenuous positions.[95]

According to Millis, the interwar years also constituted a period of inventions and new thinking that spawned a fourth revolution in militaries—the Scientific—that would be evident in World War II. Exploiting this revolution, Germany appeared to have solved the problem of reinjecting tactical and even operational mobility into land warfare with its *Blitzkrieg* combined arms doctrine—through the application of new technology, with its modern aircraft and vehicles, tactical radios, radar and sonar, and even industrial processes. Until late in the war, however, Germany mobilized only a fraction of its population and industry, partly because of racial and gender ideology. This decision essentially negated the advantages they gained through the industrial revolution in warfare. Although German leaders gained their publics' loyalty through propaganda and terrorism, they could have capitalized on Germany's historic leadership of the military managerial revolution. They did not win because Germany's military and its war efforts were isolated from the largest portions of the population for too long.

What proved most significant in warfare's scientific revolution were creativity and intellect, as well as industrial mobilization, outstanding military leadership, and cooperation among allies. The Allies capitalized on the realization that creativity, intelligence, and the mobilization of human and material resources should not be limited by race and gender. Not everyone immediately accepted this proposition, but our most effective leaders understood that brains and ability did not come in a particular color or sex. Women and minority men made their commitments to the nation and the military despite the fact that they did not yet enjoy first-class rights and benefits. They made sacrifices in every field, even in the face of some remaining official—and much unofficial—prejudice and discrimination. Intentionally and unintentionally, they pushed boundaries in war that were more pliant than they had been in peacetime.

Those most prescient leaders—and others who witnessed the skills and dedication of our marginalized citizens in action—started to publicly support the movement for their increased participation in military and civil arenas. This support was not garnered through feminist brainwashing; it was born of pragmatism and commitment to right. Some leaders were believers before the war but were not committed to action; others were converted later. Most, however, eventually realized that in modern war the talents and efforts of more than half of America's population (women and minority men) could not be ignored. Not all went so far as to make the next leap—that if persons contributed their utmost to the nation in time of need there should be no barrier to their political, economic, or social participation in peacetime—but the outlines of future trends already were visible.[96]

The nations in most dire need—such as France, Italy, Poland, China, and the Soviet Union—mobilized whole populations. Individuals were enlisted in any occupation in which they were mentally and physically skilled enough. Women served as resistance fighters and in combat forces. The United States and Britain, by accident of geography, had the luxury of maintaining some barriers in the short term, but forward-thinking leaders anticipated the breakdown of more of these barriers. Britain eventually drafted women—and the American Congress seriously considered doing so just as the Allies turned the corner to victory in late 1944.

What we learned in this ideological, bureaucratized, industrialized, and scientific conflict was that "near-total" wars require us to more closely match our political philosophy with reality—that our outmoded cultural ideology did not reflect reality and severely hampered our ability to defend that philosophy against totalitarian enemies.[97] General Eisenhower and President Truman predicted that future war would require all of our nation's talents in another ideological, industrial war of total mobilization. Both supported the conscription of women. Their convictions about future security requirements would not by themselves make men of color equal or completely accepted in our armed forces, however, nor would they make women more than emergency draftees in a crisis. President Truman recognized that integrating these groups was both right and militarily necessary, and took the next steps.[98] He issued an Executive Order to desegregate the military and signed the law that allowed women to serve as regular, permanent members in our armed forces.[99]

Not all military leaders agreed that future war would require the resources of an entire nation in an apocalyptic conflict of attrition. They focused on the scientific revolution, as Germany had, and envisioned a scientific war that would be based on new technologies of annihilation with strategic nuclear weapons. Leaders such as the Air Force's Curtis LeMay did not foresee that we would use more women in the military; in fact, in the 1950s he advocated being rid of all of them. He would not have admitted that dropping bombs or launching ICBMs does not require men. From the late 1940s to the 1960s, women could have fought that kind of war, just as they would have been the targets in such a war—although very few people would have proposed it.[100] Women certainly would have been at no greater risk as nuclear warriors; Cold War targeting sought to threaten civilian targets in strategies of Massive Retaliation and Mutually Assured Destruction.

People who thought we would totally mobilize to throw massive land armies into the Fulda Gap and those who thought we would use waves of nuclear bombers or ICBMs were both wrong, however. Although superpower proxy and other smaller land and air wars were fought during the Cold War—which for local participants might have been "total"—our military operations were limited and did not involve exclusive use of advanced technology or total mobilization of human or material resources. For fighting in Korea, Southeast Asia, and South and Central America, we had to change our strategy to one of Flexible Response.

Through the 1950s and 1960s, women served in the armed forces and provided important administrative, intelligence, and medical support—although in small numbers; the notion that large numbers of them would be mobilized in an emergency still held, but they were not regarded as vital. The Civil Rights and women's movements, as part of the larger social context, helped to show that citizens should not be asked or obligated to serve if they were not going to be equally valued and compensated. The question of essential fairness began to come up more often in the courts.

While issues of fairness in the Services were pushed slowly forward, the limited wars of the first 25 years of the Cold War certainly did not require military leaders to be forward-thinking in terms of increasing the number of women and minority men in the Services. They did not have to consider what was right for democracy or for military necessity. In fact, there were ceilings on the numbers of minority men and women who would be inducted. These ceilings—inaccurately called "quotas" since early in our history—were luxuries afforded by nuclear deterrence strategies and the draft.[101]

In 1973, as a result of growing public anti-war sentiments and the obvious unfairness of the Selective Service System, the U.S. military transitioned to an all-volunteer force (AVF). We quickly realized that middle-class, white men were not going to join in large enough numbers, and even the Cold War strategy of Flexible Response demanded a force structure that would require more women and more minority men. This new realization did not mean that the Services in the 1970s were free from prejudice or discrimination (neither was civil society), but more and more women and minority men were willing to enter a system that relied on their sacrifices and skills, although it still did not afford them equal access or opportunities.

Although many leaders were forced by social movements and the courts to be more fair in the apportionment of rewards and privileges, again our more forward-thinking political and military leaders began to realize that morale and cohesion, and therefore effectiveness, suffered under discriminatory rules and regulations. Senior military men such as Admiral Elmo Zumwalt and Lieutenant General Maxwell Thurmon, who had the opportunity to work with women, realized that the Services were being denied the talents and skills of a large segment of our society by outmoded practices and barriers.[102] Others—military members and civilians—continued to rebel against the removal of those artificial and outmoded barriers. Ignoring social, cultural, and demographic trends, they claimed that enough intelligent, middle-class, white men would have enlisted in the volunteer forces if women (and, by implication, minority men—whom many still considered inferior) had not been brought in. These opponents of a fully integrated military claimed that women and minority men could be inducted only by lowering standards. They ignored the fact that there was no need to lower real job standards; all exercises and studies (e.g., REFWAC and MAXWAC) showed that mixed-gender units performed at least as well as all-male units and that in conflict and other operations, American forces were as effective as they had ever been.[103] In claiming that feminists and social engineers were ruining national security, opponents resorted to emotional and visceral attacks without factual or historical support. As they shifted their arguments from one stereotype to another, each myth was successively debunked, and integration continued to move forward.

This approach, so easily refutable through careful analysis, ironically could have spelled the approaching end for gender barriers; during the final decade of the Cold War, however, anti-feminists gained a sympathetic friend in the White House. Ronald Reagan won the presidency, and his administration sought to turn back gains made under the Civil Rights and women's movements. Leaders of the military—active duty and civilian—who had been seeking not only to keep women from moving into more military specialties but to turn back their advances finally had high-level support. The Carter administration's previous projections for increasing the number of military women, increasing the number of women in nontraditional military career fields, and opening even more fields to women were either stopped or reversed in a conservative reaction.

During the "womanpause" that started in 1980, more government studies were sponsored in attempts to collect the data that opponents had always lacked; they wanted to prove that women (who at the time constituted 10 percent of the force—a ceiling that included the largely female nurse corps) damaged military effectiveness.[104] They expected to uncover data that would show that "unqualified" women were brought in or that women who met the allegedly lowered standards could not perform their duties as well as men. They wanted to prove that even if women could perform required duties, they diminished the necessary aggressiveness of their male counterparts or damaged the soldierly bonding that is required for victory in combat. Military leaders commissioned more and more studies as they threw each successive one out because the studies proved that these emotional appeals were simply unsupported by the facts.

While servicewomen's detractors went about this expensive and fruitless business, they failed to recognize that they were undermining the very bonding and morale they ostensibly were defending. During this period, military women realized that they were under attack, that a significant number of male leaders did not want them around, and that they lived under a microscope while these leaders and anti-women activists watched and waited for their smallest failures. Many of the men these women had to work for had served in a military in which women were seldom seen or heard, except when they took care of the pesky paperwork, provided medical attention, or served as recreational outlets. For the most part, these men wanted to be able to continue to use women in such tasks—but only those who would not insist on equality as military officers or enlisted personnel and did not expect to receive the privileges and benefits of veterans. Finally, they wanted women to be managed and taken care of by other women.

The force these men had grown up in was largely a younger, unmarried, white, male (98 percent) force that was insulated on military posts and served overseas. The few women in support positions served in separately managed units. Men could fool themselves that because they wanted women only on the periphery, and they were convinced our soldiers would someday fight in the Fulda Gap or on the Korean Peninsula in large armored and infantry units, this segregation made sense in the interest of national security—even though, as in World War II Germany, their preferred force did not reflect reality, society, or our political ideals.[105]

These resisters could not reverse women's gains, however, and their Cold War never became hot. Instead, Americans deployed to the Middle East in peacekeeping forces, and to Grenada and Panama, and we bombed terrorist-sponsoring regimes such as Libya—and all of these operations included women. Things did not go smoothly in every aspect, of course. In each instance, problems with mixed-gender forces arose regarding which rules applied to whom, and how combat rules applied in "operations other than war."[106] The resulting confusion among units that did not know whether they were supposed to deploy their women is well documented; this confusion was partly related to the backlash created by the "womanpause" efforts. These issues with initial deployments of mixed-gender units were minor, however, given that most of our planning centered not on conflicts like these but on the big wars we thought we would fight—or wanted to fight. Luckily, our force structure was always, almost by accident, up to the task. In none of these operations did any data show that integrating women had cost lives or resources. In every instance, the soldiers in the field acquitted themselves well and bravely, even if the bureaucracy did not. Males and females all got the job done together.

Finally, in 1989, with the end of the Cold War, military planners realized that the Fulda Gap battle probably would never occur and that responding to multiple SSCs around the globe might be the most taxing—and most common—circumstances our forces would have to be structured and trained for. Still, we remained prepared for a major land campaign; in 1990, for Desert Shield, we deployed for one. By all measurements, in DESERT STORM we had the most effective and disciplined fighting force we have ever fielded. It also was the most gender-mixed force any nation ever sent to war. The heavy forces we had built our Cold War tactics around turned out not to be the forces that we most required—nor have they been since. In fact, taxpayers and Congress continually ask whether, for any foreseeable future, we will ever again need (or be able to deploy) such heavy and cumbersome forces.[107]

Desert Storm was a turning point for women as the war's experiences were added up, and in 1991 Congress and the Bush administration asked whether the continuing combat restrictions had any relevance or meaning in the current cultural or social milieu. Opponents continue to debate, but the official answer was and remains: probably not.[108] Even the stacked conservative Congressional commission focused most on the possibility of capture, rather than on women's strength or emotional limitations. After Desert Storm, Congress and the Services opened many remaining military occupations to women—beyond those recommended by the commission. Opponents clearly were outnumbered as many senior military and political leaders, academics, and other citizens praised our returning forces, complimented servicewomen, and voiced surprise that the public had not reacted to women's service, captivity, or deaths with the shock and abhorrence they expected. Although decisions to lift some combat restrictions were not unanimous, any claim that a clear majority of our military and civilian leaders and citizens had been brainwashed by radical feminists or that they sold out their honor and integrity to "political correctness" does not even warrant a response.[109]

What does deserve serious consideration is what the next war or other military operation will require of us. We must capitalize on all of our experience, examine historical and more recent trends, and review mistaken past predictions to design and build a force now for the future—or at least for the next two decades. We need only look at how inaccurate many "professionals" have been in their efforts to do just that over the past two centuries to understand how difficult this task is.

Today, well-meaning and intelligent military thinkers disagree about whether we are in the midst of another "revolution in military affairs" (RMA). Whether we are experiencing an actual revolution or not, the Joint Chiefs of Staff intend to capitalize on very significant changes in warfare and the international environment, as evidenced in the National Military Strategy. Examining what this strategy might mean for future force structure and the type of soldiers we recruit is useful to this discussion on the integration of women. The Department of Defense does not want to continue to "fight the last war," as it so often is accused of doing, but it must be prepared for a difficult-to-imagine future. The process by which we develop our strategy and design our forces is interesting and laborious; it brings together current intelligence and an analysis of trends to determine which threats are most likely and which are most dangerous, as well as which military capabilities will be required to meet the demands of the future international security environment.

Each year, Joint Staff Strategy personnel and Service Planners, along with the intelligence community, conduct a classified Joint Strategy Review (JSR). The resulting document summarizes the thoughts of the best and brightest on trends and threats—from economic globalization and the spread of democracy to asymmetric threats and ethnic conflict.[110] Developers of the report might posit the chances for the emergence of a peer competitor or a regional near-peer, threats to the homeland or economic dislocation, or mass migrations resulting from famine or complex natural disasters. The JSR report does not suggest a strategy to address these trends or advocate that the military is always the right tool to use. Instead, it examines a range of possible situations that might threaten national security and that call, at least in part, for a military response, whether unilateral or in coalition with others.[111]

The JSR Report informs the efforts of the National Security Council as it writes the NSS and the military as it writes the NMS. These two documents outline national priorities and give broad direction for how the Services and Combatant Commanders are to address a range of possible threats.[112] The usual approach is to assume that the military is best used for "fighting and winning the nation's wars"—with other partners when we can, alone when we must. We also recognize, however, that although force might not be necessary in addressing certain cases, the military may be the only organization with the resources to respond to operations other than war. These operations include situations that are more serious than police can deal with but somewhat less than what we might consider "warfighting." We do not have another organization to deal with these circumstances.[113]

Some experts have complained in recent years that we are frittering away our military resources on those "less important" cases; others claim that these operations are exactly what we must design and train the current and future force to do. The consensus in official circles has become our national strategy of engagement and our military strategy of constantly shaping the environment to be conducive to our security and interests, responding to the entire spectrum of military operations as necessary, and preparing now for the future. We have defined our security interests more broadly in our new international context, and over the past decade we have come to see the value in this approach.[114] We can examine the aspects of this strategy to help us predict what kind of military the United States will need.

We shape the international security environment in many ways, including our presence overseas, combined education and training, and security assistance programs. Our military is basically charged with "role modeling" civil-military relations for nascent and emerging democracies. We try to show exactly what military sociologists propose for a healthy relationship—a military that reflects its society and carries out the mandates of the civilian leadership as prescribed in a constitution. Our military also models pluralism and diversity in such missions. The fact that 50 states with sometimes very different political, economic, and social concerns have come together in a union in which we resolve our differences without force of arms is something Americans tend to take for granted. Successful interpersonal interaction between different races, genders, and religions—not to mention regions, families, and classes—is another dynamic that we can model. This dynamic is relevant in, for instance, Eastern European countries that are emerging from communism, particularly in view of the fact that so many have suppressed ethnic and cultural issues of their own to resolve.[115]

Our pluralistic and civilian-controlled military forces also can provide powerful examples to the people of Africa, Asia, and South America. We should be conscious in every situation about whether we "walk the walk" as we "talk the talk" of democracy. To our military men and women's credit, during operations in the Balkans over the past two years that were aimed at stopping ethnic violence in a volatile region, nary a word made the press about racial, religious, or gender problems among our forces during the Macedonian peacekeeping mission, the Kosovo air campaign, or the ongoing Kosovo mission. I do not mean to suggest that we did not experience a single problem in any of these areas, but the fact that none made the papers or created a public uproar means to many outside observers—as it should to us—that whatever problems we may experience are uncommon and are being handled by our leaders in mostly satisfactory ways.

We can see the third aspect of the NMS in these recent military operations: preparing now for an uncertain future. There are at least three pieces to this leg of the strategy. First is our move toward building a flexible, capabilities-based force rather than a force built for a specific future threat. Second is the "business plan" for how to procure the equipment to enable our forces to perform these missions. Third is the recruiting and training required to build a force of quality people who can use the equipment to accomplish the missions.[116]

Joint Vision 2010 (JV2010), as well as the follow-on thinking about the next decade, proposes that technology will enable our forces to better to achieve Dominant Maneuver, Focused Logistics, Precision Engagement, and Force Protection. We can argue about how high-tech our enemies will be, but we have clearly started down the road to using technology in a new and increasingly information-centered world to maximize our military advantages. While we keep in mind that we may be fighting less-advanced non–nation-states, terrorist entities, or ethnic or religious warriors in urban environments, the prevalent thinking is that we will use all of the advances in information technology to our advantage. Information Superiority is the enabler for these aspects of JV2010.[117]

With information technology and an appropriate integrating doctrine, we can find out more about the adversary before conflict arises; we can shape perceptions among groups and individuals who would oppose our security interests; we can maintain our own command and control while denying an adversary theirs; and we can analyze, make decisions, and act more quickly than our opponents. We will use our information systems to find out what our materiel needs are and supply them quickly. We will be able to move more forces more rapidly, track them constantly, control them en route, and even disperse them while massing their effects on our objectives. When we engage enemy forces or terrorists, we will use all available and affordable technology to do so as precisely as possible to ensure economy of force while minimizing collateral damage.

Part of what the "business plan" addresses is how much of the technology we require we can afford; the commitment to design, equip, and train such a force is well along, however. We are developing a force that is lighter and much more flexible than we have ever had before. We want our forces to be based at home to the greatest extent possible yet be able to work well in coalitions and to respond at a moment's notice to all levels of crisis at home and abroad—from Y2K-like civil challenges to massive migration flows across our borders to missile attacks against us. We will ask our soldiers to fight terrorists, religious warriors, and warlords; to defeat near-peer armor, air, and sea forces; to defend against threats from nuclear, chemical, and biological weapons; and to combat ethnic hatred, diseases, famine, and natural disasters.

In truth, these challenges are not new, not nontraditional, and not improper for our military. Although some military leaders and thinkers, as well as politicians, have rejected such actions as unfitting for our armed forces, over the more than two centuries of our existence our civilian leaders and citizens often have called on our military to carry out exactly these kinds of missions. Because we often have rejected these missions, philosophically and rhetorically, as outside the proper purview of our regular forces, however, we have not appropriately equipped, planned, or trained for them. Not surprisingly to those who have served, our forces have always made do and succeeded anyway. We can only imagine how much better they could perform if we only admitted the necessity up front and planned accordingly.

The third aspect of this discussion about our future force focuses on the people who have succeeded in the military arena in the past and must succeed in the future—our sons and daughters. In the past, we did not ask for much in the way of qualifications. Revolutionary and Civil War soldiers did not have to pass strength or fitness tests. They generally were like their adversaries: mostly young, mostly male, and, in our case, mostly white. As military forces became more professionalized, we started to demand more education of officers and more general health and fitness of all members.

We often have changed standards for induction over the past two centuries. In general, however, we have been able to demand a higher level of physical fitness and intellectual development during peacetime or economic downturn, whereas in wartime we have been willing to accept volunteers or to draft conscripts who do not meet peacetime standards. We must ask ourselves: If we repeatedly acknowledge that these broader standards are appropriate for wartime forces, why should we not adopt the same standards in peacetime if preparation for war is the peacetime forces' real purpose? To use another sports analogy, "We must practice as we'll play."

Although some opponents use the term "lowered standards" to refer to the inclusion of women and minorities, historically we have neither lowered nor raised standards where mission accomplishment is concerned. Mostly we have changed them—as firefighters changed the height of ladder supports—without changing the requirement to be strong enough to hold a fire hose or carry an unconscious person. Consider a woman who is tactically brilliant and a man who is fantastically strong: Saying that we lowered standards to allow the stronger man into the service makes as much sense as suggesting that the woman's relative weakness represents a deficiency in the force. As the aircraft maintenance example demonstrates, having some people who can carry fifty-pound toolboxes and some people who can crawl inside engines is beneficial. The fact that the military has constantly changed standards and conditions of service only tells us that our ideas of requirements change as warfare changes—or that we really have very little idea what we need.

What do we need? All of our planning and strategy documents say we need the highest-quality force we can get. We recognize that we judge quality by aggregates of different attributes—strength, intellect, marksmanship, leadership, eyesight and hearing, character, and so on—and that judging the real potential of young individuals by counting the number of pushups they can do or the numbers of figures they can compute in their heads alone is difficult. Yet we also recognize the need to set real fitness and job standards, recruit individuals who meet intellectual and physical requirements, and then enforce performance. We also know how difficult all of this is when we cannot easily struggle free of our cultural context to predict the future of warfare.

Nonetheless, we try. We predict that SSCs will continue to be the most likely missions we will have to conduct, but we must remain prepared for the most dangerous threats as well: nuclear, biological, or chemical attacks on the United States. Successful prosecution of these various missions demands a flexible and diverse force that we can multitask. Our forces must be able to respond to a spectrum of operations, from humanitarian relief operations (HUMROs) and noncombatant evacuation operations (NEOs) to MTWs.

Clearly, we are going to need the most intelligent, fittest team players with character that the nation can provide. Equally clearly, our demographics will not support an all-male military of the size we need with the level of quality that we believe is best for all of our varied missions without an ongoing active draft (which our nation will not countenance). We know that our allies and our adversaries will mobilize their entire populations—sometimes routinely, but certainly when dire situations demand it. We know also that our soldiers, sailors, airmen, and marines must be disciplined, dedicated, and emotionally mature to do the things we ask them to do, from fighting to role modeling.

To enable our armed forces to do all these tasks well, we must call on our greatest national strength, the very characteristic we demonstrate around the world when we assist other peoples in developing democratic civil society with a subordinate military: diversity and pluralism, which are strengths in and of themselves.[118] Our servicemembers come from and must relate to an increasingly diverse society; they must work within a more diverse military and increasingly within a complex interagency setting that seeks synergies between all our tools for national security. Our armed forces also will try to attain security multipliers by working as much as possible within very diverse coalitions around the world. We will do our military members a huge disservice if, because of narrow thinking, we do not give them the best training and tools for operating in this environment. They do not simply need excellent, advanced equipment. They need the training, co-workers, and leadership to meet and match the global environment that continually affects our national security.

To meet our future security needs, then, the bottom line is this: We must not fall back on emotionalism, nor can we rely on the accuracy of our predictions about the specifics of the future battlefield. The former has never gotten us very far in supporting our real security needs, and we do not have a successful track record with the latter. I submit that instead of fear-mongering and crystal ball gazing, we should rely on the political ideology that we say we believe in to shape a force we can trust. We must accept all Americans who meet real standards and who are willing to serve. In fact, I argue that all citizens should serve in some capacity.

Historical monographs on military history, women's history, and minorities' history show that although we usually trot out our cultural vision of a "warrior" for these debates, that vision generally has not matched the people we recruit. We recruit whomever we need at the time—and sooner or later, we need just about everybody. Who would have expected, for instance, that one of the critical cadres of World War II would be a bunch of brilliant mathematicians, stereotypically envisioned with hair wildly askew, scribbling on chalkboards and mumbling in the trenches? Indeed, we did not need them in the trenches but at their chalkboards, breaking the enemy's communications codes and designing weapons of mass destruction. In the same arena, men who spoke English only as a second language—the Navajo talkers—provided us with an unbreakable code.

Similarly, historical stereotypes of women and women's "place" hamper our debate on the integration of women into the armed forces. Real women and the work that they have been involved in—not to mention their participation in war—seldom have fit the stereotype, yet the stereotype informs our historical memory.[119] In fact, we remember what fits our cultural ideology better than we remember reality.[120] Twentieth-century American history really shows that women's place, socially and culturally, has changed over time. Women are not only involved in more occupations; they also have even more responsibilities in the home than they had at the turn of the 20th century or in the 1950s. Few people would argue that the way we treated minorities at those times is the way we should treat them in the armed forces today. Likewise, women's role in the military has reflected changes in the larger society: Their roles have expanded to include more kinds of work, as well as more dangerous and heavier labor in industry, police forces, fire departments, and high-technology business.

By the same token, if women could be in the Navy, why not on ships? If they could be on ships, why not on "combat" ships? If women could be soldiers in Combat Service Support, why not in Combat Arms? If they could fly fighters for training in the Navy, why not in combat for the Air Force? If they could fly heavy cargo aircraft and civilian airliners, why not heavy bombers?

Just as with the integration of African Americans, we see transition as a series of steps that slowly overtakes white male privilege. First, bar "out groups" from the nation-state's defining institution. When they are needed, bring them in—but without full benefits and only in low-prestige jobs; through that process, some jobs become feminized (e.g., administration and personnel) and some racialized (e.g., ship's steward and EEO counselor), so that white men largely reject these career fields. When the out groups are needed more urgently and the unfairness of their treatment is exposed, integrate them only to the level of the defining jobs of the particular service—combat ships in the Navy; combat aircraft in the Air Force; infantry, armor, and artillery in the Army; and as little as possible in the Marine Corps because almost all Marines are combat soldiers. Once the core leadership positions are effectively locked out, we revert to arguments such as those in the first part of this paper—women and minorities ruin team cohesion and cannot lead—which are more difficult to refute when no women or minorities are allowed on critical teams or into the jobs that define leadership; as a result, these arguments are pursued largely on the basis of uninformed opinion rather than evidence.

Therefore, the measure of quality in servicemembers should be based not on group stereotypes but on individual merit and the obligations of citizenship. I think we would all agree, black and white and male and female, that we want to be judged as individuals by our performance, not by group stereotypes. That is what our political philosophy demands. The obligations and the benefits of citizenship must extend equally to us all. Just as parents, teachers, or coaches may treat each child, student, or player according to his or her different abilities and emotional dispositions, our best military leaders treat service members in a way that elicits their best efforts and ensures equality of opportunity as they seek to guarantee a quality outcome—in this case, successful performance in military operations and national security.

Privilege is not given up easily, however. We have undermined the quality of our force by preventing capable women from serving in the core functions of our Services. Arbitrarily barred from these functions, they cannot truly be a part of the team, nor can they contribute their full skills and capabilities. Although we should not pretend to know the particulars of what future warfare will bring, we do know that any future war will require us to field a quality force. The integrity of our society and its ideals require that the force we field represents the society it defends—and the society it defends believes in civil equality. These ideals are not mutually exclusive; they cannot be. We know women can do the job. We know society will call for them to do it when the chips are down because it always has. We know that every skill is needed and that anyone who can perform the required tasks is a valuable asset. The time has come to proceed to the discussion that really matters: Do citizens have a right or an obligation to serve?

❏ OUR QUESTIONABLE COMMITMENT TO DEMOCRACY: THE VIABILITY OF OUR POLITICAL PHILOSOPHY

As we have seen, the debate about integrating women into the military—or integrating them further—has been a "moving target." We can gather data about women's physical and intellectual abilities, and we can argue about their emotional and cultural suitability. We can debate endlessly about tomorrow's national security needs, and we can imagine future warfare and the types of people we will need for military operations. All of these arguments have been dealt with repeatedly in historical debate. Tenuous concerns about close quarters or bathrooms (e.g., on submarines) will evaporate as repeated deployments demonstrate that military effectiveness—and the very old, tried-and-true method of a simple reversible sign on the door showing who is in the latrine—is more important than obsession with "sex in the trenches." Increasing reliance on stand-off operations, nonlethal technologies, peacekeeping and -shaping missions, and information warfare will further blur the definitions of *combat* and *warrior* and complicate the skills these roles require. Pragmatic predictions about the continuing expansion of women's volunteer service roles do nothing to resolve what many observers regard as the foundation of inequality between the sexes in the U.S. military—the civic obligations of citizens embodied in the draft.

The discussion of citizenship that follows shows that it, too, has been a "moving target" in history. Rights and obligations have been variously defined over the more than 200 years of our national existence. Beyond simply historicizing this debate, therefore, we must decide what citizens can expect from the nation if they fulfill their obligations, and we must pin down what we want those civic obligations to be.

First, we must undertake a historical review of definitions of citizenship as they have been formulated around race, gender, and other categories. Several outstanding historical and legal works can inform this exercise.[121] This review will bring us to a philosophic milestone at which we must examine our ideology and decide whether we can live by it in the real world—or whether it has been and will be a comforting fiction that exists only on paper and in our minds. Will our cultural biases win out over our political philosophy? Or can national security be achieved through liberal democracy? Are pluralism and military effectiveness mutually exclusive? We have only tentative answers because we have not explicitly addressed the issue of women's military participation and the civic implications from this perspective in the courts or in legislation.

To begin, we should define our terms. Unfortunately, people usually speak about citizenship and the practice of democracy as if our definitions of these concepts have been consistent and clearly understood. Neither is the case. Citizenship has been a "moving target" not only for women and minorities but for white, heterosexual men as well. Of course, this lack of a settled definition creates problems at the very heart of a debate on the further integration of women in the military. Nevertheless, a discussion about what constitutes first-class political, social, and economic status is essential if we are to move forward with a national security policy that is based on our ideals, rather than our emotional baggage of mythical pasts and imagined futures.

Historian Peter Riesenberg and others have written extensively on the historical construction of citizenship and military obligation. Riesenberg verifies that military service has been connected to the concept of citizenship since its origins in Sparta—the first Greek *polis* to develop the practices of citizenship. He tells us that "citizenship developed against the backdrop of war . . . civic virtue [was] defined in terms of absolute military efficiency."[122] Athens added jury service and voting to the definition of citizenship; Rome offered male commoners citizenship in exchange for emergency defense service. No matter what the historical reality, culturally men were defined as the warriors and women as the protected; women could not be part of the political community because their first loyalty was constructed to be to their family.[123]

Some Renaissance thinkers muted the connection between arms-bearing and citizenship. To Machiavelli, however, the connection was central: Only men who owned property had a stake in the state's defense and sovereignty. Citizenship was limited to these men; women did not belong to the body politic. Later, English writers such as James Burgh expanded the connection to include freemen. Freemen bore arms in the republican tradition; all other men were "slaves," and women were objects to be protected.[124]

Central to our discussion, historian Linda Kerber traces the history of arms-bearing in the American colonies, where it shifted between right and obligation. Householders were required to defend their communities. Interestingly, infirm men and widows who headed their own households were required to pay for substitutes; we do not know whether the widows were allowed to turn out with weapons instead if they so chose. Utopian writers also constructed the defense of the community as the responsibility of "freeholders." Some went farther: Sir Thomas More's *Utopia* posited that men and women alike would not only fight but also train, "should the need arise." More also believed that children should accompany fathers and mothers to war to support their parents. By the 18th century, bearing arms was a right—as a check on government power—and an obligation, to help to preserve peace in the community. In any case, Kerber's research shows that at least as early as the 16th and 17th centuries, discursive spaces existed in which to think of women as equal citizens with regard to bearing the burden of the defense and security of the community.[125]

Our nation was born in a debate about the disenfranchisement of the colonies' male citizens in relation to the citizens of England. Not all the members of the colonies who fought for independence or supported that fight were enfranchised through our Revolution, however; many new rights pertained only to white men of property. Women and minorities had to fight for many years for rights that supposedly and rhetorically belonged to all human beings in the Lockean political thought on which we based our Constitution. As our Declaration of Independence states, a government is rightly formed by, gains power from, and rests on the consent of the governed. Even if we limited our discussion to life, liberty, and the pursuit of happiness—leaving aside the vote and property ownership—we would see that these supposedly inalienable rights, which we claimed were inherent in humanity, did not accrue to everyone who lived in the new states. As under English common law, women were still considered property under the principle of coverture, in which they had no independent political or economic existence apart from their husbands or fathers.

With the spectacle of veterans being denied suffrage because of property requirements and the destabilizing influence of being in the New World, away from traditional authorities, there was room for new conceptions of citizenship. In part, the new Republic would define being a part of the polity by "allegiance." This definition allowed for expansion of the franchise to white immigrants and even left room for discussion about including women. Some advocates, such as Mary Wollestonecraft, argued for women's competence to participate as first-class citizens. Others argued that childbirth was women's reciprocal obligation to bearing arms. Still others discounted women by calling them noncitizens, based on the principle of coverture. Several post-Revolutionary legal cases decided that a woman could not swear allegiance to the new nation separately from her husband. Kerber concludes that "the Revolutionary generation passed on complex and sometimes contradictory understandings of the meaning of citizenship."[126]

Within these complex understandings, first-class American citizenship—at this time including the right to vote—often was connected with military service and national defense. Nine of the original states' constitutions included the "duty of the citizen to render military service" and compelled *him* to do so if necessary. Although the political and legal language of the day often used the terms "persons" and "citizens," most often the words meant only white men.[127] On the other hand, we all know the story of the long fight for the vote for black men and all women. Black men fought during our Revolution and in the American West before they were given the right to vote (and we know their ability to exercise that right was further infringed for many years after it was supposedly guaranteed by law). Women not only supported the regular forces in these conflicts but also took up arms, either in disguise or to protect their homesteads.

Connections between service and citizenship continued to be complex. As early as 1812, some opponents of the draft tried unsuccessfully to detach citizenship from arms bearing, arguing that Congress did not have the power to conscript. In 1856, Chief Justice Roger Taney ruled that Dred Scot did not have constitutional rights partly because African American men were excluded from the obligation to serve in the militia—even though disabled white men were not obligated but were still considered citizens. During and after the Civil War, the link between the obligation to bear arms and the rights of citizenship grew stronger; even before the passage of the Thirteenth Amendment, the Emancipation Proclamation merged the two for black soldiers. The rhetoric that they had bought their rights with blood (combat service) entered constitutional and Reconstruction debates.[128] It is difficult to imagine that citizenship and service could still be restricted after this experience, but it was. Obviously our political philosophy allowed for expansion of both concepts; just as obviously, cultural ideology held us back.

Kerber argues that after the Civil War, with the link between service and citizenship strengthened racially, the distinction between persons who bore arms and those who did not grew more invidious. As veterans claimed political and economic entitlement, there was an increasing sense that individuals who did not fight were not politically equal. In 1870, the New York *World* made the link explicit: "Woman, being exempted by her sex from military duties and responsibilities, holds all her rights by sufferance. . . . " Claiming that men showed the strength of their character in military service, the newspaper called for "female soldiering" if there was to be equality between the sexes.[129]

Kerber found that from 1865 to 1930, suffragists responded to such arguments connecting equal obligations to soldier and equality of citizenship with combinations of four claims. One was that women risked their lives for the country in childbirth. John Stuart Mill insisted instead that women had always fought in wars (openly or in disguise), which proved their fitness for citizenship. Third, some people claimed that voting and arms bearing were not linked at all: Men between the ages of 18 and 21 could fight but not vote; men who were over military age did not lose their right to vote; and women could be exempt (like Quakers), pay substitutes, or support war efforts in nursing or industry. Finally, more and more suffragists rejected female arms bearing in favor of juxtaposing women's pacifism to men's military service—women's political power would provide a voice of reason to dissuade men's warlike passions.[130]

As Kerber shows, by accident and intent the government, public, courts, and military leaders came to equate military service not only with basic rights such as voting but also with privileges and benefits such as education and housing loans and health care. Some of the privileges associated with military service were less tangible—such as being valued by one's community or gaining favor in elections for sacrifices made on behalf of the nation. Veterans have always "defended sovereignty and safe borders" and embodied wisdom and strength gained through adversity; military service also has symbolized discipline and dedication. Whether they were willing (volunteered) or compelled (drafted) to risk their lives for the collective good, men have been given a little something extra as citizens, tangibly and intangibly.[131]

The leaders of the movements for minority and women's enfranchisement understood this connection between military service—particularly in wartime—and full citizenship. Leaders in both struggles debated whether citizens should sacrifice first and ask for rights after the conflict or whether the government and public ought to recognize their status first to merit their sacrifices for rights that white men apparently inherited at birth. The question, really, was whether such an inheritance should pertain to all born or naturalized citizens, without any further requirement, or whether there should be some test to pass. Obviously, there was a double standard. White men were born with privileges to vote, serve on juries, enjoy equality before the law, and own property. In return, they were obliged to follow the law, serve in the armed forces if called upon, and pay taxes, at a minimum. Yet minority men had to fulfill these same obligations, repeatedly and over time, to earn the basic privileges that were white men's birthright. Women did not gain the right to vote until they had served (outside the nurse corps) in our first mass, industrialized, foreign war, as well as on the homefront in critical war industries.

A review of our political and legal history shows that we have awarded full citizenship only to persons who were expected to serve—even though we specifically prevented other groups from serving. In other words, we told women and minority men that they could not serve, then used their lack of service as partial justification for denying them all the benefits of citizenship, though we still expected them to abide by the law and pay their taxes.

This history is particularly ironic in that "taxation without representation" was one of the first issues to crystallize our political philosophy. Although white male colonists aimed at breaking England's paternalistic control over them, women and minority men were considered to be "children" who were politically represented by the master/husband—or not to be persons in their own right at all. It should come as no surprise that people who were denied civil rights and privileges in earlier periods focused on military service as a way to earn the rights that others inherited by virtue of their race and gender. It also is not surprising that other still-marginalized groups, such as homosexual Americans, have drawn the same conclusions and are pursuing honorable service opportunities. Whether constructed as a right, an obligation, or a privilege, service in the armed forces has been the measure of true personhood in this country since its inception. In fact, for the purposes of this discussion, it has been the measure of "manhood."

We have tended to equate all military service with citizenship, whether individual men served two years or twenty, in peacetime or wartime, in combat or desk jobs. Even more interesting, the mere fact that men might be vulnerable to a draft or even registration for a draft made them that much more politically and socially "equal" (in the Orwellian sense) than women. This construction blithely ignored the fact that even men who might be subject to registration, if drafted, might gain deferments or be disqualified for any number of reasons. Yet because of combat restrictions that continue to be the basis for barring women from certain career fields, the unconscious public assumption remains that all men have served or are vulnerable to serve in combat, whereas no women are vulnerable—reinforcing the social, political, and economic privilege men "deserve" because of ostensible risk to defend the nation.[132]

Interestingly, this debate is changing somewhat as politicians in the past several elections have found it useful to distinguish between men who served and those who avoided service (Bush versus Clinton) and particularly those who served in combat (especially if injured) and those who avoided service (Dole versus Clinton). Ironically, although the fire was aimed at Democrat Clinton, several conservatives had to run for cover or make excuses when their own records of service were found to be lacking because of educational deferments (which only our upper classes could afford) or medical reasons, real or contrived—among them Newt Gingrich, Phil Gramm, and even radio demagogue Rush Limbaugh. The use of military service as a litmus test for public office further underlines the link between military service—more particularly, dangerous military service—and citizenship. We have lately drawn distinctions not only between those who were subject to military obligation and those who did not serve but between those who served but appear to have gotten off lightly, with assignments to the Reserves or National Guard—such as Dan Quayle, George W. Bush, and Bill Bradley—and those who actually went to Vietnam.[133] Now there is a further distinction drawn between Al Gore's service (perceived as not dangerous) as a military journalist in Vietnam and John McCain's experience of combat and brutalization as a POW.[134]

In addition, the news media did mention that Elizabeth Dole did not serve in the military. They did not mention that she did not have the same opportunities to serve (2 percent enrollment ceiling at the time), nor would her service have been socially acceptable during the ages when she would have been available. Nor did the press equate her Red Cross service with armed service, which further suggests (however much we deny it) that some service is more equal than others in validating full citizenship. The message: Risk counts.

Our popular culture, in fiction and in the news media, has associated maleness with the supreme sacrifice. This myth ignores the historical fact that civilian and military women have volunteered and served in harm's way during conflict and that many men have not—either intentionally or because they were denied entry. In our cultural imagination, all men are warriors and all women are civilians to be protected. We can find abundant evidence in two of our most popular news organs, the *Washington Post* and the *New York Times,* in which there have been many calls for *all* citizens to defend their country. Only a few of these calls to arms explicitly limited this call to men; most assumed it was understood.[135]

This history, of course, raises the question of why do we not deny full citizenship to those who do not serve because they refuse to when we deny it to those who cannot serve because they are barred. This inconsistency in our political rhetoric and practice is exhibited repeatedly in our history. The disconnect between our cultural ideology—which is not the reality for most Americans—and our political ideals is obvious if one simply looks at the historical evidence of our public debates, from those on Universal Military Service to those on the Equal Rights Amendment. The unreality of our cultural ideology must be exposed and the practical implications of our political ideology debated from an historically informed perspective if we are to move ahead.

Besides Kerber's excellent treatment of the subject, several other historical and political works add to our knowledge and ability to grasp and redefine the terms of this debate on full citizenship and military obligations. Jean Elshtain's *Women and War* is an enduring examination of the cultural construction of a polarity between male warriors and female nurturers that persists even in the face of real evidence that this division is a fiction. Other reputable works have tried to call our attention to the inconsistencies between our historical memory and reality. Notable among these efforts are Stephanie Coonts's *The Way We Never Were* (specifically regarding the 1950s) and William Chafe's essays in *Women and Equality.* Coonts demonstrates that an in-depth look at the 1950s shows that there was no idyllic era when women did not have to work outside the home and families self-actualized in the suburbs. Chafe shows that although there may be some grounds to dismiss certain historical comparisons between racial and gender-based discrimination, black men and all women have suffered from discrimination based on readily obvious physical characteristics.[136]

More recent works inform our discussion even more. Richard Kohn has edited a volume of essays, *The United States Military under the Constitution of the United States, 1789–1989.* In this volume, Kohn and Richard Morris examine the origins of our Constitution and its relationship to national security. Allan Millet looks at the Constitution and our concept of the citizen-soldier, and Bernard Nalty explores the Constitution in relation to black servicemen. Finally, Jonathan Lurie offers a review of how the Supreme Court has exercised "Civil Rights Supervision" over the armed forces.[137] Several other notable authors have written about civil-military relations to examine the military's connection, or lack thereof, to our civil society and to propose approaches for deciding who should serve and how their service operates in social and political ways.[138]

David A. J. Richards makes a legal argument that relates our rights to the Constitution. Richards reminds us of the legal basis of our political philosophy and the rights contained therein; he addresses specifics about military service. Richards presents a compelling case for how injustices today are related to historic struggles for equality. He specifically draws on rights-based dissent, abolitionism, and antebellum feminism in a solid interpretation of the 13th and 14th amendments.

In keeping with our Lockean political and intellectual roots, Richards argues, "All political power . . . could be legitimate only if it met the requirement of extending to all persons subject to such power nationally enforceable standards of respect for inalienable human rights and the use of power to pursue the public interest."[139] Richards further claims that this position must include "the demand that all persons subject to the burden of allegiance to the political power of the United States be accorded both their natural rights as persons and their equal rights as citizens, based on the fundamental egalitarian requirement of politically legitimate government stated by the equal protection clause."[140]

Richards's argument is based on a conception of American revolutionary constitutionalism as a test of the legitimacy of political power by respect for inalienable human rights. He uses the U.S. Constitution and the Reconstruction Amendments as the basis for his argument that legal and political views that are based on originalism or majoritarian democracy are historically misguided. These two approaches are inconsistent with our political philosophy of basic respect for fundamental and inalienable human rights and the suspectness of gender as a category that abrogates equal treatment under the law. Richards calls into question any socially or culturally constructed classification of individuals as the basis of legitimate state concern with equal rights. His argument insists on proper historical contextualization, and, in an appeal to our constitutional conscience, he challenges all Americans to fulfill a responsibility "to demand that their law and public and private culture conform to their best critical understandings of American ideals and traditions."[141]

These works on our cultural heritage and historicization of our political philosophy—not to mention the constitutional basis of our armed forces—ultimately are important. For our discussion, however, we should return to two more specific arguments in Kerber's *No Constitutional Right to be Ladies*. In her work, Kerber writes explicitly about female citizens and how women's rights and obligations have been constructed over time—especially how their participation in citizenship has differed from men's. Looking specifically at obligations rather than rights, she reviews these differences by gender, race, and class exploring treason, vagrancy, taxation, and jury service. Her final chapter is most relevant to this discussion; she investigates how, beginning in the 1970s, the courts have been asked to examine how veterans' preferences have operated in employment; whether female servicemembers should have equal benefits for their families; whether pacifism could keep a woman from gaining American citizenship; and how the question of conscription should inform debates over civil rights.

What Kerber finds is that the principle of coverture, in substituting duties to family and spouse for civic duties, acted on American women implicitly much longer than it did explicitly. This principle had been repeatedly eroded, but not until 1992 did the Supreme Court rule that men no longer had power over the bodies of their wives (*Planned Parenthood of Pennsylvania v. Casey,* 112 S.Ct. 2791). She suggests that this ruling opened the doors for the wider debate we seek here. Because the courts also found that women have no "inherent right" to be excused from obligations of citizenship—including the risky service of the military—Kerber also maintains that, far from being a privilege, this "right to be ladies" negatively affected women's ability to exercise other rights such as trials by juries of one's peers.[142]

Historically, however, even without being obligated, women served the military and in the military—with few if any benefits. As armies became industrialized and bureaucratized state institutions, they more successfully excluded women who tried to disguise themselves as men, as well as camp followers, and officially included only nurses and laundresses. Military service did not bring equal benefits even for these women, however. Even though white nurses were an official part of the military, they received only "relative rank"—and only after 50 years of struggling for some military status. Another world war and another couple of decades were required for nurses to receive real rank and commensurate benefits. Female Signal Corps recruits who had served with the Army overseas did not gain military benefits at all, even though they had been subject to courts martial and military regulations. Black women were limited in their participation in the Nurse Corps, and in the World War II WAC, they did not receive the same benefits as white women. During that war, they were completely excluded from the Navy, Coast Guard, and the Women's Air Service Pilots (WASP). Black and white women were limited in pay, rank, opportunities, and benefits. In fact, when women were first accepted into the Army's auxiliary corps (WAAC), they were not provided any benefits or even reemployment rights after discharge. Even after WAAC members transitioned to the WAC, benefits would extend for only six months after the duration.[143]

Limitations arising from confusion about how to construct a citizen's obligation to defense and security are evident at every turn. Although female military leaders stressed women's willingness to fulfill citizenship obligations, they did not press for rights or benefits. Like nurses, other servicewomen held "relative rank," so no one would confuse them with actual soldiers. Even after attaining "real" rank they could not serve in command positions, or even supervisory positions over men, until after 1967. Female veterans were not allowed membership in the Veterans of Foreign Wars organization, even if they had served overseas. Finally, even though WASPs risked their lives and some gave their lives, they received no veterans' status or benefits until the late 1970s—and then only after a long legal fight.

From the end of World War II to the ERA debate of the 1970s, there was little discussion of women in the forces or the conscription of women; they served in very small numbers. Women were treated very differently even as a complex set of circumstances moved us to the AVF in 1973. Only after military planners decided they could not recruit enough middle-class white men and the Civil Rights and women's movements changed the public's conceptions of fairness in employment and opportunity did the Services turn to women.[144] Because more women were needed, military leaders sought nontraditional arenas in which they could contribute—the most nontraditional being combat positions. As we know, many nontraditional occupations have been opened to women over the past 20 years. The law only barred women from combat vessels and aircraft in the Navy and Air Force; the Army excluded women from combat positions by policy. Definitions of combat positions have been as fluid as the definition of combat itself. For example, men in Vietnam were denied combat pay and awards in the early years of that conflict because we did not want to admit to people on the homefront that we were at war.

More recently the combat distinction has been called a "social marker rather than a substantive boundary."[145] Our doctrine and tactics, as well as our strategy, recognize that in modern warfare there is little distinction between combatants and noncombatants; all are at risk. None of the 13 women who were killed in the Gulf War were in combat positions, and many men in combat occupations were at little risk.[146]

From military and veteran's general benefits we come to a more specific consideration. The issue of veterans' preferences is very important in showing how the previous limits on female military participation kept women from equal opportunity in the civilian job market. The public and judicial debate about these preferences, especially those for disabled veterans, are evidence that despite historical evidence that women did serve and were injured and killed in military service, the public generally does not remember their sacrifices and constructs all women as civilians. In addition, the preference debate shows that although women's service was restricted by numbers and occupation, and those who did participate were volunteers, these facts get lost as people viscerally address how male veterans sacrificed for their nation. An indication of the degree to which women's military contributions were considered inferior to men's is the fact that women veterans were placed in the lowest category of veterans' preference—behind wives and mothers of disabled and deceased male veterans. The legal cases Kerber reviews demonstrate that civilian privilege does come from military service—but only for white men.[147]

Kerber traces the way veterans' status generally has operated to provide privilege. From the Civil War pension system for a generation of "'righteously privileged,' largely middle-class Northern white men" to the expansive GI Bill after World War II, men gained social insurance, education, home ownership, and jobs. These preferences did not work the same way for men and women. Neither husbands of disabled female veterans nor widowers were included in the 1944 Act.[148]

When some states sought to limit veterans' hiring preferences, conservatives fighting to maintain the system of "absolute preferences"[149] argued under the assumption that all veterans served under fire—and that women did not contribute to the war effort at all. A news columnist in Massachusetts wrote, "I'll tell you what's unconstitutional; it's unconstitutional to give those juicy Civil Service jobs away to panty-waists and shirkers who never marched proudly in the uniform of their country." Ignoring the limits on women's service, other editorials and columnists attacked women who "had excused [themselves] from military obligation."[150] The press also tried to inflame public emotions by linking women's claims for equal opportunity and benefits for service with gay rights and funding for abortion.

In the late 1970s, as women fought for reconsideration of "absolute veteran's preferences," the Supreme Court asked the question, "Is it also discriminatory to bar women from combat and then make combat service the basis of the preference?" Despite the question, in 1979 the Court ruled in favor of maintaining these preferences. The dissenters, Thurgood Marshall and William Brennan, wrote that "the absolute-preference formula has rendered desirable state civil service employment an almost exclusively male prerogative. . . . this consequence follows foreseeably, indeed inexorably, from the long history of policies severely limiting women's participation in the military"[151] (*Personnel Administrator v. Feeney*, 442 U.S. 256, 283). The majority pointed out that the state did not intend discrimination, and the preference system affected male nonveterans as well. They did not acknowledge, however, that there was no ceiling on men's service. Historian Sheila Tobias confirms in her study of the postwar careers of veterans what we have observed: that "service in war gives [male] veterans a stock of political capital" that they can use as evidence of experience, patriotism, and claims to "competence in matters of foreign and military policy."[152]

Beyond benefits and preferences, however, Kerber argues that in the 20th century the connection between citizenship and military obligation most often has been debated in the context of the draft—and it is here that "citizenship" has most often been unconsciously equated with "male." Defending the World War I draft, the Supreme Court expressed this connection: "[T]he highest duty of a citizen is to bear arms at the call of the nation. . . . [T]he very conception of a just government and its duty to the citizen includes the reciprocal obligation of the citizen to render military service in case of need and the right to compel it" (*Selective Draft Law Cases*, 245 U.S. 366, 368, 278–80, 290 [1918]).[153] When the draft was reinstituted in 1940, the fact that it applied only to men did not obviate the justification that it was the obligation of "every citizen."[154] In the cases Kerber examines, we see how obvious is the disjuncture between rhetoric and practice. Because we can say "all citizens" but mean men, we can believe that we grant all citizens equal status when we do not. Our expectations for service and benefit have been different for men and women.

Even when there was no active draft, the nation anticipated one. The Supreme Court in 1929 ruled that Rosika Schwimmer, a famous pacifist who also was over military age, could not become a citizen because she would not affirm on her naturalization questionnaire or in court that she was "willing to take up arms in defense of this country." This ruling came in spite of the fact that natural-born citizens who were pacifists were not required to take the oath or to bear arms. More important, women were specifically barred from service and combat. The Court's majority asserted that "it is the duty of citizens by force of arms to defend our government against all enemies whenever necessity arises is a fundamental principle of the Constitution" (*U.S. v. Schwimmer*, 279 U.S. at 648, 650).[155]

Legislative attempts to change this nonsensical requirement in the naturalization process were repeatedly rejected, as were attempts to try to match rhetoric with reality by allowing women to serve. Even foreign female conscientious objectors, who had served in noncombat roles in World War

I, were rejected for citizenship for refusing to agree to bear arms. During the congressional hearings on their cases, women representing patriotic societies testified against the prospective immigrants: "[T]he mothers of the men who have fought for this country beseech you not to give the great privilege of American citizenship to men and women who are not willing to bear arms and to pay the debt of devotion they owe to this country."[156] Not until 1946 did the Court reverse itself and allow conscientious objectors to serve in other ways; the 1950 naturalization law allowed for an alternate oath.[157] Nevertheless, the rhetoric connecting citizenship and service did not change; our belief system did not necessarily track with the Court and the law.

According to Kerber, the idea of the citizen-soldier was vigorously deployed during World War II. The 1940 Selective Training and Service Act was based on a concept of universal obligation: "In a free society the obligations and privileges of military training and service should be shared generally."[158] American women were still excluded, however. There was a discussion about drafting white women nurses in 1942 and 1944, but enough of them volunteered that this step was not taken. Even more consideration was given to drafting women for war industry, and Republicans proposed "universal registration" for national service that would include women who did not have children younger than eighteen living with them. Kerber quotes Undersecretary of War Robert Patterson: "[T]he democratic way is to recognize the equality in obligation of all to serve . . . in the way that will best serve the Nation."[159] Some women's groups opposed the idea of registering women, claiming that "women are naturally and rightly the homemakers. . . . They play their part during the war by 'keeping the home fires burning' . . . and by carrying on the services that hold the community together."[160] Members of the War Manpower Commission disagreed, however, criticizing these naysayers for "thinking entirely in terms of the privileges and freedoms which a democracy is created to protect, but [ignoring] completely the fundamental obligations on which the success of any democracy rests."[161]

Kerber argues that the consensus that emerged after the war was that only dictatorships sought to militarize women—despite the fact that other democracies conscripted women; in democracies, women were supposed to fulfill their obligation within their homes.[162] To take Kerber's argument even further, this attitude denied history and recent reality: We had won the war in part because of the mobilization of a large number of women into industry and services, not to mention the military. At the same time, the government and the press had criticized women who stayed at home even though they struggled with child care, transportation, and inequitable pay and benefits.[163]

Kerber does show that in 1948, following the Soviet detonation of an atomic bomb, the debate on Universal Service was revitalized. General Dwight Eisenhower testified that women would have to be drafted in the next war because any future war would be "total war." Aside from Eisenhower's statement, gender was barely mentioned in the renewed debate, and when the term *citizen* was used it obviously referred only to men. The nation did consider drafting female nurses again for the Korean and Vietnam conflicts, however.[164]

Kerber points out that the link between service obligation and citizenship was dampened but not obviated by the Vietnam experience. Draft resisters who fled the country lost the benefits of citizenship by doing so. Although the AVF ended the draft and discussions of obligation in 1973, the modern debate about the Equal Rights Amendment soon brought the issue center stage again, as the elites argued about whether the amendment would require equal military service and risk for women. Opponents defined the terms of the debate, and proponents could not move them off the specter of the nation drafting half of its combat forces from the ranks of women and making all women use coed restrooms. The anti-ERA forces would countenance no discussion of deferments, exemptions, and qualifications. If the ERA had passed it might have made different age, marital, and educational standards for women illegal in one fell swoop, but opponents persisted. The emotional arguments won a huge victory for Phyllis Schlafly and the forces of conservatism and anti-feminism.

In fact, the place where we see "military obligation" operate most differently in relation to gender is in the draft debate during the Vietnam conflict and during the ERA debate of the 1970s. Several draft-eligible men brought court cases against the draft and registration. They primarily believed that citizens should have the right to question war's purposes. Their lawyers, however, used the "kitchen sink" approach in their briefs; they threw in the argument that men bore the citizenship obligation disproportionately in this arena. In an irony of history, the 14th Amendment—which was written to protect minorities—was used by the dominant group in society as white, middle-class men claimed they were denied equal protection. After the courts rejected questions about whether the war was illegal or whether the state had the right to conscript, gender discrimination was the only remaining point of contention.

As in the immigration cases, the state reserved the right to require even female citizens to carry arms. The fact was that many men were exempt from the draft—131 for every 100 inducted. In every previous case that questioned the draft on the basis of gender discrimination, however, the courts had ruled that as long as Congress offered a rational basis for a male-only draft, the courts would not interfere with the legislative prerogative. The language of some of the decisions would seem obviously wrongheaded today, however: Judges repeatedly equated men's military service with women's childbearing responsibilities as reciprocal obligations to the state. These arguments continued to ignore childless women or men who were judged unfit for service.[165]

By far the most important case challenging the male-only draft in the period during and after Vietnam was Robert Goldberg's. When Goldberg first became draft eligible in 1968, he had a medical student deferment, and the unequal treatment of men and women was increasingly being questioned. The legal context of unequal treatment was still pervasive, however. Military women were limited to traditional occupations. By the time the case made it to court in 1975, men had to register, but there were no draft calls. By then, Goldberg's lawyers could point out that old precedents had been undermined or overturned, and the traditional language of protection in civil affairs had eroded significantly. Women were coal miners and Merchant Marines and even Marine Corps tank mechanics. Several legal rulings indicated a significant change from earlier findings that a woman's place was in the home and her obligation to the state as a citizen was centered exactly there. If women's civic obligation was no longer to stay at home, however, what was it?

The Supreme Court had finally ruled in 1975 that men and women were equally obligated for jury duty.[166] Goldberg's lawyers also cited a 1973 finding against the military, when the Court ruled in favor of Sharron Frontiero's claim for equal benefits from the Air Force for her civilian husband. Although this case concerned benefits rather than obligation, and the Court treated gender discrimination as less serious than racial discrimination, the bench came closer to naming gender a "suspect classification" requiring "the discriminator to show not merely that discrimination was 'reasonable' but that it was *necessary* to achieve a constitutional objective." Furthermore, a Montana District Court had ruled against a male-only draft. Judge W. D. Murray wrote, "[T]he requirements of serving in the armed forces will undoubtedly be an unpleasant experience for many women; but it is an equally unattractive experience for many men . . . the sexual distinctions in the legislation which make him subject to induction are suspect classifications. . . . Women, just as men, are persons and citizens, and in the scheme of government under the Constitution they must be treated as equals of men both as to their rights and obligations. It does not suffice under the Constitution to treat women kindly because we love them. We must treat them rightly. The burdens of citizenship must be borne by all citizens."[167] Unfortunately, Murray's decision was overturned on appeal.

Most people probably had not heard of the Goldberg case when President Jimmy Carter proposed universal draft registration after the Soviet invasion of Afghanistan, spurring the public debate again. Although President Carter had been opposed to the draft more generally, he also was suspect of the military's gendered traditions—of which he had some knowledge as a Naval Academy graduate and veteran. Although most Democrats really wanted the AVF to survive, they agreed that if a draft were necessary, women as well as men should be registered. Defense officials acknowledged that women added to the quality of the force by relieving the Services of the need to draw from the bottom of the male applicant pool; they also acknowledged that women performed "impressively." Statistical indicators showed that women were doing so well that military leaders asked the Services to recruit more women than the 10 percent ceiling allowed and asked Congress to repeal combat exclusions. Congressional committees demurred.[168]

In the interest of maintaining the AVF, Richard Danzig, Secretary of Defense for Manpower, wanted to develop a coed registration plan for crisis mobilization. Instead, President Carter decided on actual coed registration. Although Carter supported equality for women, he was most focused on responding to the Soviet Union. The central issue for the public and in the congressional debate, however, became women in the military and in combat. The executive branch was convinced that women were essential to the AVF, but opponents made the argument that women in combat would be the logical consequence of increasing the numbers of women in the forces through a coed draft. Eventually, a male-only draft was retained when President Carter accepted a political deal that gave him the show of force he wanted.

During the debate, Danzig discounted a proposal for a "parallel female draft" for noncombat positions instead of a coed draft. He maintained that the draft worked that way in practice anyway: People were drafted for the jobs the military needed to fill—combat and noncombat. Only members who were "qualified" for certain positions were put in them. Kerber points out though that President Carter's formal statement on reinstituting registration redefined the debate. Carter said that universal registration reflected the changing times, including women's entry into many other professions, and that registration was an obligation. He also linked coed registration not only to women's increased willingness to meet the "responsibilities of citizenship" but also to the ERA: "There is no distinction possible, on the basis of ability or performance, that would allow me to exclude women from an obligation to register. . . . Just as we are asking women to assume additional responsibilities, it is more urgent than ever that the women in America have full and equal rights under the Constitution. Equal obligations deserve equal rights."[169] Nevertheless, Carter recognized that women's inclusion would be based on the Services' ability to use individuals' skills appropriately, leaving room for some or most women to be combat exempt and certainly not drafted in numbers equal to men.[170]

As the public debate on draft registration continued, congressional resistance grew, focusing almost exclusively on gender and the prospect of women serving in combat. Opponents ignored the fact that as with men who were required to register but might later be found unfit for service or apply for exemption under numerous categories, women would have access to various "outs." When Congress passed the male-only draft, Goldberg's anti-draft court case took center stage, and the ERA debate remained in the spotlight. This debate finally focused at least a little on women's obligations of citizenship and roles in the military.

Phyllis Schlafly, Jesse Helms, and Jerry Falwell, along with the Eagle Forum, the Moral Majority, and other organizations, claimed that President Carter was part of a feminist conspiracy to first repeal the combat exemption, then register women for the draft, and finally to draft women into combat positions. Actually, most feminists opposed the draft, war, and the military generally. If forced into an ideological corner, however, they would admit that the Constitution legitimated a draft. Therefore, if military service was an obligation of citizenship, it should rest on women equally. Judy Goldsmith of the National Organization for Women (NOW) testified to Congress, "Those who oppose the registration and draft for females say they seek to protect women. But omission from the registration and draft ultimately robs women of the right to first-class citizenship and paves the way to underpaying women all the days of their lives. Moreover, because men exclude women here, they justify excluding women from the decision making of our nation." She went on to point out that because of military training and education and veteran's benefits, the exclusion of most women, "far from protecting them, serves to continue their second-class citizenship, pay and opportunity." Goldsmith asked if women could be more readily victimized if they were constantly told they were unable to protect themselves and were not trained to do so. She asked if a man was less likely to attack a woman if he knew she had been trained as a Marine.[171]

Schlafly's associate, Kathleen Teague, responded that the purpose of the military was not upward mobility but the defense of the country. She argued that the "right" to be excluded from the draft was a right "which every American woman has enjoyed since our country was born," and she asked what women would get in return for giving up their "constitutional right to be treated like American ladies." Assistant Secretary of Defense Robert Pirie responded, "Since women have proven that they can serve successfully in the Armed Forces, equity suggests that they be liable to serve as draftees if conscription is reinstated." Kerber adds that although Teague emphasized the notion of "difference" as embedded in traditions of chivalry and religion, these ideals did not pertain to most women historically. Teague further averred, "Motherhood is not fungible with fatherhood . . . our daughters are not fungible with our sons. The drafting of wives is not fungible with the drafting of husbands. . . . Our young women have the right to be feminine, to get married, to build families and to have homes. Our daughters should not be deprived of rights which every American woman has enjoyed since our country was born."[172]

Teague continued by painting a barbaric picture of the military—on the basis of which one would have had to question the sanity of women who served as volunteers as well as the behavior of all military men: "We don't want our daughters subjected to the Army environment where there is little or no privacy, where the rape rate is considerably higher than in civilian life, where there is open toleration of immoral sex . . . where illegitimate births receive equal honor and financial rewards with legitimate births."[173] One wonders why anyone would have let their sons join or why Teague would not have insisted on a quarantine of soldiers from civil and civilized society.

Schlafly and Teague claimed that people who argued for equal rights and equal obligations were in the minority and were aberrant, accusing opponents of being "a handful of women, unhappy with their gender, [who] want to be treated like men."[174] Today's opponents use a similar argument; they propose that if a majority of women do not want combat positions opened or coed draft registration, this attitude somehow would allow them to abrogate the obligations of citizenship. Perhaps if a majority decided they should not pay taxes or serve on juries, such behaviors would be permissible as well.

In response to the Eagle Forum position, Goldberg's lawyer, Donald Weinberg, set out to show through technical considerations and historical material that the male-only draft was less a matter of reasonable congressional prerogative than flat-out sexual discrimination. Weinberg pointed out that women already were operating anti-aircraft weapons and servicing front-line tanks—and that the Congress had passed the ERA and was sending it to the states for ratification. He also questioned why men had to prove ineligibility for the draft, whereas it was presumed for women; he maintained that this different treatment was just as wrong as presuming women to be dependent but making men prove it (*Frontiero v. Richardson*, 411 U.S. 677 [1977]). The Justice Department countered that women "could not fight" and that "every nation in the world" subscribed to that policy.[175] Weinberg replied that women could fight and had fought and that other nations had used women fighters.[176]

Previously, on the case's way to the Supreme Court, the Pennsylvania District Court had ruled that "classifications based upon gender, not unlike those based upon race, have traditionally been the touchstone for pervasive and often subtle discrimination." The District Court would not accept "outdated stereotypical notions" or "administrative convenience" (as the military had argued in *Frontiero*); it ruled that the argument that women needed to be "protected" was equally suspect. Judge Edward Cahn wrote, "It is incongruous that Congress believes on the one hand that it substantially enhances national defense to constantly expand the utilization of women in the military, and on the other hand endorses legislation excluding women from the pool of registrants available for induction."[177] This court found that the Military Selective Service Act of 1980 violated the Fifth Amendment.[178] The Supreme Court reinvigorated the public debate on women and the draft, women in combat, and women in the military more generally by accepting the appeal. The issues of citizenship and the ERA would continue to be a part of the public debate for the time being.

In the appeal, opponents to a universal draft testified that the legislative branch possessed the power to determine military strength and that some religions (in this case Orthodox Jews) would not let women register. The Eagle Forum brought 16 draft-age young women forward to testify that they did not want to be drafted, go to war, or serve in the military. The young women who testified also expressed fears of sexual abuse and being captured by the enemy. The Forum claimed that women's exemption was like that of clergy in that women, too, upheld the American family, and serving would violate their modesty and "nature as a woman."

The suit was not about women, however. Kerber shows us the ironies involved as the case of the all-male draft was argued. Men brought suit, men served as lawyers, and the bench was all male. The issue in this case was discrimination against men. The focus was on the relationship between Congress and the military, not on women's obligations. The question for the justices was whether Congress was being reasonable. Weinberg argued that gender discrimination should be treated as race discrimination was, on the basis of the 1976 *Craig v. Boren* ruling that "classification by gender must serve important government objectives and must be substantially related to the achievement of those objectives."[179]

In the Goldberg case, however, the justices overruled the Pennsylvania court and decided that registration and drafting women should be a decision for Congress, starting from the proposition that the administration and the plantiffs denied—that the purpose of the draft was only to obtain combat troops. Under that assumption, because women were not used in combat, they did not need to be drafted or even to register. Justice White dissented, writing that Congress had not concluded that every position in the military, no matter how far removed from combat, had to be filled with combat-ready men. Therefore, not all military men were fungible, and not only did the armed forces utilize women, they drafted and utilized noncombat qualified men and conscientious objectors.

In a different vein, Justice Brennan signed on to Justice Marshall's dissent. Marshall objected on the basis of equal civic obligation; he believed that the Court was avoiding its "constitutional obligation" to judge congressional acts by the standards of the Constitution as they involved equal protection of the laws. Marshall wrote, "The Court today places its imprimatur on one of the most potent remaining public expressions of 'ancient canards about the role of women,' . . . [differential registration] categorically excludes women from a fundamental civic obligation."[180]

Kerber points out, through a review of this and other cases, that there still is no consensus on a citizen's responsibility to bear arms. Changes over time show that there has been no such thing as a static conception of how gender operates or "women's place." Moreover, although men previously have monopolized agencies of state violence that are internal (police) and external (military/combat) to the nation state, this monopoly has eroded—as has the distinction between combat and noncombat assignments.[181]

Kerber maintains that even if women have served in combat unofficially, and even if under current regulations they could be ordered into combat, there is no consensus that women have an equal obligation to serve or to bear arms. When we eventually gain that consensus, Kerber believes that many women will blame feminists for having to take on this obligation in exchange for intangible rights and equalities that they may not think they want or need. As Jean Elshtain, Judith Stiehm, and Kerber agree, however, women eventually will have to give up their cheerleader or sideline critic status to take an active part in the decisions and actions of the state, even when they entail violence. Women cannot avoid these responsibilities forever.

Kerber and Elshtain agree that although rights are pleasing to contemplate and obligations are not so pleasing, "democracy requires for its social glue a mode of participation with one's fellow citizens that is animated by a sense of responsibility for one's society." They add that citizens should not be denied the opportunity to exercise that responsibility for increasingly suspect categorizations.[182] At the same time, if all citizens fulfilled their responsibilities freely, the state would have no need for compulsion. We should not have the option of limiting ourselves to the duties we pick and choose.

Kerber's central argument is that women's obligations and rights have been confused. She argues that the "wages of gender" are not privilege and not the result of an immutable biological or religious destiny but the residue of an historic and constructed system of domestic relations. Specifically, although we would not overtly continue the system of coverture, we unwittingly do so every day that inequities that are based on group membership rather than individual merit exist. As much as we want to believe that we are intellectually and politically advanced, not until the 1970s did the courts recognize that difference was not privilege for women. "Privilege" left women vulnerable if they no longer had a male protector or if the men in their lives failed to protect and provide for them. Despite the Supreme Court's ‾1992 *Casey* ruling, Kerber maintains that the principle of coverture survives in attempts to keep qualified women out of the military and out of certain jobs by arguing that women need, and have a right to, male protection.

At the beginning of the 21st century, Kerber and others recognize that the debate is still very much alive, albeit in different forms. Feminists will be blamed for trading insecurities for abstractions—but only by people who ignore the history of civic obligations. When opponents ask what women will get in return for giving up the right to exclusion, Kerber avers that women have not been exempt; their obligations have simply varied over time in form and object. Attaching femininity to exclusions from civic obligation is historically twisted; as Kerber notes, poor and minority women could never claim this fictional right to be "treated like ladies."[183]

Kerber's closing is pointed and challenging: "Whether one is male or female, racially marked in a system that treats Caucasians as 'normal,' married or single, heterosexual or homosexual, continues to have implications for how we experience the equal obligations of citizenship. How one is taxed, whether or not one's loyalty to the state is filtered through one's marital partner, whether one owes the state risky military service—all vary by gender." She argues although we are entitled to equal protection under the law, "there is no constitutional right to be a lady or a gentleman, excused from obligations borne by ordinary women and men." Equality is a great principle, and in Anglo-American legal traditions equality has always meant simultaneously common law and equity. What is experienced as obligation has shifted over time as social relations between men and women have shifted. In other words, "The principles remain steady, but the work of maintaining them in our lives will have no end."[184]

☐ CONCLUSIONS: REASON OR REACTION?

David Richards guides us to the Constitution and the Reconstruction amendments for the principles of our political philosophy and discussions of rights. Linda Kerber cites the Declaration of Independence and the Gettysburg Address as containing the principles and obligations to which we should be dedicated. The bottom line is that we have not clearly defined the rights, obligations, or privileges of citizenship. This failure makes our debate on women's military participation unstable and allows opponents to be evasive—to talk as if we have an agreed and static definition, instead of a dynamic one. They use this definition to keep people out of the military or out of certain positions or to deny them rights and privileges, as they variously define citizens' obligations. This "moving target" of our definition of citizenship must be brought into focus. History can illuminate the past, and it sheds light on how shifting and malleable arguments abuse facts and maim logic.

One part of this newly focused debate, informed by intellectual and cultural history, will be for us to define what we really mean by political democracy in the here and now. Then, as Kerber and Richards have done, we must analyze our behavior in comparison with our political philosophy. Where there are disconnects, we must decide which is stronger—our cultural ideology or our commitment to our political philosophy. Sorting out cultural myth and wishful conservative thinking from verifiable history, as Stephanie Coonts has done, also is helpful. We know that "myth is hardly sound footing" for strategic planning and force structure decisions in the 21st century.[185]

When all is said and done, we are left with a more important debate: whether our political philosophy and military effectiveness are mutually exclusive. I believe that they are not. I believe that our democracy can protect itself and be true to its principles. I believe—as the Director of Central Intelligence, George Tenet, does—that diversity is a strength in and of itself rather than merely a political ideology or goal. Secretary of the Navy Richard Danzig says that he is "animated by the fundamental perception that we are a democracy. The character of our country is changing. As the character of the country changes, so must the character of our military."[186] This republic embodied the ideological changes in 18th-century warfare, organized and managed mass armies of citizen-soldiers by adapting the organizational principles of the bureaucratic revolution in the 19th century, and equipped our military better than any other in the 20th century by capitalizing on the industrial revolution. I have no doubt that in the 21st century this republic can continue to lead the way through the information revolution to build and maintain the most diverse and the most effective military force in the world.

In this uncertain future, I do not believe that we can continue to protect our interests and our sovereignty if any of our citizens choose—or are forced—to sit on the sidelines, as apathetic observers and distanced critics or even as enthusiastic cheerleaders. We all must accept our civic responsibility to be engaged to the limits of our ability.

Our democratic political philosophy is based on the principle of individual merit. I question opponents who would exclude groups, especially on the basis of biological determinants. I also question the commitment to democracy of people who do not believe that our political philosophy can work within our defining national institutions or when the going gets tough. That is exactly where and when democracy must meet the test.

The debate about women in the military will not go away until we resolve our definition of civic responsibility. Until we do that, our discussion of women's military roles will sink to the level of Fred Reed, Elaine Donnelly, Brian Mitchell, or Phyllis Schlafly—and each time one of them writes something emotional and flippant, another group of young (or old) soldiers will flock to them to articulate their general post–Cold War, *fin de siècle* malaise. In addition, I can predict with near certainty that without this resolution almost every editorial, op-ed, and letter to the editor decrying the problem of military readiness will continue to emote its way to the suggestion that women are the problem.[187]

Meanwhile, our young women continue to face the reality of trying to serve their country while being rejected in its public forums and within one of its defining institutions. Over the past 20 years, I have continually asked myself (in a variation of Freud): What do the opponents of women really want? Would they turn back the clock? They would not find their fantasy in history, as we have seen. Nor can they make a mythical past into a future reality. Military and civilian leaders have made their decisions clear—women are a crucial part of America's armed services today and will remain so in the foreseeable future. People who argue against military women do not support national security, enhance military effectiveness, or contribute to cohesiveness. With their diatribes, they damage morale, sustain harassment and prejudice, and create divisiveness.

Should we really portray white, middle-class men as victims in the evolution of our democracy? Is this debate really about feminism and culture wars, or is it about the future of the nation and world? Can we continue to lead the world toward what we hope will be a better future politically, economically, and socially if we have a military that does not reflect our philosophical values and our civilian population?

This issue really is a question of leadership. I would like to see the leaders of our armed forces at every level embrace in their policies the view of democracy they espouse in their oaths of office. To respond to myth and prejudice as quickly and strenuously as they respond to disparaging comments about the F-22 or a new carrier battle group, however, our most senior leaders (and we) will have to get smarter about our history and our political philosophy.

This series on public controversies, dedicated to public education and information, is an essential effort. In addition, organizations such as the Alliance for National Defense (AND) and Defense Advisory Council on Women in the Services (DACOWITS) remain dedicated to research and investigation on behalf of an engaged citizenry. These educational efforts and organizations can strengthen our public institutions and civic commitment, rather than ripping the fabric of our connections to each other and our communities.[188]

With the commitment of our leadership, appropriate education, and accurate information, we can enter a constructive and informed—rather than destructive and visceral—debate. We can fix our sights on a clear discussion of the historical evidence; we can highlight relevant historical and current data on women as casualties and POWs, as well as the dynamics of bonding. We can focus debate on the future of the nation-state and war, as we do continuously within government and the military—asking our best intelligence specialists and analysts to predict the future. We also can learn a great deal by engaging academics and the citizenry in a public debate outside the confines of government and the military.

In the end, we must admit that although we can forecast as we do with the weather, we can never fix with certainty what form war will take and what kind of force structure we will need. Whether we return to mass industrial armies or leap forward to a future described in science fiction and some visionary military theories as information- or cyber-warfare, we will need our smartest and most capable citizens. Guessing which scenarios are most dangerous and which are most likely, we must do our best to build a flexible force and strategy that support our national security and reflect our political philosophy.

Beyond the visceral and the mundane and beyond our imagined futures, we must fix the target of our debates on the practice of citizenship in this democratic nation, and we must truly decide whether we believe in the liberal promise of our Revolution as it has evolved through more than two centuries. This concept has been a "moving target"—and often forgotten; if we do not resolve the issue, however, we can only continue to evolve haphazardly as our changing context slowly but inevitably forces us to reexamine our biases and paradigms. If we avoid the issue of civic obligation and debate women's military participation more narrowly, we may feel as though we have fixed the problem. I believe, however, that we will soon realize that we have neglected a much more important discussion. If we decide that women will not face the same civic obligations as men, then how should we treat our economically and educationally disadvantaged citizens, our physically and mentally challenged citizens, our homosexual citizens, and our immigrants? Where will the next nexus of debate on rights, responsibilities, and privileges be? How will those next debates intersect with the demand that all citizens be liable for national defense and that all citizens warrant first-class status? How will our conceptions of civic obligation change as our understanding of the nation-state changes and we are asked to provide more blue helmets to international forces under the United Nations?

This is not a discussion in the interest of a fictional political correctness.[189] We must resolve this question of civic obligation so that we are better prepared for the future. Failure to do so now is an insult to our heritage and all our people. Delay is inappropriate to our history and a handicap to our future.

Even as late as 1999, well-known military sociologist and specialist on conscription Charles Moskos—in a debate on continued funding for the Selective Service System—could make the comment that men would not know they were citizens if they did not have to register for the draft, saying, "it will mean a cutoff of citizenship responsibility. . . . This is the one time in his life a man has to sign a document saying he has a citizenship obligation."[190] No one reacted to what was missing. How will young women validate their citizenship or fulfill their obligation?

Without intention or recognition, Moskos crystallized the debate we must have for our nation at the start of the 21st century. Civic obligation is the basis of action and treatment in every other sphere of our community. Now we must decide what it is, and for whom. How will we fulfill our obligations as citizens?

NOTES

1. The views expressed herein are those of the author and do not reflect the official policy or position of the U.S. Air Force or the Department of Defense. I thank my friends and colleagues Larry Morton and Cynthia Wright for their invaluable assistance. Through their own service experience and education, they helped to sharpen my thinking and added important insights to mine. I also thank Lynn Dawson and Gayla Crabtree for letting me try out my ideas on them. Discussions with them and other co-workers—including Amy Ryder, Sean O'Brien, Anthony Nicholson, Delores McCook, and Kermit Quick—moved this project toward completion. Finally, I could not have completed this essay without the help and support of my friend Monique Mansoura and my mother, Elizabeth Fenner. Despite all their best efforts, however, mistakes or omissions are strictly my own.

2. Georgia Sadler, "Open MLRS and Special Operations Forces Helos!" and "Women's Assignments to Submarines: Has the Time Come?" *Alliance Advocate* 1, no. 2 (October 1999): 3–4. In addition, see the coverage of the Fall 1999 DACOWITS Conference in *Alliance Advocate* 1, no. 4 (December 1999): 3–6.

3. See John T. Correll, "Lessons Drawn and Quartered," *Air Force Magazine* (December 1999), and James A. Kitfield, "Another Look at the Air War That Was: An Eaker Institute Panel Weighs the Implications of Operation Allied Force," *Air Force Magazine* (October 1999). There are thousands of other examples; see, e.g., Joel Garreau, "Reboot Camp: As War Looms, the Marines Test New Networks of Comrades," *Washington Post,* 24 March 1999, C1 (on the Marine Corps), and Bradley Graham, "Army's Big Gun Must Lose Some Weight: Crusader Tests Vision of Leaner, More Agile Force," *Washington Post,* 25 November 1999, G1.

4. Brian Mitchell, *Weak Link: The Feminization of the American Military* (Washington, D.C.: Regnery Publishing, 1989) and *Women in the Military: Flirting with Disaster* (Washington, D.C.: Regnery Publishing 1999); Phyllis Schlafly (for example, see her Eagle Forum online column, "No Longer Trying To Be All You Can Be," 6 October 1999); and Elaine Donnelly (for example, see her Center for Military Readiness questionnaire for presidential candidates, December 1999) are some of the foremost proponents of this school of thought. These ideas also are reflected in the columns of Fred Reed for the online *Armed Forces News*, as well as in recent letters to the editor of *Proceedings*, the journal of the U.S. Naval Institute. See also Mona Charen, "Eight Good Reasons to Oppose Women in the Military," *Boston Globe,* 27 August 1997, 21, and Cal Thomas, "Crashes: Symptom of Weakened Military?" *Long Island Newsday,* 23 September 1997.

5. There are a growing number of credible historical works on this subject; the best is the latest edition of Jeanne Holm's groundbreaking work, *Women in the*

Military: An Unfinished Revolution, rev. ed. (Novato, Calif.: Presidio, 1992). The newest credible and substantial work that is broader and deeper in scope is Linda Grant Depauw, *Battlecries and Lullabies* (Norman: University of Oklahoma Press, 1988).

6. See Lorry Fenner, "Ideology and Amnesia: The Public Debate on Women and the American Military, 1940–1973," Ph.D. diss., University of Michigan, 1995, and "'Either You Need These Women or You Do Not': Informing the Debate on Military Service and Citizenship," *Gender Issues* 16, no. 3 (summer 1998), among others.

7. Several well-written monographs cover women and war historically, and more generally, including DePauw, *Battlecries and Lullabies;* Jean Elshtain, *Women and War* (New York: Basic Books, 1987); and Cynthia Enloe, *Does Khaki Become You? The Militarisation of Women's Lives* (Boston: South End, 1983).

8. Fenner, "Ideology and Amnesia." See also "Military Readiness: Women Are Not a Problem," RAND Research Brief, available at <http:\\www.rand.org/publications> (documented in Margaret C. Harrell and Laura L. Miller, *New Opportunities for Women: Effects on Readiness, Cohesion, and Morale,* forthcoming).

9. See Morris J. MacGregor, Jr., *Integration of the Armed Forces, 1940–1965* (Washington, D.C.: Center of Military History, 1981); Alan M. Osur, *Blacks in the Army Air Forces during World War II: The Problems of Race Relations* (Washington, D.C.: Office of Air Force History, 1986); and Alan L. Gropman, *The Air Force Integrates, 1945–1964* (Washington, D.C.: Office of Air Force History, 1985). Measurement of minority men's performance often was conducted in noncontrolled experiments. For example, untrained and in segregated units, black men performed weakly in combat. By any objective measurement, however, when these minority servicemembers were properly trained and led, they proved more than adequate in every military capacity.

10. Fenner, "Ideology and Amnesia." dissertation. Since at least the 1940s, American popular culture sources show that the arguments used by opponents of women in the services shifted over time from the physical to the emotional to the intellectual. Opponents argued that moral weakness, lack of leadership ability, and women's rampant immorality would prove the Services' undoing. In every case they were wrong. For arguments that the Services have not lowered standards for women, particularly at the Service academies, see Richard F. Ballard, "Marching to the Same Drummer," *Washington Post Education Review,* 28 July 1996, 5, and Shelley Davis, "Whirly Girls," *Retired Officer* (November 1998), 64–70. Davis points out that Jerrie Cobb met all of the standards for NASA's astronaut training in 1961 but still was not accepted into the program. See also coverage of minority men and women in popular print media between 1940 and 1980 for apt comparisons.

11. In several cases, the Services have added physical tests for specialties after they were opened to women. For instance, the Air Force added a weightlifting requirement for pilots after women were accepted for fighter and bomber aircraft. Previously there had been no upper-body strength test, and women had been flying larger cargo aircraft for the Air Force and Navy fighters for years without taking such a test. Foreign military women also had been flying American-made fighter aircraft.

12. For example, Linda Kerber, in *No Constitutional Right to be Ladies* (New York: Hill and Wang, 1998) cites a 1970 legal finding (reminiscent of language used in a 1957 trial) that was based on group membership rather than individual merit, in a case specifically based on physical characteristics and assumed male superiority in strength. The judge found that " . . . for the most part physical strength is a male characteristic, and so long as this is so, the United States will be compelled to establish and maintain armed forces of males which may at least physically be equal to the armed forces of other nations, likewise composed of males, with which it must compete" (*U.S. v. Cook,* 311 F.Supp. 618, 622 [W.D.Pa. 1970], item 12). This ruling assumes that men always would be fighting one-on-one in hand-to-hand combat—mistakenly creating a comparative standard rather than an occupational standard. The Services have never measured the physical strength of other nations' soldiers to create U.S. military strength standards. This finding also assumed that our adversaries would/will never use military women—completely ignoring the fact that other nations, allies as well as enemies, have used women in their militaries.

13. As told by Capt. Georgia Sadler (USN, Retired), former head of women's programs for the U.S. Navy starting in 1980. When the Navy began to assign women to ships in 1978, the physical strength of women again became an issue.

14. As recounted by a female graduate from the U.S. Air Force Academy in a panel discussion at the 1996 20-year reunion of the first female Academy entrants. Her husband served in this fire department.

15. Linda Bird Francke, *Ground Zero: The Gender Wars in the Military* (New York: Simon & Schuster, 1997), 217–19. The stigma against helping female colleagues operates differently. The stigma against men who need help also is different. In addition, the whole group of men is never tarred by one man's (or some men's) failure in the way that women or minorities are tarred by the failures of individuals in those groups. For more on women at the Service academies, see Carol Barkalow, *In the Men's House* (New York: Poseidon Press, 1990); Sharon Hanley Disher, *First Class: Women Join the Ranks at the Naval Academy* (Annapolis, Md.: Naval Institute Press, 1998); and Judith Hicks Stiehm, *Bring Me Men & Women: Mandated Change at the U.S. Air Force Academy* (Berkeley: University of California Press, 1981).

16. As told by Jill McCall, USAF and USAFR, about her own experience as a USAF B-52 mechanic.

17. See Shelley Saywell, *Women in War: From World War II to El Salvador* (New York; Penguin, 1986), for women in nontraditional military capacities from World War II to the Falklands War (the Malvinas Islands); and Bruce Myles, *Night Witches* (Chicago: Academy, 1981), and Anne Noggle, *A Dance with Death* (College Station: Texas A&M University Press, 1994) about the Soviet Union's World War II female pilots. For another story of nurses in harm's way, see Agnes Jensen, *Albanian Escape: The True Story of U.S. Army Nurses Behind Enemy Lines* (Lexington: University of Kentucky Press, 1999).

18. Sociologists and psychologists have developed tests, which have changed as we have learned more within those disciplines and as society has changed. A popular test that is now used in Professional Military Education (PME) programs, the Myers-Briggs personality survey, does not have different measurements for gender and race, nor do researchers using this measurement usually differentiate by those categories. Myers-Briggs surveys show that military personnel, male and female, generally test as "ENFJ" (extroverted and disciplined). These tests do not tell us, however, whether this personality type yields not merely *an* effective fighting force but the *most* effective. If men and women profile similarly, what attributes do we want for occupations that remain closed to women? Do any women possess these attributes?

19. See Barton Hacker, "Women and Military Institutions in Early Modern Europe: A Reconnaisance, *Signs* 6 (1981): 643–71, and DePauw, *Battlecries and Lullabies,* among others. For our Civil War, see Lauren Cook Burgess, *An Uncommon Soldier* (New York: Oxford University Press, 1994), and Phyllis Raybin Emert, ed., *Women in the Civil War: Warriors, Patriots, Nurses, and Spies* (Lowell, Mass.: Discovery Enterprises, 1995).

20. See Hacker, "Women and Military Institutions"; Holm, *Women in the Military;* Saywell, *Women in War;* DePauw, *Battlecries and Lullabies;* June Wandrey, *Bedpan Commando* (Elmore, Ohio: Elmore Publishing Co., 1989). See also William B. Breuer, *War and American Women: Heroism, Deeds, and Controversy* (Westport, Conn.: Praeger, 1997), and Mattie E. Treadwell *The Women's Army Corps* (Washington, D.C.: Office of the Chief of Military History, 1954). This point also is supported by Holocaust sources, including Dalia Ofer and Lenore J. Weitzman, eds., *Women in the Holocaust* (New Haven, Conn.: Yale University Press, 1998), and Carol Rittner and John K. Roth eds., *Different Voices: Women and the Holocaust* (New York: Paragon House, 1993).

21. In 1999 DACOWITS asked DoD to investigate whether the ASVAB measures experience or aptitude. Many women, because of high school curricula and socialization, do not test well on the mechanics and electronics portion of the ASVAB; their selection of a job in these areas, however, should not be based on lack of experience if they have aptitude. Similarly, many men have not tested well in foreign languages but could have outstanding aptitude. The Services have tried to design a method to test language aptitude rather than knowledge by constructing a fictitious language for students to use for grammatical exercises. The Services also separately test for job-specific language capability. The GAO also has studied DoD's use of the ASVAB; see Georgia Sadler, "GAO Study—Occupations: Change is Slow," *Alliance Advocate* 1, no. 3 (November 1999): 3 (full report available at <http://www. gao.gov>). Also see Rick Maze, "Aptitude Test Redesign Would Ease Gender Bias," *Air Force Times,* 4 October 1999, 22. DACOWITS continues to work on this issue in 2001.

22. According to Col. Mark Pizzo, USMC (a faculty member at the National War College), evidence shows that combat soldiers in Category IV (of very low intelligence) have a higher combat casualty rate. Note that there is no study that correlates survival potential to physical ability (i.e., the number of push-ups a soldier can perform). The real problem in arguing these standards is that they have been applied differently at different times, in different Services, for different people, and for a variety of reasons. For example, today one must be an officer to be an Air Force pilot, and all officers have bachelor's degrees. During World War II, college degrees were not required, and enlisted members served as pilots. Helicopter pilots in the Army today do not necessarily have degrees (most are warrant officers).

23. Women in my own military cohort group had to score higher on the AFOQT than male applicants in 1979 and 1980 to enter Air Force Officer Training School.

24. We should discuss why women do not get promoted and recognized at a much higher rate if intellectual criteria are so important and women are in higher categories.

25. Col. Mark Pizzo, USMC, faculty member at National War College, note 22.

26. The reality is that intellectual standards are a luxury; they also are very malleable. Intelligence is only one of many criteria, and intellectual standards are adjusted for recruiting as dictated by demographics (See, e.g., Roberto Suro, "Military Confronts Trends in Recruiting, *Washington Post,* 5 October 1999). In fact, if standards were not "lower" for men, more women could be inducted. Women do not gain advantage from a "social experiment," affirmative action, or some suspect "politically correct" quota; far from it, their numbers are capped.

27. See Gropman, *The Air Force Integrates.* In Black History Month presentations to the National War College and in classes at the Industrial College of the Armed Forces (both part of the National Defense University at Ft. Leslie J. McNair, Washington, D.C.), Gropman reads from student and faculty research projects from the Army War College of the 1930s and 1940s. In their papers, these senior military leaders claim that black men completely lack the necessary attributes for military leadership and combat. See also Fenner, "Ideology and Amnesia," and "Either You Need These Women or You Do Not."

28. Kerber, *No Constitutional Right to Be Ladies,* 265, and Holm, *Women in the Military,* 192–202.

29. Elizabeth Becker, "Motherhood Deters Women From Army's Highest Ranks," *New York Times,* 29 November 1999, A1 and A16; Diana West, "Military Maternity: Colonel Accepts Mission at Home," *Washington Times,* 3 December 1999; Suzanne Fields, "Colonel Mom: She Didn't Try to Make General," *Washington Times,* 2 December 1999, A21; "Don't Demote Motherhood" (editorial), *Washington Times,* 5 December 1999, B2; "Mothers at Sea," *Wall Street Journal,* 3 December 1999, W17.

30. Fenner, "Ideology and Amnesia."

31. Numerous studies have shown this. See Fenner, "Ideology and Amnesia," and Holm, *Women in the Military,* among others. In an example of how some of the physical rules work, in 1990—when I was on the faculty at the U.S. Air Force Academy—a female cadet was told, without supporting rationale, that if her ovarian cyst required removal of an ovary she would not be allowed to fly. Having two ovaries obviously is not a pilot qualification in general. For an example on commentary criticizing military women for pregnancy, see David Hackworth, "Commentary: Thanks to the Ranks," 24 November 1999, available at <http://www.hackworth.com> and <http://rlmcmahon.freeyellow.com>.

32. Wayne E. Dillingham, "The Possibility of American Military Women Becoming POWs: Justification for the Combat Exclusion Rules?" *Federal Bar News & Journal* (May 1990), and "The Possibility of American Women Becoming Prisoners of War: A Challenge for Behavioral Scientists," *Minerva: Quarterly Report on Women and the Military* 8, no. 4 (winter 1990): 17–22.

33. See Fenner, "Ideology and Amnesia," and "Either You Need These Women or You Do Not," for lengthier discussions of this topic.

34. Army Generals Hale and Maher retired and were demoted in 1999 for violating the UCMJ. Both had sexual relations with subordinates' civilian wives.

35. See Saywell, *Women in War*. (Part of this discussion also is from a 1997 interview with a married military couple.)

36. Marie E. deYoung, "Why I Back Berry," *Air Force Times*, 13 September 1999, 55. None of these arguments should lead us to the conclusion that women (or, specifically, military women) are at fault or that if they were removed from the situation we would have no further problems. In addition, the expenses that deYoung mentions existed before military women arrived on the scene and still apply to all-male units. Where is the evidence that would clearly demonstrate that military women were responsible for these issues? deYoung claims that "thousands of defense dollars" are wasted "as a consequence of inappropriate relationships"—implying that these costs are related primarily to relations between military men and military women who are not married to each other. She says that these expenses include family counseling, psychiatric hospitalizations after suicide attempts, treatment for HIV and other sexually transmitted diseases, and legal expenses for divorces.

37. See Treadwell, *U.S. Army in World War II*, 195–218; Holm, *Women in the Military*, 51–54 (on the World War II "Slander or Whisper" campaign against WAACs); Enloe, *Does Khaki Become You?*; Saywell, *Women in War*, on World War II as well. See Fenner, "Ideology and Amnesia," for more cases.

38. Fenner, "Ideology and Amnesia," 494–99.

39. Ibid. See also Charles C. Moskos, "A Sociologist Appraises the G.I." *New York Times*, 24 September 1967, section VI, 32. See also Elizabeth Kier, "Homosexuals in the U.S. Military: Open Integration and Combat Effectiveness," *International Security* 23, no. 2 (fall 1998): 5–39; David Gress, "Multiculturalism in World History," *Footnotes* (Foreign Policy Research Institute Newsletter) 5, no. 8 (September 1999).

40. To this assessment, I bring more than 20 years of service in the coed military, as well as three decades of experience playing on and coaching women's, men's, and coed athletic teams.

41. Samuel Huntington, *The Soldier and the State* (Cambridge, Mass.: Harvard University Press, 1957), and Morris Janowitz, *The Professional Soldier* (New York:

Free Press, 1971). In the 1950s, Huntington's seminal work prescribed isolation and political insulation for the professional officer corps, so they could exercise their functional imperative—the wielding of violence for the nation-state. Janowitz's proposition is that unless the armed forces are firmly situated in society they will be a danger to the state. There is much discussion and concern today about the perceived growing gap between the military and civilian worlds in the United States. See Richard H. Kohn, ed., *The United States Military under the Constitution of the United States, 1789–1989* (New York: New York University Press, 1991), and Don M. Snider and Miranda A Carlton-Carew, eds., *U.S. Civil-Military Relations: In Crisis or Transition?* (Washington, D.C.: Center for Strategic and International Studies, 1995). See also Garry D. Ryan and Timothy K. Nenninger, eds., *Soldiers and Civilians: The U.S. Army and the American People* (Washington, D.C.: National Archives and Records Administration, 1987), for several insightful essays. In addition, see Russell F. Weigley, "The American Military and the Principle of Civilian Control from McClellan to Powell," *Journal of Military History* 57 (special issue, October 1993): 27–58, and Richard H. Kohn, "Out of Control: The Crisis in Civil-Military Relations," *The National Interest,* no. 35 (spring 1994): 3–17.

42. Linda K. Kerber, "'A Constitutional Right to be Treated Like Ladies': Women, Civic Obligation and Military Service," *University of Chicago Law School Roundtable* (1993), 95–128.

43. The best-known—and currently subscribed to—probably are the 19th-century Prussian Carl von Clausewitz, *On War,* edited and translated by Michael Howard and Peter Paret (Princeton, N.J.: Princeton University Press, 1976), and the ancient Chinese Sun Tzu, *The Art of War,* translated by Samuel B. Griffith (London: Oxford University Press, 1963).

44. See Deborah Tannen, *Talking From 9 to 5: Women and Men and the Workplace: Language, Sex, and Power* (New York: Morrow, Williams and Co., 1995) and Carol Gilligan, *In a Different Voice: Psychological Theory and Women's Development* (Cambridge, Mass.: Harvard University Press, 1982) for arguments regarding essential differences between men and women. Although I would argue that we are moving to a more androgynous culture, Tannen's and Gilligan's arguments generally remain relevant today. See also Kier, "Homosexuals in the U.S. Military," on the military's efforts toward cohesion and those that are counterproductive to stated aims.

45. See "Exploding the Myths, Exploring the Facts" (proceedings from the 1992, 1994, 1996, and 1998 conferences of the Women's Research and Education Institute), available at <http://www.wrei.org>. See also Kerry Segrave, *Policewomen: A History* (Jefferson, N.C.: McFarland & Co., 1995).

46. In 1997, a female sociologist spent a few days in the field with her boyfriend's special forces unit and concluded that because men bond over "sex talk," women will not be able to bond with men—nor serve in special forces units effectively.

47. Kier, "Homosexuals in the U.S. Military."

48. Ibid.

49. From U.S. Air Force Academy (USAFA) Behavioral Science Department briefings to the Department of History faculty between 1986 and 1990.

50. Fenner, "Ideology and Amnesia."

51. From a 1997 interview with Major Marty Stanton (USAF, Ret.) on her experiences in Vietnam. Also see Breuer, *War and American Women,* 72–79 and Saywell, *Women in War.*

52. From interviews with female aircrew members and male and female USAFA graduates who went through the unabridged SERE training. Also from a 1999 interview with former cadet SERE trainer (now Maj., USAF) Anthony Nicholson. See also Franke, *Ground Zero,* 81–83 and 87–91.

53. For a similar but more recent British study, see Kate Rounds, "Clippings," *Ms. Magazine* (December 1999/January 2000), 29.

54. Department of Defense Inspector General, *Tailhook 91: Events at the 35th Annual Tailhook Symposium,* 1993.

55. See Francke, *Ground Zero,* 97–103, and Holm, *Women in the Military,* 457–59.

56. Kenneth Allard, *Somalia Operations: Lessons Learned* (Washington, D.C.: National Defense University Press, 1995).

57. Former Air Force Colonel and lawyer Charles L. Dunlap, Jr. wrote an award-winning essay ("The Origins of the American Military Coup of 2012") proposing this scenario while he was at senior PME at the National War College in 1992. Since then he has recycled the same idea in numerous other pieces and presentations.

58. TISS Project on the Gap Between the Military and Civilian Society, Peter Feaver and Christopher Gelpi, co-principal investigators, 1999 (<http://www.poli.duke.edu/civmil>).

59. We can make the argument that for some people, choices are circum-scribed by socioeconomic conditions that also affect their educational level and intellectual development. The American public at large does not seem to register these conditions and contexts, however, during the debates about the AVF. These conditions for exercising choice also pertained to the draftee Army we maintained during the Vietnam era. Men from white, middle- and upper-class families could choose college and resulting deferments, or college and the officer corps or National Guard service, or the Air Force or Navy to avoid ground combat positions.

60. Leslie Smith, "Courage Under Fire in Battle Knows No Barriers of Gender," *Air Force Times,* 22 March 1999, 58. Dillingham also makes a very strong argument for women as adults exercising free will in the Kantian sense, informed and choosing their own fate, rather than subjecting them to government or patriarchal protection-ism. In a luncheon address to the Industrial College of the Armed Forces, National Defense University, in November 1999, Edvard Luttwak joked that one is safer flying combat missions in American aircraft (Kosovo) than flying on foreign civilian aircarri-ers in peacetime.

61. A December 1999 fire in Massachusetts that cost the lives of six firefight-ers is a recent example.

62. Fred Reed, "Recruiting and Gender," *Armed Forces News*, 18 November 1999, and "Group Therapy vs. National Defense," *Armed Forces News,* 8 October 1999 (both available at <http://www.armedforcesnews.com>).

63. See "In Memoriam," *Alliance Advocate* 1, no. 2 (September 1999): 7, on Captain Jennifer Jill Shafer Odom, USA.

64. See Kate Rounds, "Clippings," *Ms. Magazine* (December 1999/January 2000), 28. For one example of the reaction, see E. J. Dionne, Jr., "The Wrestler on Religion," *Washington Post,* October 5, 1999, A17.

65. Fenner, "Ideology and Amnesia," on historical amnesia. Not only is there no outcry over female casualties, there is hardly any memory of them.

66. Ibid.

67. Francke, *Ground Zero,* 46–72.

68. For the first Women's History Month presentation at The Citadel, March 1999, my talk was titled, "Women's Military Participation: Right, Privilege or Obligation." I reviewed American women's historical contributions in wartime and discussed racial and gender aspects of citizenship through our history.

69. The claim that we abhor women committing violence—we should oppose allowing women into combat positions because we generally regard women as nurturers and therefore, presumably, must protect them from becoming killers, to avoid upsetting the gendered balance (or polarity) of our society—also is a cultural myth. Another myth is that women do not commit violence or participate in war. To the contrary, women have been called upon by publics and nation-states to take up arms repeatedly. People do not know that we have trained allied forces' women at our Euro-NATO fighter pilot school in Texas or that they have participated in the Balkan wars. For example, the Joint Task Force commander for Bosnia told a National War College class about a Danish female tank commander who fired a large number of rounds into a suspect building. When he asked her why she had fired that number of rounds, she answered that those were all she had. He commented that he had no doubt that women possessed the required amount of aggression for war. The United States has repeatedly demonstrated that we will use women in warfare when we need them. When we need them, somehow we know they are capable, and asking them to do violence for the community or state will not destroy our culture. There is little public outcry against them. Whether we want to believe it or not, our adversaries, far from disrespecting us for integrating women warriors, have used their own women to fine effect. See the works of anthropologist Margaret Mead, including "What Women Want," *Fortune* 34 (December 1946), 173, and *Male and Female: The Classic Study of the Sexes* (New York: Morrow, William and Col., 1996); see also Gerda Lerner, especially *The Creation of Patriarchy* (New York: Oxford University Press, 1986). See also Elshtain, *Women and War*, and Kerber, *No Constitutional Right to Be Ladies.* According to scholars of gender difference in ancient cultures, women were supposed to give life, and men were to take life if necessary to protect women—primitive men were afraid that if women could both give and take life, women would gain a dangerous autonomy and men would lose their place in society—and become superfluous. At the beginning of the

20th century, men and women were culturally assigned to separate spheres and separate obligations to the nation: If a man's obligation to the community and state was constructed to be one of armed defense, potentially taking life and losing his own in the struggle, women were to fulfill their reciprocal obligation by bearing children, thereby giving life—potentially dying in childbirth. In both cases, societal obligations were so serious that the loss of one's life in support of these roles was an accepted, if not routine, risk. See, among others, Antonia Fraser, *The Warrior Queens* (New York: Alfred A. Knopf, 1989); Tim Newark, *Women Warlords* (London: Blandford, 1989); Nadezhda Durova, *The Cavalry Maiden* (Bloomington: Indiana University Press, 1989); and Anne Noggle, *A Dance with Death: Soviet Air Women in World War II* (College Station: Texas A&M University Press, 1994). Many people might suggest that this cultural anthropology has very little relevance to military effectiveness and efficiency today. What is significant, though, is that we know that these historical roles were based on mythology or social construct. Reality has seldom reflected this strict polarity, particularly if we add considerations of social class to the discussion. See William H. Chafe, *Women and Equality: Changing Patterns in American Culture* (Oxford: Oxford University Press, 1977); Elshtain, *Women and War;* and Kerber, *Women of the Republic* and *No Constitutional Right to Be Ladies.* In fact, men are not always suited to be warriors, and many show great compassion; women are capable of great violence—from frontier women protecting their homesteads to women in modern war, terrorism, and rebellion.

We easily forget ancient women warriors, of which there are examples in nearly every culture, but the more recent should not be so remote to us—the World War I Russian Women's Battalion of Death, World War II British women who served in anti-aircraft units, Europeans in resistance movements, Soviet pilots, or Israeli fighters. Even in public sports and entertainment, from women in martial arts to women in boxing, women are aggressive and can fight. There should be a study of the profits made from female mud wrestling and the interest in the stereotypical "cat fight"—indeed, most popular culture vehicles that include women usually feature at least one case of physical or mental combat between women. In our imagined futures, our most popular mass-market science fiction and fantasy literature features warriors such as Linda Hamilton in the *Terminator* films, Sigourney Weaver as Ripley of *Aliens* fame, and Lucy Lawless as Xena, among others—not to mention the brave police officers or crazed and violent female villains on nightly television. See Sherrie A. Inness, *Tough Girls: Women Warriors and Wonder Women in Popular Culture* (Philadelphia: University of Pennsylvania Press, 1999) and the several works on popular culture by Susan Jeffords. Some observers would include Demi Moore's portrayal of a female SEAL in *GI Jane* in the category of fantasy; this movie also included the typical "cat fight" with Anne Bancroft as the female legislator.

The comments on NATO women refer to a nonattributable remark to the National War College class of 1999 and Major Sarah L. Garcia, USAF, "Women in the NATO Armed Forces," presentation Interallied Confederation of Medical Reserve Officers, July 1998; reprinted in *Minerva* 17, no. 2 (summer 1999): 33–82.

The United States has repeatedly considered the military necessity of drafting women and placing women in combat positions, and the armed forces have routinely waived combat restrictions or reclassified billets for women in support positions who are sent into hostile fire zones. This reclassification usually is done without adequate time for preparation and training, thereby dooming these women to perform less well than they otherwise would. The same thing happened repeatedly with black soldiers before their full integration—most notably at the beginning of the Korean conflict, when ships stewards were thrown into combat because of mounting casualties; see Fenner, "Ideology and Amnesia"; Morris J. MacGregor, Jr., *Integration of the Armed Forces, 1940–1965* (Washington, D.C.: Center of Military History, 1981); Alan M. Osur, *Blacks in the Army Air Forces During World War II: The Problem of Race Relations* (Washington, D.C.: Office of Air Force History, 1986); and Alan L. Gropman, *The Air Force Integrates, 1945–1964* (Washington, D.C.: Office of Air Force History, 1985).

70. Sally Hayton-Keeva, *Valiant Women: In War and Exile* (San Francisco: City Lights Books, 1987), and Saywell, *Women in War*. See also Frank Van Riper, "At War: Fact and Fiction," *Washington Post*, 23 April 1999, 73, on a photography exhibit at Washington D.C.'s Troyer Gallery—especially one of the photographs ("Partisans Entering Pistoia, Italy, 1944") showing heavily armed female Italian partisans—and John Pomfret, "A Long March to Respect: Chinese Military Polishes Reputation," *Washington Post*, 2 October 1999, A15–16, with accompanying photograph of a large unit of female soldiers.

71. Hayton-Keeva, *Valiant Women,* and Saywell, *Women in War.*

72. World Jewish Congress, "Female Combatants," *Dateline*, October 1999, 5. The Israeli Defense Forces plan to train women for border force duty and establish pilot programs in armored and artillery forces. These women were to deploy with their units in Lebanon, before the Israelis withdrew. We can assume that women will accompany the units if they redeploy.

73. During Operation DESERT STORM, when military members revealed that they were homosexual, they were still sent to the war, with the promise of being removed from duty once they returned (if they returned). The United States has a problematic record with regard to accepting sacrifice from citizens but not affording them first-class citizenship in return. During World War II, Nisei women served while their families resided in internment camps. African American POWs of the North Koreans were lectured about the Declaration of Independence and Constitution to show them that the United States had not fulfilled the promise of liberty and equality for blacks in our society in the 1950s. Private Sarah Keys, USA, was jailed in North Carolina for refusing to move to the back of the bus a month prior to Rosa Parks's ride. In 1999, a Republican member of the Arizona legislature and Reserve Army officer admitted that he was gay in a public debate on state laws. He was sent to Kosovo with his unit. The Army Reserve attempted to discharge him for admitting his homosexuality publicly, but he fought dismissal. The Army will allow him to finish his enlistment based on his promise not to seek reenlistment. (His public admission violated the "don't ask, don't tell" policy.) On Private Keys and the Nisei WACs, see Brigadier General Evelyn Foote, "From the President . . . ," *Alliance Advocate* 1, no. 4 (December 1999): 1.

74. Fenner, "Ideology and Amnesia," 50–217. See examples of American military leaders who were converted by serving with women, seeing them perform militarily, or having daughters who entered the military. In addition, the German Minister Albert Speer observed that the Allies won World War II in large measure because they mobilized military and civilian women sooner and more extensively than Germany did.

75. There are numerous general monographs on women's history (see Selected Bibliography, especially works by Evans, Chafe, and Flexner). See also histories of race relations in America and during the Civil Rights movement.

76. Fenner, "Ideology and Amnesia."

77. Historical examples abound. Napoleon exercised superior leadership until his luck and resources ran out and his enemies formed coalitions against him. During World War I, Germany did not have the resources to fight all of its opponents. The British Empire expanded to the point that its resources could not maintain it. Germany and Japan did not have the resources in World War II to compete with either the mobilized Soviet Union or United States, not to mention these two powers combined with the other Allies.

78. See Joint Vision 2010, the Air Force's Strategic Plan "Global Engagement," and monographs such as Alvin and Heidi Toffler, *War and Anti-War: Survival at the Dawn of the 21st Century* (Boston: Little, Brown and Co., 1993). See also Gary Hart and Warren B. Rudman, "New World Coming," available at <www.nssg.gov/Reports/New_World _Coming>. See also the "1999 Annual Forecast: A New and Dangerous World," *Global Intelligence Update,* 4 January 1999. On civil-military relations, see Peter D. Feaver and Christopher Gelpi, "How Many Deaths Are Acceptable? A Surprising Answer," *Washington Post,* 7 November 1999, B3; Richard H. Kohn, "Out of Control: The Crisis in Civil-Military Relations," *The National Interest* no. 35 (spring 1994): 3–17; Russell F. Weigley, "The American Military and the Principle of Civilian Control from McClellan to Powell," *Journal of Military History* 57 (special issue, October 1993): 27–58; Don M. Snider and Miranda A. Carlton-Carew, eds., *U.S. Civil-Military Relations: In Crisis or Transition?* (Washington, D.C.: Center for Strategic and International Studies, 1995); Tom Ricks, *Making the Corps* (New York: Simon and Schuster, 1998), and "The Great Society in Camouflage," *Atlantic Monthly* 278 (December 1996): 24–38, among others.

79. In 1996, as Director of Military History at USAFA, I gave an end-of-year capstone lecture to all students in the sophomore core military history course titled "The History of Future War." This lecture reviewed the semester's material by looking at some of the most prominent military theorists and practitioners—those who studied the past and anticipated the future well and, more often, those who misjudged past lessons and future requirements. I ended with a challenge to our students to study well and anticipate wisely by trying to transcend the paradigms of the present.

80. See Howard and Paret's edition of *On War*. The most useful discussions I have had on Clausewitz's theory of war were guided by Professor Thomas Keaney, formerly of the Air Force and a fellow faculty member at the National War College. Dr. Keaney is now at Johns Hopkins University School for Advanced International Studies. As our course director for "The Fundamentals of Military Strategy" at NWC, he had faculty and students read the Howard and Paret work in the order in which Clausewitz actually wrote and polished it. Understanding this dynamic, as well as gaining insight into the intellectual context in which it was written from my own historical studies and discussions with other faculty members (namely Professors Ilana Kass and David Tretler), has been crucial to the development of my ideas. I also was asked to teach the faculty workshops at the National War College on Clausewitz and his contemporary Antoine Jomini in 1998.

81. Casper Weinberger and Colin Powell set conditions for American military involvement that were based largely on the Vietnam experience. These conditions included the public's support, a well-defined mission, and the intent to use "overwhelming" force. See John T. Correll, "The Use of Force," *Air Force Magazine* (December 1999), 38.

82. Peter Grier, "New World Coming," *Air Force Magazine*, December 1999, 59–62; Hart and Rudman, "New World Coming."

83. Walter Millis, *Arms and Men: A Study in American Military History* (New Brunswick, N.J.: Rutgers University Press, 1984). For other discussions of patterns of strategic development, see Basil H. Liddell-Hart's works, including *Deterrent or Defense: A Fresh Look at the West's Military Position* (New York: Praeger, 1960), and *Strategy* (New York: Penguin Books, 1991); see also J. F. C. Fuller, *The Conduct of War, 1789–1961: The Study of the Impact of the French, Industrial, and Russian Revolutions on War and Its Conduct* (London: Methuen and Co., Ltd, 1972).

84. Hacker, "Women and Military Institutions in Early Modern Europe."

85. For the purposes of this discussion, I concentrate on European and American developments. Significant advances and influences did come from other parts of the world, but in the interest of space I paint the general outline of military development in the Western context. In addition, we obviously have a history of earlier democracies whose male citizens represented the polis and fought as part of their obligation as citizens. I also am omitting a discussion of guerrilla fighters, as in Spain's war against Napoleon. That episode is specifically interesting, however, because it informed the theorists of the day—Clausewitz embraced the phenomena as one aspect of war to consider, whereas Jomini rejected it as not real war—and because women fought in that people's army.

86. Burgess and Holm, *Women*.

87. See Dennis Showalter and others on the American Civil War and the Franco-Prussian War.

88. Michael Howard, "Men Against Fire: The Doctrine of the Offensive in 1914," in *Makers of Modern Strategy: From Machiavelli to the Nuclear Age,* edited by Peter Paret (Princeton, N.J.: Princeton University Press, 1986), 510–26.

89. Air theorists include Guilio Douhet, Billy Mitchell, and Hugh Trenchard. For naval forces and aviation, see H. T. Bartlett and Wiliam A. Moffet, and for amphibious warfare see Earl H. Ellis and Dion Williams in Russell F. Weigley, *The American Way of War: A History of United States Military Strategy and Policy* (Bloomington: Indiana University Press, 1977).

90. Professor John Shy of the University of Michigan taught military history with this method. See also Bruce D. Porter, *War and the Rise of the State: The Military Foundations of Modern Politics* (New York: Free Press, 1994).

91. There are many excellent, more modern history texts that recognize that political and military histories take place in specific social, economic, and cultural contexts. There also are outstanding histories of the early Civil Rights movement. For the advance of black men in the armed forces see MacGregor, *Integration in the Armed Forces;* Gropman, *The Air Force Integrates;* Osur, *Blacks in the Army Air Forces;* and Bernard C. Nalty, *Strength for the Fight: A History of Black Americans in the Military* (New York: Free Press, 1986). On black women in the WAC, see Charity Adams Earley, *One Woman's Army: A Black Officer Remembers the WAC* (College Station: Texas A&M University Press, 1989). Finally, for the women's suffrage and rights movements, see the works of Evans; Patricia Hollis, *Women in Public: The Women's Movement, 1850–1900* (Boston: George Allen and Unwin, 1981); and Eleanor Flexner, *Century of Struggle: The Woman's Rights Movement in the United States* (Cambridge, Mass.: Harvard University Press, 1975). For a discussion of the public debate about civil and political rights and military service for women and minority men from 1940–1973, see Fenner, "Ideology and Amnesia."

92. The best secondary source reference on women's growing participation in the armed forces is Holm, *Women in the Military.* For women's participation in the Revolution, see DePauw, *Founding Mothers* and *Battle Cries and Lullabies,* and Kerber, *Women of the Republic;* for the Civil War, see Burgess, *An Uncommon Soldier.* There also are several excellent histories of the Nurse Corps.

93. U.S. Navy Yeomen (F), Marines, and Pershing's civilian Signal Corps women.

94. See MacGregor, *Integration of the Armed Forces,* and Holm, *Women in the Military.* For women Marines in World War I, see the official USMC history: Linda L. Hewitt, *Women Marines in World War I* (Washington, D.C.: History and Museums Division, Headquarters, U.S. Marine Corps, 1974).

95. For women's history in the period, see Evans, *Born for Liberty,* and Linda K. Kerber and Jane Sharron De Hart, *Women's America: Refocusing the Past* (New York: Oxford University Press, 1995) generally, as well as Dorothy M. Brown, *Setting a Course: American Women in the 1920s* (Boston: Twayne Publishers, 1987), and Susan Ware, *Holding Their Own: American Women in the 1930s* (Boston: Twayne Publishers, 1982). See also Lois Scharf and Joan M. Jensen, eds., *Decades of Discontent: The Women's Movement, 1920–1940* (Boston: Northeastern University Press, 1987). There are several excellent books on women and flying, including biographies of Amelia Earhart (Ware's biography is the best for context) and Jacqueline Cochran

(Brinley is probably best). See also Judy Lomax, *Women of the Air* (New York: Dodd, Mead & Co., 1987).

96. See note 73 on Nisei WACs, African Americans, and homosexuals.

97. The best book on World War II is Gerhard Weinberg, *A World at Arms: A Global History of World War II* (Cambridge: Cambridge University Press, 1994). For women on the home front and in the military, besides Evans, *Born for Liberty*, and Kerber and De Hart, *Women's America*, see Allan M. Winkler, *Home Front U.S.A.: America During World War II* (Arlington Heights, Ill.: Harlan Davidson, 1986); Susan M. Hartmann, *The Home Front and Beyond: American Women in the 1940s* (Boston: Twayne Publishers, 1982); D'Ann Campbell, *Women at War with America: Private Lives in a Patriotic Era* (Cambridge, Mass.: Harvard University Press, 1984); and Doris Weatherford, *American Women and World War II* (New York: Facts on File, 1990). For the official history of the WAAC and the WAC, see Treadwell, *U.S. Army in World War II*. For the history of black men in the military in World War II, see MacGregor, *Integration of the Armed Forces*, and Nalty, *Strength for the Fight*. On the public debate on women's participation in the military, see Fenner, "Ideology and Amnesia."

98. Treadwell, *U.S. Army in World War II*, 759–61. See also Holm's discussion of women's integration in *Women in the Military*.

99. Executive Order 9981, 26 July 1948, called on the armed forces to desegregate. Of course, integration was not automatic or quickly achieved. Congress passed P.L.625 on 2 June 1948 to regularize women's service.

100. In World War II, women had flown all of the types of aircraft that would have been used. They ferried fighters and bombers and towed targets. As the latter, they were literally "moving targets" for anti-aircraft crews.

101. The fact that we called ceilings "quotas" for so long causes a problem in the modern use of the terms. Anti-affirmative action proponents point to historical quotas to imply—or claim outright—that this arrangement allowed for unqualified women and minority men to enter the service or particular fields within the service. Instead, these individuals usually had to score higher on entry qualifications than white men because the Services took so few of them. The only time some less-qualified women and minorities entered was when recruiters reached the number of applicants allowed under the ceilings through a "first-come, first-served" approach and thereby rejected more-qualified women and minorities who tried to enlist later in the year. (See Fenner, "Ideology and Amnesia," for the details of how the system of ceilings worked.)

102. Holm, *Women in the Military*, and Breuer, *War and American Women*.

103. Holm and Breuer differ in their interpretation of these two studies and the Women in the Army (WITA) study, as well as the results of all three. Holm served as WAF director through part of this period; Breuer takes most of his support from popular culture sources (newspapers and magazines) and writings by Brian Mitchell.

104. Holm, *Women in the Military*, 387–90.

105. Ibid., 381–437.

106. Ibid., 404–405, 426.

107. Garreau, "Reboot Camp," and Graham, "Army's Big Guns Must Lose Some Weight."

108. Presidential Commission on the Assignment of Women in the Armed Forces, *Women in Combat: Report to the President,* 15 November 1992.

109. Holm, *Women in the Military,* 470–86 (largely based on Department of Defense, "Conduct of the Persian Gulf Conflict," interim report to Congress, 10–12).

110. I served on the Joint Chiefs of Staff/J5, Strategy Division, Concepts Branch in 1997. I also served on the faculty at the National War College from 1997 to 1999, where I taught the process of strategy formation in our system and the content of our national and military strategies. As a member of the Joint Staff, I also participated in writing the 1997 Quadrennial Defense Review (QDR) report.

111. Having served in J5, Joint Chiefs of Staff, I have specific experience with the Joint Strategy Review (JSR), National Security Strategy (NSS), National Military Strategy (NMS), Joint Vision 2010, and the QDR.

112. See the current NSS and NMS. The *JSR Report* is classified.

113. Although several national security analysts complain that we are using our military for too many small things, others promote flexible forces to deal with all contingencies. The Marine Corps prides itself on being the "911" force to call in any emergency. See "The 21st Century Army: A New but Risky Sort of War," *Economist,* 2–8 January 1999. Male and female Marines train for a "three-block war": fighting rebels, distributing food and medicine to civilians, and quelling riots—all in the space of three city blocks. They train with nonlethal munitions and are taught to recognize and react to the block they are in at any given time.

114. The public supports using the military more than the leaders of the Services or even government leaders. See "A Busy Military: Public Supports Using the Military," *Air Force Times,* 29 November 1999, and Steven Kull and I. M. Destler, "U.S. Foreign Policy: What Do Americans Want?" *Chronicle of Higher Education,* 3 September 1999, B8.

115. David Finkel, "The Face of Hate," *Washington Post Magazine,* 12 December 1999, 14. Dana Priest, "Waging Peace in Kosovo," *Washington Post,* 23 November 1999, 1.

116. QDR report, 1997.

117. *Joint Vision 2010.*

118. Among others, see George J. Tenet, Director of Central Intelligence, DCI Diversity Strategic Plan, October 1999. Universities also are defending diversity as a strength in and of itself. See Ben Gose, "A Sweeping New Defense of Affirmative Action," *Chronicle of Higher Education,* 18 September 1998, A46; Peter Schmidt, "U. of Michigan Turns to Scholars to Bolster Its Defense of Affirmative Action," *Chronicle of Higher Education,* 2 April 1999, A38; and William G. Bowen and Derek Bok, "Get In, Get Ahead: Here's Why (Why Diversity Matters in College Admissions)," *Washington Post,* 20 September 1998, C1. As of December 2000, the University of Michigan had won its case in support of the use of race as one category for consideration in admissions to support diversity in education; the ruling was overturned and the appeal continues.

119. Chafe, *The American Woman*, 18–19.

120. Fenner, "Ideology and Amnesia," and Andrea Press, *Women Watching Television: Gender, Class, and Generation in the American Television Experience* (Philadelphia: University of Pennsylvania Press, 1991).

121. Kier, "Homosexuals in the U.S. Military"; Kerber, *No Constitutional Right to Be Ladies*; Kohn, "Out of Control"; David A. J. Richards, *Women, Gays and the Constitution: The Grounds for Feminism and Gay Rights in Culture and Law* (Chicago: University of Chicago Press, 1998); James F. MacIssac and Naomi Verdugo, "Civil-Military Relations: A Domestic Perspective," *U.S. Civil-Military Relations: In Crisis or Transition*, edited by Don M. Snider and Miranda Carlton-Carew (Washington, D.C.: Center for Strategic and International Studies, 1995). Also Captain Rosemary Mariner (USN, Retired) lectures and e-mail "Re: Women in Combat," 23 January 1999.

122. As explained and quoted in Kerber, *No Constitutional Right to Be Ladies*, 236–37.

123. Ibid., 236–38.

124. Ibid., 238.

125. Ibid., 239.

126. Ibid., 242.

127. Ibid.

128. Ibid., 243.

129. Ibid., 243, 221–36, 252–60.

130. Ibid., 244–45.

131. Fenner, "Ideology and Amnesia," and Kerber, *No Constitutional Right to Be Ladies,* 221–36, 252–60.

132. This privilege operates differently for men of color, as well as—even if less obviously so—for gay men and men of certain religious groups and moral beliefs.

133. Fenner, "Ideology and Amnesia," chapters 2–9. In addition, a key statistic cited for the growing "crisis" in civil-military relations is that fewer and fewer federal legislators are veterans. Again, little distinction is made between length of service, combat, and wartime status. We also ignore that fewer citizens in general have served since World War II—and even fewer since the end of the draft and the Vietnam conflict. Finally, we ignore the fact that with more women in Congress, who had less opportunity to serve, there would be a smaller percentage of veterans. Perhaps that situation will change—the first female veteran, Heather Wilson (R.-N.M.), has been elected.

134. Among others, see E. J. Dionne, Jr., "Two for Glory," *Washington Post,* 10 December 1999, A47.

135. Fenner, "Ideology and Amnesia," chapters 2–9.

136. Chafe, *Women and Equality*, 45–78.

137. Richard H. Kohn, ed., *The United States Military under the Constitution of the United States, 1789–1989,* (New York: New York University Press, 1991), 1–14 . Writers in this volume amplify and expand on themes discussed in Kerber, *No Constitutional Right to Be Ladies.* Richard B. Morris reminds us that the overriding purpose of the Constitution was to preserve liberty, and the standing army was one of the most dangerous institutions to that liberty. Military thinkers today debate whether the all-volunteer military is becoming more socially and politically isolated and less like the American population. Allan Millet points out that a key issue from our colonial past is that all able-bodied males of military age would be enrolled by local organizations to fight in time of need. Even though Millet specifies "men" in this part of the discussion on citizen-soldiers, he also refers to "masses of citizens" and "people" when discussing our Revolutionary roots and current practice. Bernard Nalty extends the debate to black men, showing that although "military service was seen to be a fundamental obligation of citizenship . . . this obligation did not flow in reverse, . . . service did not bring full equality under the Constitution. . . . " Black men were not considered citizens and were denied the opportunity to serve except in emergencies. Individual black men gained from their service, but their service did not translate into constitutional rights and basic liberty for all black Americans. In addition, segregation damaged efficiency by denying black men a combat role (and training); civil political pressure, the votes of black Americans, and the Civil Rights movement were required to change society's racial ideas and practices and abolish segregation in the military. (Nalty does not mention black women.) Finally, Jonathan Lurie shows that the courts have avoided intervention even into broad oversight of civil rights in the military. Until 1951, military members did not enjoy the same rights and protections as other Americans while they lived under military jurisdiction. In the past 50 years, however, the military has increasingly recognized those rights and aligned the military system with the civilian judicial system. This evolution is increasingly important as individuals inside and outside the military seek to gain recognition of their rights as citizens.

138. See Feaver and Gelpi, "How Many Deaths are Acceptable?"; Weigley, "The American Military and the Principle of Civilian Control"; and others as cited above. Also see William Matthews, "Political Gap Between Public, Military Growing, Survey Says," *Air Force Times,* 6 December 1999, 23, and Bradley Graham, "Civilian, Military Seen Growing Apart Study Finds Partisan Armed Forces 'Elite,'" *Washington Post,* 18 October 1999, A17.

139. Richards, *Women, Gays, and the Constitution,* 16.

140. Ibid.

141. Ibid., 6–7.

142. Judith Youngman, "A Must Read" (review), via e-mail, 6 February 1999. Karen J. Winkler, "Constitutional History With a Difference: Studying Women's Civic Obligations," *Chronicle of Higher Education,* 18 September 1998, A17–18. Kerber, *No Constitutional Right to Be Ladies,* 307, 380.

143. Kerber, *No Constitutional Right to Be Ladies*, 264.

144. Ibid., 265. Kerber also confirms that Morris Janowitz, too, argues that there was greater reliance on volunteer forces in the international context during this period.

145. Kerber, *No Constitutional Right to Be Ladies*, 267.

146. Edvard Luttwak told a joke recently at an Industrial College of the Armed Forces alumni lunch. He decried the military's current casualty aversion, saying that flying in civilian foreign carriers was more dangerous than flying in our Air Forces in war. As an example of how combat restrictions worked in DESERT SHIELD/STORM, Breuer's numbers add up to the following: 6.8 percent of the American forces were female; women were then overrepresented as POWs at 11.8 percent (2 of 17) and underrepresented in deaths at 3.6 percent (11 of 305)—unless one considers that women were supposedly zero percent of the combat forces.

147. Kerber, *No Constitutional Right to Be Ladies*, 221–36, 252–60.

148. Ibid., 251.

149. Absolute preferences consisted of a lifelong and complete advantage in the scoring systems for Civil Service jobs.

150. Kerber, *No Constitutional Right to Be Ladies*, 255.

151. Ibid., 258–59, 370.

152. Ibid., 257–59.

153. Ibid., 246, 366.

154. Ibid., 246–48, 285.

155. Ibid., 247, 367.

156. Ibid., 248, 367.

157. Ibid., 248.

158. Ibid.

159. Ibid., 249.

160. Ibid.

161. Ibid., 249–50.

162. Ibid., 250. See also Fenner, "Ideology and Amnesia," 50–101.

163. Fenner, "Ideology and Amnesia," 50–101.

164. Kerber, *No Constitutional Right to Be Ladies,* 250; Fenner, "Ideology and Amnesia," 102–48.

165. Kerber, *No Constitutional Right to Be Ladies*, 271–72.

166. Ibid., 276.

167. Ibid., 276–77.

168. Ibid., 279.

169. Ibid., 281.

170. Ibid.

171. Ibid., 284–86.

172. Ibid., 287.

173. Ibid., 290–91.

174. Ibid., 287.

175. Ibid., 290–91. Sharron Frontiero challenged the Air Force to provide spousal/dependent benefits for her husband on the same basis that it provided benefits to the wives of servicemen. The Air Force insisted that male spouses of Air Force personnel prove that they were more than 50 percent dependent on their Air Force wives before they would be afforded benefits such as commissary privileges, hospital care, and housing; wives of servicemen did not have to prove "dependency." The Air Force argued that requiring all men to prove that their wives were "dependent" would be a problem; because there were relatively few servicewomen, however, it could require them to prove their husbands' dependency. The Court ruled against the Air Force's use of administrative expediency for discrimination (*Frontiero v. Richardson,* 411 U.S. 677 [1973]).

176. Kerber, *No Constitutional Right to Be Ladies,* 290–91.

177. Ibid., 291.

178. Ibid.

179. Ibid. In addition, as VMI fought against admitting women, the Supreme Court found that women could not be restricted because of unproven and untested generalizations about the effects of having women around, based on unproven and unfounded generalizations drawn from historical perceptions of women and men. In addition, the Court found that the fact that not all women would seek an opportunity and not all women could meet performance standards should not restrict women who were interested and could meet standards from access or opportunity. The majority argued that we do not apply the "all" standard to men; therefore, women would be denied equal protection. I am indebted to Dr. Judith Youngman for this information (e-mail, 22 January 1999). Youngman also recommends a MacArthur Scholar Series Paper by Lucinda J. Peach, "Women at War: The Ethics of Women in Combat," reprinted in *Minerva: Quarterly Report on Women of the Military* 12 (winter 1994): 1–64.

180. Kerber, *No Constitutional Right to Be Ladies,* 299.

181. Ibid., 300.

182. Ibid., 304; Elshtain, *Women and War.*

183. Kerber, *No Constitutional Right to Be Ladies,* 303–10.

184. Ibid., 309–10.

185. Feaver and Gelpi, "How Many Deaths are Acceptable?"

186. George Tenet and Georgia Sadler, "Women's Assignment to Submarines: An Update," *Alliance Advocate* 1, no. 1 (September 1999): 3.

187. The examples are endless; in addition to those cited previously under Reed and Schlafly, see also Fred Reed, "Group Therapy vs. National Defense," *Armed Forces News,* 8 October 1999, and "Recruiting and Gender," *Armed Forces News,* 18 November 1999; William Murchison, "Boomer Ethic is Hostile to Military," *Dallas Morning News,* 24 February 1999 (Murchison sees the military as a "guy thing"); and William C. Moore, "The Military Must Revive its Warrior Spirit," *Wall Street Journal,* 27 February 1998, 22.

188. The Alliance for National Defense (AND) was started in August 1998 by a concerned group of military and civilian citizens. AND is a nonprofit "educational forum to encourage and promote the vital roles played by military women in our national defense" (Evelyn P. Foote, AND President, *Alliance Advocate* 1, no. 1 [September 1999]). DACOWITS is an official government organization. Although many opponents have painted DACOWITS as a feminist organization from beginning to end, it is not now, nor did it start that way. Some are calling for its disbanding, which I believe would be a mistake. President Truman started the Committee because of the military's hope for support from civilian women, particularly during the Cold War. With the advent of the AVF, DACOWITS helped the armed forces learn how to best recruit and integrate women in the interest of military effectiveness. Although its advice has not always constituted what the Services wanted to hear, it was exactly what the military asked for from such a body. Over time, DACOWITS also has become an advocate for military women, but its activities have benefited military men and families as well.

189. Someone should do a study on the evolution of the term "politically correct." I remember that in the early 1980s, liberal communities used the term as a sarcastic comment to police their own ranks—not the ranks of those with differing politics. In other words, a vegetarian might be chided for wearing leather or an animal rights advocate could be criticized for eating veal. The term was not used by vegetarians to attack meat eaters as not politically correct, nor against conservative politicians for not supporting women's rights. By the 1990s, the conservative right had captured this term and turned it on those who were already marginalized, rhetorically standing the hierarchy on its head. The marginalized community did not have the political power to enforce "correctness." Blaming dispossessed people for wielding discriminatory authority and power over the most political and financially powerful people in our society reverses victimhood. Under the current use of the term, middle-class white men claim that they are victims of reverse discrimination and prejudice.

190. Jessica Lee, "Draft Agency's Number May Be Up," *USA Today*, 24 August 1999, 6.

SELECTED BIBLIOGRAPHY

Air Force Magazine, Air Force Association, 1998–1999.

Air Force Times, 1998–1999.

Allard, Kenneth. *Somalia Operations: Lessons Learned.* Washington, D.C.: National Defense University Press, 1995.

Alliance Advocate, Alliance for National Defense, 1999.

American Women and the U.S. Armed Forces: A Guide to the Records of Military Agencies in the National Archives Relating to American Women. Washington D.C.: National Archives and Records Administration, 1992.

Anonymous. *WAAC: The Woman's Story of the War.* London: T. Werner Laurie Ltd., 1930.

Barkalow, Carol, and Andrea Raab. *In the Men's House.* New York: Poseidon Press, 1990.

Becraft, Carolyn. *Women in the U.S. Armed Services: The War in the Persian Gulf.* Washington, D.C.: Women's Research and Education Institute, 1991.

Binkin, Martin. *Who Will Fight the Next War? The Changing Face of the American Military.* Washington, D.C.: Brookings Institution, 1993.

Binkin, Martin, and Shirley Bach. *Women and the Military.* Washington, D.C.: Brookings Institution, 1977.

Bracken, Jeanne Munn. *Women in the American Revolution.* Carlisle, Mass.: Discovery Enterprises, 1997.

Breuer, William B. *War and American Women: Heroism, Deeds, and Controversy.* Westport, Conn.: Praeger, 1997.

Brinley, Maryann Bucknum. *Jackie Cochran: The Story of the Greatest Woman Pilot in Aviation History.* New York: Bantam Books, 1988.

Brodie, Bernard. *War & Politics.* New York: MacMillan, 1973.

Brown, Dorothy M. *Setting a Course: American Women in the 1920s.* Boston: Twayne Publishers, 1987.

Burgess, Lauren Cook, ed. *An Uncommon Soldier.* New York: Oxford University Press, 1994.

Campbell, D'Ann. *Women at War with America: Private Lives in a Patriotic Era.* Cambridge, Mass.: Harvard University Press, 1984.

Chafe, William Henry. *The American Woman: Her Changing Social, Economic, and Political Roles*, 1920–1970. New York: Oxford University Press, 1972.

Chafe, William H., *Women and Equality: Changing Patterns in American Culture.* Oxford: Oxford University Press, 1977.

Coontz, Stephanie. *The Way We Never Were: American Families and the Nostalgia Trap* (New York: Basic Books, 2000).

Cott, Nancy. *The Grounding of Modern Feminism.* New Haven, Conn.: Yale University Press, 1987.

D'Amico, Francine, and Laurie Weinstein, *Gender Camouflage: Women and the U.S. Military.* New York: New York University Press, 1999.

DCI Diversity Strategic Plan: A Functional Plan that Supports the DCI's Strategic Intent. October 1999.

Degler, Carl. *Women and the Family in America from the Revolution to the Present.* New York: Oxford University Press, 1980.

Department of Defense Inspector General. *Tailhook 91: Events at the 35th Annual Tailhook Symposium*, 1993.

DePauw, Linda Grant. *Battle Cries and Lullabies: Women in War from Prehistory to the Present.* Norman: University of Oklahoma Press, 1998.

———. *Founding Mothers: Women of America in the Revolutionary Era.* Boston: Houghton Mifflin Co., 1975.

Dever, John P., and Maria Dever. *Woman and the Military: A Hundred Notable Contributors, Historic to Contemporary.* Jefferson, N.C.: McFarland & Co., 1994.

Dillingham, Wayne E. "The Possibility of American Military Women Becoming POWs: Justification for the Combat Exclusion Rules?" *Federal Bar News & Journal.* May 1990.

———. "The Possibility of American Women Becoming Prisoners of War: A Challenge for Behavioral Scientists," *Minerva: Quarterly Report on Women and the Military* 8, no. 4 (winter 1990): 17–22.

Disher, Sharon Hanley. *First Class: Women Join the Ranks at the Naval Academy.* Annapolis: Naval Institute Press, 1998.

Dunlap, Charles L., Jr. "The Origins of the American Military Coup of 2012." In *Essays on Strategy X*, edited by Mary A. Sommerville (Washington, D.C.: National Defense University Press, 1993), 3–43.

Durova, Nadezhda, translated by Mary Fleming Zirin. *The Cavalry Maiden: Journals of a Russian Officer in the Napoleonic Wars.* Bloomington: University of Indiana Press, 1989.

Earley, Charity Adams. *One Woman's Army: A Black Officer Remembers the WAC.* College Station: Texas A&M University Press, 1989.

Ebbert, Jean, and Marie-Beth Hall. *Crossed Currents: Navy Women from WWI to Tailhook.* Washington, D.C.: Brassey's, 1993.

Elshtain, Jean Bethke. *Women and War.* New York: Basic Books, 1987.

———. *Meditations on Modern Political Thought.* University Park: Pennsylvania State University Press, 1992.

Emert, Phyllis Raybin, ed. *Women in the Civil War: Warriors, Patriots, Nurses, and Spies.* Lowell, Mass.: Discovery Enterprises, 1995.

Enloe, Cynthia. *Does Khaki Become You? The Militarisation of Women's Lives.* Boston: South End, 1983.

———. "The Politics of Constructing the American Military Woman Soldier as a Professionalized 'First Class Citizen': Some Lessons from the Gulf." *Minerva: Quarterly Report on Women and the Military* (spring 1990).

Evans, Sara M. *Born for Liberty: A History of Women in America.* New York: Free Press, 1989.

Feaver, Peter D., and Christopher Gelpi. "How Many Deaths Are Acceptable? A Surprising Answer." *Washington Post,* 7 November 1999, B3.

Fenner, Lorry. "'Either You Need These Women or You Do Not': Citizenship and Women in the Military." *Gender Issues* (summer 1998).

———. "Ideology and Amnesia: The Public Debate on Women and the American Military, 1940–1973." Ph.D. diss., University of Michigan, 1995.

Flexner, Eleanor. *Century of Struggle: The Woman's Rights Movement in the United States.* Rev. ed. Cambridge, Mass.: Harvard University Press, 1975.

Francke, Linda Bird. *Ground Zero: The Gender Wars in the Military.* New York: Simon & Schuster, 1997.

Fraser, Antonia. *The Warrior Queens.* New York: Alfred A. Knopf, 1989.

French, Marilyn. *The War Against Women*. New York: Summit Books, 1992.

Friedl, Vicki L., compiler. *Women in the United States Military, 1901–1995: A Research Guide and Annotated Bibliography*. Westport, Conn.: Greenwood Press, 1996.

Golar, Martha L. et al. "The Combat Exclusion Laws: An Idea Whose Time Has Gone." Association of the Bar of the City of New York Committee on Military Affairs and Justice, 1 April 1991.

Goldman, Nancy Loring. *Female Soldiers—Combatants or NonCombatants?* Westport, Conn.: Greenwood Press, 1982.

Gordon, Linda. *U.S. Women's History*. Washington D.C.: American Historical Association, 1990.

Gordon, Marilyn A., and Mary Jo Ludvigson. "A Constitutional Analysis of the Combat Exclusion for Air Force Women." *Minerva: Quarterly Report on Women and the Military* 9, no. 2 (summer 1991).

Griffith, Samuel B., trans. *The Art of War* (original by Sun Tzu). London: Oxford University Press, 1971.

Gropman, Alan L. *The Air Force Integrates, 1945–1964*. Washington D.C.: Office of Air Force History, 1985.

Hacker, Barton. "Women and Military Institutions in Early Modern Europe: A Reconnaissance," *Signs: Journal of Women in Culture and Society* 6, no. 4 (1981): 643–71.

Hansen, Ellen, ed. *Principles of Democracy: The Constitution and The Bill of Rights*. Carlisle, Mass.: Discovery Enterprises, 1995.

Hartmann, Susan M. *The Home Front and Beyond: American Women in the 1940s*. Boston: Twayne Publishers, 1982.

Haskell, Molly. *From Reverence to Rape: The Treatment of Women in the Movies*. 2nd ed. Chicago: University of Chicago Press, 1987.

Hayton-Keeva, Sally. *Valiant Women in War and Exile*. San Francisco: City Lights Books, 1987.

Hewitt, Linda L. *Women Marines in World War I*. Washington, D.C.: History and Museums Division, Headquarters, U.S. Marine Corps, 1974.

Hine, Darlene Clark. *The State of Afro-American History: Past, Present, and Future*. Baton Rouge: Louisiana State University Press, 1986.

Holm, Jeanne M., ed. *In Defense of a Nation: Service Women in World War II*. Washington, D.C.: Military Women's Press, 1998.

———. *Women in the Military: An Unfinished Revolution*. Rev. ed. Novato, Calif.: Presidio, 1992.

Hollis, Patricia. *Women in Public: The Women's Movement, 1850–1900*. London: George Allen & Unwin, 1981.

Howard, Michael, and Peter Paret, eds. and trans. *On War* (original by Carl von Clausewitz). Princeton, N.J.: Princeton University Press, 1976.

Hunter, Anne E., ed. *On Peace, War and Gender: A Challenge to Genetic Explanations*. New York: The Feminist Press at CUNY, 1991.

Huntington, Samuel. *The Common Defense: Strategic Programs in National Politics.* New York: Columbia University Press, 1961.

―――. *The Soldier and the State.* Cambridge, Mass.: Harvard University Press, 1957.

Inness, Sherrie A. *Tough Girls: Women Warriors and Wonder Women in Popular Culture.* Philadelphia: University of Pennsylvania Press, 1999.

Janowitz, Morris. *The Professional Soldier: A Social and Political Portrait.* New York: Free Press, 1971.

Jeffords, Susan. "'The Battle of the Big Mamas': Feminism and the Alienation of Women." *Journal of American Culture* 10, no. 3 (1987): 73–84.

―――. *Hard Bodies: Hollywood Masculinity in the Reagan Era.* New Brunswick, N.J.: Rutgers University Press, 1994.

Kaledin, Eugenia. *Mothers and More: American Women in the 1950s.* Boston: Twayne Publishers, 1984.

Katzenstein, Mary Fainsod. *Faithful and Fearless: Moving Feminist Protest inside the Church and Military.* Princeton, N.J.: Princeton University Press, 1998.

Kelly, Joan. *Women, History, and Theory.* Chicago: University of Chicago Press, 1984.

Kerber, Linda. *Toward an Intellectual History of Women.* Chapel Hill: University of North Carolina Press, 1997.

―――. "'A Constitutional Right to be Treated Like . . . Ladies': Women, Civic Obligation and Military Service," *University of Chicago Law School Roundtable,* 1993, 95–128.

―――. *No Constitutional Right to be Ladies: Women and the Obligations of Citizenship.* New York: Hill and Wang, 1998.

―――. *Women of the Republic: Intellect and Ideology in Revolutionary America.* New York: W. W. Norton, 1980.

Kerber, Linda, and Jane Sherron De Hart. *Women's America: Refocusing the Past.* New York: Oxford University Press, 1995.

Kier, Elizabeth. "Homosexuals in the U.S. Military: Open Integration and Combat Effectiveness," *International Security* 23, no. 2 (fall 1998): 5–39.

Kohn, Richard H. "Out of Control: The Crisis in Civil-Military Relations," *The National Interest,* no. 35 (spring 1994): 3–17.

―――, ed. *The United States Military under the Constitution of the United States,* 1789–1989. New York: New York University Press, 1991.

Lerner, Gerda. *The Creation of Patriarchy.* New York: Oxford University Press, 1986.

Lomax, Judy. *Women of the Air.* New York: Dodd, Mead & Co., 1987.

MacGregor, Morris J., Jr. *Integration of the Armed Forces, 1940–1965.* Washington, D.C.: Center of Military History, 1981.

MacKinnon, Catherine A. *Feminism Unmodified: Discourses on Life and Law.* Cambridge, Mass.: Harvard University Press, 1987.

―――. *Toward a Feminist Theory of State.* Cambridge, Mass.: Harvard University Press, 1989.

Mangerich, Agnes Jensen. *Albanian Escape: The True Story of U.S. Army Nurses Behind Enemy Lines.* Lexington: University of Kentucky Press, 1999.

Marshall, S. L. A. *Men Against Fire.* New York: Morrow, 1947.

Matthews, William. "Political Gap Between Public, Military Growing, Survey Says," *Air Force Times,* 6 December 1999, 23.

May, Elaine Tyler. *Homeward Bound: American Families in the Cold War Era.* New York: Basic Books, 1988.

McGuire, Phillip, ed. *Taps for a Jim Crow Army: Letters from Black Soldiers in World War II.* Lexington: University Press of Kentucky, 1993.

Millett, Kate. *Sexual Politics.* New York: Avon, 1969.

Millis, Walter. *Arms and Men: A Study in American Military History.* New Brunswick, N.J.: Rutgers University Press, 1984.

Mitchell, Brian. *Weak Link: The Feminization of the American Military.* Washington, D.C.: Regnery Gateway, 1989.

———. *Women in the Military: Flirting with Disaster.* Washington, D.C.: Regnery Publishing, 1999.

Morden, Betty J. *The Women's Army Corps, 1945–1978.* Washington, D.C.: U.S. Army Center of Military History, 1990.

Morris, Madeline. "By Force of Arms: Rape, War and Military Culture." *Duke Law Journal* 45 (1996): 651.

Moskos, Charles. "Army Women," *Atlantic Monthly,* August 1990.

———. "Women in Combat: The Same Risks as Men?" *Washington Post,* 3 February 1990.

Muir, Kate. *Arms and the Woman: Female Soldiers at War.* London: Sinclair-Stevenson, 1992.

Myles, Bruce. *Night Witches: The Amazing Story of Russia's Women Pilots in World War II.* Chicago: Academy Chicago Publishers, 1990.

Nalty, Bernard C. *Strength for the Fight: A History of Black Americans in the Military.* New York: Free Press, 1986.

National Military Strategy of the United States of America. Shape, Respond, Prepare Now: A Military Strategy for a New Era, 1997. Washington D.C.: Joint Chiefs of Staff.

National Security Strategy 1999. Washington D.C.: National Security Council.

"The Netherlands' Female Fighter Pilots," *WMA News* (summer/fall 1984).

Newark, Tim. *Women Warlords: An Illustrated Military History of Female Warriors.* London: Blandford, 1989.

Noggle, Anne. *A Dance with Death: Soviet Air Women in World War II.* College Station: Texas A&M University Press, 1994.

Norton, Mary Beth. *Founding Mothers and Fathers: Gendered Power and the Forming of American Society.* New York: Knopf, 1996.

Ofer, Dalia, and Lenore J. Weitzman. *Women in the Holocaust.* New Haven, Conn.: Yale University Press, 1998.

O'Neill, William L. *Everyone Was Brave: The Rise and Fall of Feminism in America.* Chicago: Quadrangle Books, 1969.

Osur, Alan M. *Blacks in the Army Air Forces During World War II: The Problem of Race Relations.* Washington, D.C.: Office of Air Force History, 1986.

Porter, Bruce D. *War and the Rise of the State: The Military Foundations of Modern Politics.* New York: Free Press, 1994.

Presidential Commission on the Assignment of Women in the Armed Forces. *Women in Combat: Report to the President.* Washington, D.C.: U.S. GPO, 1992.

Press, Andrea. *Women Watching Television: Gender, Class, and Generation in the American Television Experience.* Philadelphia: University of Pennsylvania Press, 1991.

Preston, Richard A., and Sydney F. Wise. *Men in Arms: A History of Warfare and Its Interrelationships with Western Society.* New York: Holt, Rinehart and Winston, 1979.

Reed, Fred. "Recruiting and Gender," *Armed Forces News,* 18 November 1999.

————. "Group Therapy vs. National Defense," *Armed Forces News,* 8 October 1999.

Richards, David A. J. *Women, Gays and the Constitution: The Grounds for Feminism and Gay Rights in Culture and Law.* Chicago: University of Chicago Press, 1998.

Rittner, Carol, and John K. Roth. *Different Voices: Women and the Holocaust.* New York: Paragon House, 1993.

Rogen, Helen. *Mixed Company: Women in the Modern Army.* New York: Putnam, 1981.

Rosenberg, Rosalind. *Beyond Separate Spheres: Intellectual Roots of Modern Feminism.* New Haven, Conn.: Yale University Press, 1982.

Rupp, Leila J., and Verta Taylor. *Survival in the Doldrums: The American Women's Rights Movement, 1945 to the 1960s.* New York: Oxford University Press, 1987.

Ryan, Garry D. and Timothy K. Nenninger, eds. *Soldiers and Civilians: The U.S. Army and the American People.* Washington, D.C.: National Archives and Records Administration, 1987.

Saywell, Shelly. *Women in War.* New York: Penguin Books, 1986.

Scharf, Lois, and Joan M. Jensen, eds. *Decades of Discontent: The Women's Movement, 1920–1940.* Boston: Northeastern University Press, 1987.

Schmidt, Peter. "U. of Michigan Turns to Scholars to Bolster Its Defense of Affirmative Action," *Chronicle of Higher Education,* 2 April 1999, A38.

Schneider, Dorothy, and Carl J. Schneider. *Sound Off! American Military Women Speak Out.* New York: Paragon House, 1992.

Scott, Joan Wallach. *Gender and the Politics of History.* New York: Columbia University Press, 1988.

Seeley, Charlotte Palmer, compiler. *American Women and the U.S. Armed Forces: A Guide to the Records of Military Agencies in the National Archives Relating to Women.* Washington D.C.: National Archives and Records Administration, 1992.

Segal, David R. *Recruiting for Uncle Sam: Citizenship and Military Manpower Policy.* Lawrence: University Press of Kansas, 1989.

Segrave, Kerry. *Policewoman: A History.* Jefferson, N.C.: McFarland & Co., 1995.

Shilts, Randy. *Conduct Unbecoming: Gays and Lesbians in the U.S. Military.* New York: St. Martin's Press, 1993.

Snider, Don M., and Miranda A. Carlton-Carew, eds. *U.S. Civil-Military Relations: In Crisis or Transition?* Washington D.C.: Center for Strategic and International Studies, 1995.

Stiehm, Judith Hicks. *Bring Me Men and Women: Mandated Change at the U.S. Air Force Academy.* Berkeley: University of California Press, 1981.

———. *Arms and the Enlisted Woman.* Philadelphia: Temple University Press, 1989.

———. *It's Our Military Too: Women and the U.S. Military.* Philadelphia: Temple University Press, 1996.

Toffler, Alvin, and Heidi Toffler. *War and Anti-War: Survival at the Dawn of the 21st Century.* Boston: Little, Brown and Co., 1993.

Treadwell, Mattie E. *The Women's Army Corps.* Washington, D.C.: Office of the Chief of Military History, 1954.

Walker, Keith. *A Piece of My Heart.* New York: Ballatine Books, 1985.

Wandrey, June. *Bedpan Commando: The Story of a Combat Nurse During World War II.* Elmore, Ohio: Elmore Publishing Co., 1989.

Ware, Susan. *Holding Their Own: American Women in the 1930s.* Boston: Twayne Publishers, 1982.

Weatherford, Doris. *American Women and World War II.* New York: Facts on File, 1990.

Weigley, Russell F. "The American Military and the Principle of Civilian Control from McClellan to Powell," *Journal of Military History* 57 (special issue, October 1993): 27–58.

Winkler, Allan M. *Homefront U.S.A.: America during World War II.* Arlington Heights, Ill.: Harlan Davidson, Inc., 1986.

Women in Uniform: Exploding the Myths; Exploring the Facts. Conference papers, Women's Research and Education Institute, Washington, D.C., 1998.

Women in the Military: International Perspectives. Conference Proceedings of Women's Research and Education Institute, Washington, D.C., 1992.

Women in the United States Military, 1901–1995: A Research Guide and Annotated Bibliography. Westport, Conn.: Greenwood Press, 1996.

Zumwalt, Elmo. "Equal Rights and Opportunities for Women in the Navy," Z-Gram 116. 7 August 1972.

PART TWO

Marie E. deYoung
*A Feminist Analysis in Support of
the U.S. Army Ground Combat
Exclusion for Women*

❏ INTRODUCTION

Congress established the United States Army for the sole purpose of national defense and protection of the Constitution of the United States. As an extension of the executive branch, constitutionally, the Army has been and always should be exempt from many statutory and constitutional mandates that pertain to individual or citizens' rights. The courts traditionally have upheld the Army's decisions to abrogate the individual rights of soldiers and potential recruits whenever it has proved that the requirements of national defense supersede an individual's claim to liberty. Where the civil rights of male soldiers are concerned, the invincible legal defense of the Army's right to abrogate soldiers' rights is attributed to the so-called Feres doctrine. This doctrine is invoked routinely to squelch male soldiers' pursuit of legal remedies for injustices on the part of the government, even in cases in which governmental malfeasance resulted in maiming, murder, or accidental death of soldiers (*Feres v. United States*, 340 U.S. 135, 1950).

As an institution, the United States Army is in crisis. This crisis was triggered by a systematic political thrust to change the Army's *raison d'être*— and its culture. The devolution of military strength and readiness began when legislators and activists usurped the necessary authority of military leadership to subordinate the individual rights of uniformed service members as needed to safeguard the highest standards of training and discipline. The collapse of morale and discipline that hastened the devolution of military readiness was effected by the preferential selection of particular civil rights issues for judicial, legislative, and media interference—namely, the rights of women and gay soldiers. The devolution was complete when policymaking shifted from the requirements of national security to the demands of uncompromising special interest groups to prioritize the rights of individuals over the needs or the good of the Army.

Army leadership acquiesced ceaselessly to the demands of judicial and legislative advocates who do not have, at the heart of their concern, the Army's mission to provide the strongest national defense. Instead, the dominant agenda of these groups has been the modification of personnel policy to advance feminist and gay political goals that are entirely extraneous to the Army's mission.

Although many personnel issues could be refracted through the lens of policymaking by appeasement, in this analysis I focus on one that affected me most as a female officer in the United States Army: the aggressive strategies to assign women to ground combat units. I am a feminist—that is, a woman who struggles to end sexist oppression (hooks 1984)—and a feminist scholar (that is, a woman who places women at the center, as the subjects of inquiry and as active agents in the gathering of knowledge) (Stacey and Thorne 1998). As such, I argue that the strategy to push women into combat roles to increase the political stature of women is counterproductive and inconsistent with the principles of American democracy, as well as the goal of full participation by women in American society.

In this analysis I demonstrate that too often, the reality of war fighting, ground combat, and the negative consequences for women who are assigned to ground combat training is glossed over. Harsh reality is overlooked to advance, at best, an abstract goal of improving women's political status by assigning women to combat fighting positions. Such political goals may have great appeal with an uninformed electorate that is predominantly female. I hope to show that the trend is detrimental to these same constituents—as well as to cost-effective but unsurpassable national defense. Assignment of women to near-combat and ground combat situations does not increase military effectiveness; it decreases such effectiveness, and such assignments are detrimental to women who must endure them.

Ground Combat: Definition for the Purpose of Personnel Assignment

In media and congressional debates, blithe sound-bite descriptions of modern warfare deflect the public's attention from the grave consequences of the Army's incremental policy changes that inch toward eradication of combat exclusion policies for women. In this oppositional public discourse, extremists on both sides of the issue have failed to adequately define or describe ground combat in advocating policy changes. The Presidential Commission on the Assignment of Women in the Armed Forces, for example, issued its findings concerning gender assignments in the military without ever defining the term *ground combat* in its final report (Presidential Commission 1993).

The persistent lack of definition and the lack of moral or tactical consistency in ground combat fighting strategies have made the discussion about women's place in ground combat at once complicated and confusing. Ironically, the blurred distinction between combat and noncombat roles on the tactical battlefield became the strongest argument for assigning women to units where they were never intended to serve under existing combat exclusion policies—even as combat service support soldiers.

What is ground combat? *Ground combat* as a military term is not defined in most Army training manuals other than by description and historical scenarios. To bring clarity to the discussion on women's roles, the Department of Defense sketched a clear definition of direct ground combat for the first time in 1994 (Secretary of Defense 1994). Although the Army's personnel assignment branch never honored the new definitions, they clearly provide a sound framework that, if implemented, would have averted the personnel crisis that has now overtaken the United States Army. The 1994 Department of Defense definition of ground combat was as follows:

> B. Definition. Direct ground combat is engaging an enemy on the ground with individual or crew served weapons, while being exposed to hostile fire and to a high probability of direct physical contact with the hostile force's personnel. Direct ground combat takes place well forward on the battlefield while locating and closing with the enemy to defeat them by fire, maneuver, or shock effect (Secretary of Defense 1994).

The ground combat exclusion policy was modified to accommodate this seemingly airtight definition and, at the same time, to "expand opportunities" for women:

> A. Rule. Service members are eligible to be assigned to all positions for which they are qualified, except that women shall be excluded from assignment to units below the brigade level whose primary mission is to engage in direct combat on the ground, as defined below (Secretary of Defense 1994).

Four exceptions or clear restrictions on the assignment of women were spelled out:

- Where the Service Secretary attests that the costs of appropriate berthing and privacy arrangements are prohibitive
- Where units and positions are doctrinally required to physically collocate and remain with direct ground combat units that are closed to women
- Where units are engaged in long-range reconnaissance operations and Special Operations Forces missions
- Where job-related physical requirements would necessarily exclude the vast majority of women service members.

Expanded "Assignment Opportunities" in the Army Violate 1994 Policy

With the Secretary of Defense's concise *ground combat* definition and the concomitant exceptions in place, the Services responded to the demands of women's groups and expanded opportunities for women, as Lieutenant General Theodore G. Stroup, Jr. testified to Congress (U.S. House Armed Services Committee 1994a). In accordance with the new ground combat definition, Stroup testified that Army women would be excluded from combat infantry and armor battalions because they engage in direct fight with the enemy. In his testimony, Stroup declared that women could be assigned to combat engineer battalion *headquarters* because "the headquarters does not engage in direct ground combat and does not routinely collocate with maneuver battalions." Women could be assigned to forward air defense artillery (FADA) headquarters but not to FADA batteries because the batteries are collocated with infantry and armor task forces (U.S. House Armed Services Committee 1994b).

Even before the official announcement of these policy changes, I served as a chaplain to units that were collocated with combat maneuver elements. Subsequently, every combat training unit to which I was assigned as a battalion chaplain collocated with combat line units. I address the problem of assigning women to combat battalion headquarters elements when I analyze my own experience with the combat engineers. First, however, we must look at the new policy in general terms.

From August 1993 until January 1995, I was the first woman regimental support squadron chaplain for the 2nd Armored Cavalry Regiment (ACR)—a light cavalry unit. The situation created in the 2nd ACR, intentional or not, explicitly violated the old and new ground combat exclusion rules in letter and spirit. Consequently, as a "Cav" support chaplain, I experienced firsthand the artifice that propels women into military situations for which they are not qualified.

The ACR is much like an oversized brigade, with three combat line squadrons (equivalent to battalions), one aviation squadron, one support squadron, and the regimental headquarters. By doctrine, the cavalry support squadron, to which women have been assigned since 1993, is scattered about the battlefield. The light cavalry regiment's main role is to be the main screening force (Department of the Army 1996). The regiment's responsibility in armed conflict is to keep contact with the enemy, to provide a covering force in battle. Figure 1 demonstrates the full range of combat tasks performed by armored cavalry troops (Department of the Army 1996).

The Regimental Support Area (RSA) covers the Forward Edge Battle Area (FEBA)—which, during Desert Storm, encompassed 25 square miles. Part of the regimental headquarters collocates with the support squadron. Teams from every element in the support squadron, however, are sliced off and moved to collocate with the three fighting squadrons. As Figure 1

	RECON				SECURITY						MISSIONS ASSOCIATED WITH ECONOMY-OF-FORCE ROLE					
	Route	Area	Zone	Recon in Force	Screen	Guard	Cover	Area	*Route	*Convoy	Hasty Attack	Attack	Movement to Contact	Defend Battle Position	Defend Sector	Retrograde (Delay)
ACR		X	X	X	X	X	X	X	X	X	X	X	X		X	X
-Squadron		X	X	X	X	X		X	X	X	X	X	X		X	X
-Troop	X	X	X		X			X		X	X	X	X	X	X	X
-Scout Platoon	X	X	X		X						O		O	O	O	O
-RAS		X	X	X	X			⊗	⊗	⊗	X	O	X			X
-ACT	X	X	X		X						X	O	X			X
ACR(L)		X	X	X	X	⊗	⊗	X	X	X	⊗	⊗	⊗		⊗	⊗
-Squadron		X	X	X	X	⊗		X		X	⊗	⊗	⊗		⊗	⊗
-Troop	X	X	X		X			X		X	⊗	⊗	⊗	⊗	⊗	⊗
-Scout Platoon	X	X	X		X			X			O		O	O	O	O
-RAS		X	X		X			⊗	⊗	⊗	X	O	X			X
-ACT	X	X	X		X						X	O	X			X
Armored Division Cavalry Squadron		X	X	X	X	X		X	X	X	X	X	X		X	X
-Troop	X	X	X		X			X		X	X	X	X	X	X	X
-Scout Platoon	X	X	X		X			X			O		O	O	O	O
-ACT	X	X	X		X						X	O	X			X
Light Division Cavalry Squadron		X	X		X			X	X		⊗	⊗	⊗		⊗	⊗
-Troop	X	X	X		X			X		X	⊗	⊗	⊗	⊗	⊗	⊗
-Scout Platoon	X	X	X		X			X			O		O	O	O	O
-ACT	X	X	X		X						X	O	X			X
Task Force Scout Platoon	X	X	X		X											

⊗ = METT-T dependent; may require reinforcement. Threat composition must be equal or less than unit in respect to firepower, survivability, and maneuverability.

x = Doctrinally capable.   * Application of area security.

O = Nondoctrinal but capable, given METT-T.

Figure 1. Cavalry Operations: Primary Missions by Unit (from FM 17-95)

reveals, the "slices," or support packages, are in proximity to the essential cavalry combat tasks: reconnaissance, hasty attacks, passage of lines, movement to contact the enemy, passage of lines (through enemy terrain), and more. Thus, in the RSA, the medical troop has a full medical station set up for casualties to receive initial triage and treatment, but medical ambulance teams are sent forward with the line squadrons to handle on-site medical problems and to initiate casualty evacuations as necessary. Similarly, the maintenance troop provides full maintenance in the RSA. At the same time, maintenance service teams (MSTs) are sent forward with battle line squadrons to provide repair and maintenance to vehicles and equipment that must be patched up and returned to the heat of battle.

Furthermore, the potential for participation in ground combat is not lost on any woman who serves such a ground combat support battalion. Ever since women were assigned to the 2nd Armored Cavalry Regiment, they have moved forward as members of their respective ambulance, maintenance, or other support teams. This arrangement clearly violates the combat exclusion rule and the exceptions to enforcement of this rule, which were set forth by the late Les Aspin when he served as Secretary of Defense. Because support teams move forward to line elements to service combat troops, all women who serve in the regimental support squadron have a high probability of being rotated into combat proximity while supporting the "fighting" squadrons.

Not only does the doctrinal requirement of collocating mixed-gender service teams with line squadrons compromise the integrity of the combat exclusion policy, the very assignment of women to the support squadron is an ignored violation. Because the regimental support squadron supports a combat reconnaissance mission, it serves well forward—that is, in front of the battlefield. It is always subject to enemy attack. Every support element must defend itself with crew-served weapons such as M-60 machine guns. The Defense Department's new definition of direct ground combat is "engaging an enemy on the ground with individual or crew-served weapons, while being exposed to hostile fire and to a high probability of direct physical contact with the hostile force's personnel." The regimental support squadron cannot accept the assignment of women and be in compliance with the late Secretary Aspin's prescriptions for the expanded role of military women.

I review extensive evidence to show that women soldiers, as a class of Army recruits, may be physically unqualified to contend with the rigors of combat service support training and harsh field conditions, let alone ground combat. Female soldiers are not ill-informed about the inappropriateness of placing women in ground combat, however, as surveys about women's attitudes can attest (Miller 1998). This knowledge is reflected in women's lifestyle choices on assignment to units with heavy field training and potential for collocation with ground combat units, as I experienced in the 2nd ACR support squadron and other support battalions.

Although a few women in our regimental support squadron were well-qualified to participate in support operations, the vast majority were discouraged whenever extended field duties (more than five days) were required. Our pregnancy rates skyrocketed during cycles of heavy combat support training (despite routine training on prevention of pregnancies and sexually transmitted diseases during basic training, military occupational specialty training, and regular unit prevention briefings). Statistics from my direct experience in these combat support units show that in just one squadron, the pattern of pregnancies was as follows: 2 of 2 from the communications section, 3 of 6 personnel clerks, and 12 of 15 female cooks (deYoung 1999). The pattern has repeated in all support companies I have served—from medical units that have instant access to birth control to aviation support battalions, such as the 404th in the 4th Infantry Division, that, compared to combat battalions, experience luxurious field living conditions.

My experience has led me to conclude that the mere fact of heavy field duties, not impending combat action, generally encourages women to make lifestyle choices (unplanned single parenthood) that will compromise not only the unit's readiness statistics but the completion of these women's primary career and education goals.

In addition, military attrition rates for women who are assigned to units that have heavy field training are high. The military finally has acknowledged that the overall first-enlistment attrition rate for women is 45 percent; white women register their dissatisfaction with the nature of military training at a rate of 54 percent (U.S. House Armed Services Committee 1999). Women who leave the Army by documenting a psychological or physical disability leave with full GI benefits in tact, including the ability to go directly to college. Pregnant women who remain in these support units and on active duty as single parents, however fecund, are not force multipliers, however. Pregnant soldiers are granted extensive maternity leave, exemption from their field training and primary duties for the duration of their pregnancy, and postmaternity leave, leaving their units perpetually vulnerable to disqualification as deployable assets.

The Army never needed to put women in this dilemma—or to make itself vulnerable to combat nonreadiness—by expanding the role of women in violation of Secretary Aspin's 1994 guidance. The Marine Corps interpreted that guidance with more faithfulness to the Secretary's definition when it was instructed to review its gender assignment policies. The Marines excluded women from assignment to all infantry regiments and below, artillery battalions and below, all armored units (tanks, amphibian assault vehicles, and light armored reconnaissance vehicles), combat engineer battalions, reconnaissance units, riverine assault craft units, and low-altitude air defense units (U.S. House Armed Services Committee 1994b). Because all soldiers assigned to these units would be in close proximity to combat—in a headquarters element or a combat platoon—women would continue to be excluded.

Lt. Gen. George R. Christmas noted that despite extensive coordination with the Army, the two branches were not consistent in their assignment decisions. He acknowledged the sincerity of the Army's decision to permit women in combat engineer battalion headquarters but insisted that the Marines could not follow suit because combat engineer battalion headquarters are not exempt from battlefield activity as the Army's headquarters, at least *doctrinally*, appear to be.

When the Army decided to assign women to headquarters elements for combat engineer (and now, armor and infantry) battalions, it violated the intent and spirit of Secretary Aspin's 1994 guidance. Wartime scenarios for Army engineer, infantry, and armor battalions are no different from the scenarios for the Marines. As a feminist who is keen on advancing the participation of women in all spheres of life, I never understood the error in the Army's interpretation until I personally lived and worked in engineer and other combat units that were newly opened to women. Only when I had the opportunity to test the Army's decisions through assignments to battalions that, according to General Stroup's Congressional testimony, should not place women in ground combat circumstances could I realize the fallacy and the failure of the Army's decision.

Two of the most rewarding assignments I have had as a chaplain were with combat engineer units. I was assigned first as the battalion chaplain for the 44th Combat Engineer Battalion in the Second Infantry Division in Korea. When I returned to the states, I was assigned as brigade chaplain to the 4th Infantry Division's Engineer Brigade. As engineer brigade chaplain (and for lack of other available chaplains), I also was the primary chaplain to two combat engineer battalions—the 588th and the 299th in the 4th Infantry Division. The logical and tactical failures inherent in the Army's decision to place women in combat engineer battalions or brigade headquarters was made abundantly clear to me during my tenure with these Sappers (engineers).

Engineer Battalion Headquarters Experience Ground Combat

First, the argument that women can be placed in engineer battalion headquarters without danger of exposure to direct combat because battalion headquarters elements do not collocate with their line combat companies is fallacious. The Army argued that battalion staff positions—including chaplains, medical officers, battalion commanders, and executive officers—should be open to women. This fallacy drives personnel assignment policy: The headquarters company *qua* company does not collocate with the line companies. Hence, women assigned to headquarters ought not be well forward on the battlefield. Advocates of the placement of women at headquarters argued that women would not be locating and closing with the enemy to defeat them by fire, maneuver, or shock effect. Therefore, women could be assigned to combat engineer battalion headquarters.

Only through my personal experience did I come to understand the danger this argument poses. As my last executive officer reminded me, the mission of the engineer battalion is to smash through obstacles, to shape the battlefield for the fighting force, and then to create obstacles and cover for tank and infantry forces that move onto new fighting terrain. Engineers are the first on the battlefield and the last off. True, while I was stationed with the most forward deployed combat engineer battalion in the world—the 44th Combat Engineer Battalion in the 2nd Infantry Division—the headquarters never did (and never will) deploy *as a unit* to support combat engineer companies. *Individuals* in the engineer headquarters company, however, do collocate or work closely with direct ground combat elements in each of the line companies.

The fact is that although the headquarters unit is stationary, every section in the headquarters has particular field responsibilities and direct support functions for the line companies in the fighting zone. The engineer battalion headquarters company has administrative clerks; nuclear, biological, and chemical (NBC) trainers; intelligence and communications specialists; medical staff; cooks; petroleum, oil and lubrication operators; truck drivers; and all kinds of mechanics assigned. Several staff officers and noncommissioned officers are responsible for successful operations, equipment maintenance, and effective training and discipline in the subordinate elements—the line companies. Low-ranking cooks, administrative clerks, nuclear-biological-chemical trainers, intelligence analysts, communications specialists, medics, truck drivers, and mechanics go to combat with the line companies as individuals or as part of service support teams.

Most of the senior leaders of the engineer battalion, all of whom are assigned to the battalion headquarters, also must deploy to the field. The battalion commander and sergeant major must move from site to site to provide training and tactical guidance, to enforce good discipline and health practices, to spot-check equipment, and to carry out other kinds of coordination. The executive officer may go or stay, as the style of the commander dictates. The medical officer must go to the field to supervise medics, ensure sanitation practices, and provide medical support. Intelligence officers supervise tactical intelligence operations. The chaplain must move from site to site to provide religious and moral support to squads and platoons scattered all over the battlefield. Thus, the fact that individual soldiers from headquarters companies deploy with combat elements to battlefield conditions should make obvious that assigning women to any headquarters in engineer or other combat battalions violates the spirit and intent of the DoD's 1994 assignment policy.

Headquarters' Ability to Cross-Level Is Weakened

Second, other realities about the management of personnel in combat situations also defy the argument that any woman assigned to a headquarters company would not be exposed to ground combat situations. For example, even the peacetime assignment of women to ground combat battalion headquarters weakens the battalion's organizational strength, and thus its readiness, because female soldiers cannot and should not be cross-leveled into line companies—as peacetime training scenarios and real combat conditions require. Cross-leveling is a sound management practice that helps organizations function during crises or when personnel shortages exist. If Bravo Company, a combat line unit, is short an administrative clerk or a track vehicle mechanic, a female soldier cannot be transferred into that assignment. If Charlie Company needs a heavy equipment transporter (HET) driver to move armored personnel carriers to and from tactical areas, a female driver cannot and should not be assigned. If Alpha Company needs a platoon leader, the female supply officer cannot be cross-leveled as such.

Cross-leveling is a short-term strategy to overcome personnel shortfalls. In long-term combat assignments, women cannot offer the same depth of experience, relationship, or institutional memory to the battalion team. Because women are assigned to combat battalion headquarters to do a specific job—such as cooking, clerking, or vehicle maintenance—their value to the combat organization is limited. They are not full team members who can rotate through a variety of positions for the length of their tour. Consequently, even in peacetime, combat engineer battalion headquarters assignments should be limited to other ground combatants to bring greater depth to the assigned soldier's skill bank and the battalion's institutional memory.

Personnel who are assigned to engineer brigade headquarters are not safe from the heat of battle, either. Despite General Stroup's testimony to Congress, combat engineer brigade headquarters personnel, where women now are assigned, are just as vulnerable to exposure to direct ground combat as women assigned to engineer battalion headquarters. As an engineer brigade chaplain, I noticed great similarities between engineer battalion headquarters and brigade headquarters. Although the headquarters brigade seems to focus on coordination between division and task force elements and the battalions who must do maneuvers, all of the tactical requirements for battalion headquarters staff pertain to brigade staff as well. All individuals who are assigned to front-line brigade headquarters must deploy to combat sites at one time or another. Thus, women who are assigned to deployed brigade headquarters in peacetime would be vulnerable to enemy attack in time of war. In addition, protracted ground combat scenarios require cross-leveling by all of the enlisted personnel and officers who are assigned to a brigade headquarters. From the executive officer and chaplain to the personnel clerk and communications section chief, personnel ought to be able to rotate into direct combat slots as emergencies or commonsense personnel management would dictate. Once again, when women are assigned to brigade headquarters, the organizational strength of the entire brigade is compromised because women cannot be cross-leveled into ground combat slots.

Lack of Strength Is Always an Issue

In the preceding sections, I have noted only how Secretary Aspin's 1994 assignment policy was erroneously interpreted to expand peacetime assignment of women in battalions, brigades, and regiments that clearly have direct ground combat responsibilities. One might ask, "If you and other women completed your assignments successfully, then what's the problem? Haven't you proved that women can hold their own, that they can succeed as ground combatants? Haven't you paved the way for further expansions?" The answer is no—unequivocally, no.

Without denigrating my own accomplishments or those of the other fine female soldiers who serve in direct ground combat units, the fact remains that we were and will continue to be the weakest link in the chain, a problem that seasoned combat soldiers have to work around. Men and women who are assigned to ground combat battalions and brigades will overcompensate for the misfit.

Many of the *quid pro quos* are extremely beneficial to the unit in peacetime. Women make strong contributions as classroom instructors, family counselors, technical writers, and as trainers. Although these contributions are important to the unit's morale or technical proficiency before the battalion engages in ground combat, they have no place *during* successful prosecution of direct ground combat. Second, because of women's documented lower standards of physical fitness, men overcompensate by doing the woman's fair share of heavy lifting, tent setup and breakdown, digging of fighting positions, carrying of crew-served weapons, road marching, and so forth in support battalions.

While I served the combat engineer brigades and battalions, I never found another female officer or enlisted soldier in the field during combat battalion training exercises. Arrangements routinely are made to keep the female executive officers or supply clerks in garrison. No female assigned to the headquarters element has ever complained to me about this chauvinistic protection from field duty. Through my experiences in rapid deployment forces and combat battalions, I have come to recognize that the strategy to leave women in garrison is protective on two counts. First, some untimely out-of-wedlock pregnancies are averted; second, men avoid accusations of sexual harassment when they attempt to hold women to the same performance standards as men.

Ground Combat Units Can't Afford to Pause for Sexual Harassment Investigations

The most tragic example of the tendency to conflate a sergeant's accountability session into an allegation of harassment occurred at Fort Hood, Texas, in 1996 (deYoung 2000). A first sergeant of the 299th Engineer Battalion Headquarters Company was accused of creating a hostile work environment for a pregnant soldier under his supervision because he would not move her out of the arms room once her obstetrician gave him guidance to make the working area environmentally safe for her. As other women assigned to this battalion headquarters also decided, this woman became pregnant for the sole purpose of being removed from the male combat battalion. She was outraged when her wish to be moved to a soft administrative position was not satisfied. Combat battalions can't afford to be crippled by high pregnancy rates or the "hostile environment" sexual harassment court-martial proceedings that too often are thrust upon sergeants and officers who strive to hold women to task. Thus, women are routinely left in garrison during field training assignments—which makes their presence in the headquarters duplicative.

Teaching Skills Are Not Comparable to Ground Combat Skills

There is another variation of the *non sequitur* that by virtue of placing women in combat battalions we have proved women belong there: Women who train or teach combatants and combat pilots are good enough to be combatants or combat pilots. Without intending to insult the holder of this argument, its failure can be found in the adage, "Those who can't, teach." I may be fully qualified to teach the next young Van Cliburn, even to the point of her winning a Tschaikovsky competition in Moscow, yet not be qualified at all to perform professionally or to win that competition myself. Similarly, I may be fully qualified to coach college soccer, but I may not at all qualify to play in a World Cup championship or even to play with a third-rate professional or college team. The opposite also is true: Great fighters, soldiers, artists, and sports heroes may not have the ability to teach their craft as well as they perform it in real-time conditions.

Teaching is a gender-neutral skill. Undoubtedly, military skills taught by women are gender-neutral: flying airplanes, logistics management, ethics, communications technology, supply management, personnel administration, or even, domestic violence prevention. If the ground combat exclusion is ever to be decided honestly and fairly, however, we must recognize an objective fact: The qualities of a ground combatant are not gender-neutral. Until God or genetic engineers find a way to restructure women's biology, the unequivocal fact is that men are favored with the physical traits that are requisite to ground combat survival. Military training manuals document the physiological basis for combat exclusion policies for women and gender-normed physical training standards—that is, for lower physical testing standards for women. Ironically, women have used the courts to gain access to male-only schools such as Virginia Military Academy (VMI) and The Citadel by striking at the heart of gender stereotypes and generalizations that precluded women's participation (see *United States v. Virginia et al.*, 518 U.S. 515, 1996). Yet there have been no lawsuits and feminists have not publicly advocated to remove the preferential standards, even to prepare women adequately for ground combat! Miller reports that Army women who theoretically want the ground combat exclusion lifted for women do not want gender-normed fitness standards lifted as the logical step toward the full integration of women (Harrell and Miller 1997).

In 1999, the Army had 10 active-duty divisions. A few of these divisions are restricted to stateside training missions. Most are available for deployment or are actively deployed on dangerous international borders. Thus, it is imperative to consider the consequences of violating the DoD policy for ground combat exclusion by assigning women to battalion headquarters that have a real potential for erupting into armed conflict. When I served the 44th Combat Engineers in 1995–1996, tensions between North and South Korea were extraordinarily high. The battalion headquarters is tucked away on a beautiful mountainside, but it is just as vulnerable to enemy attack as the infantry grunts that straddle the Demilitarized Zone (DMZ) with grenades and rifles pointed at the enemy. My commander's training guidance to soldiers always included the reminder: "We are 9 miles from the DMZ, within the 35 kilometer fan of field artillery fire. We will be hit first if the North decides to attack." Fortunately, we were never attacked, and the anticipated war between North and South may be forever postponed. What if the 1995 diplomacy efforts by emissaries such as Gen. Gary E. Luck or former President Jimmy Carter had failed, however, and the North did attack South Korea?

Depiction of "Safe" Headquarters Engaged in Ground Combat

What would an attack on a ground combat battalion headquarters—engineer, infantry, or armor—be like? Would women be protected from the reality of ground combat? Would men be sufficiently capable of fighting back the enemy if women were their squadmates? Army training manuals teach today's training lessons with stories from real combat scenarios. Perhaps Gen. Norman Schwarzkopf's account of his own experience in Vietnam suffices to demonstrate that although the headquarters may not collocate with direct ground combat elements, in fact, direct ground combat may be thrust upon the headquarters element, wherever its fixed location:

> We were surrounded. In the space of two days, more than forty paratroopers had died and at least twice that number were seriously wounded. . . . The next morning we carried our wounded on stretchers to the airstrip and waited. The instant his two-engine C-123 turboprop appeared, the enemy opened fire. . . . Meanwhile the airstrip came under mortar attack. More people were hurt, and we threw them on the airplane, too. . . . Meanwhile, we had no idea how big the enemy force had hemmed us in. We sent out patrols during the day,

and no matter which direction they took, they came under fire. . . . Each night we went to bed with the conviction that the camp would be overrun and we would be killed. I learned to sleep with one ear cocked, because I knew that at some point every night there would be a mortar barrage. The thunk of the rounds dropping into the mortar tubes was audible hundreds of yards away, and when I heard that sound, I knew I had maybe eight seconds to make it to a foxhole. Many nights I'd find myself sprinting for my foxhole without quite knowing why, but sure enough, explosions would erupt all around . . .

As the days went by, conditions in the camp became grim. Early on, the mortars destroyed the water tank. Although there was a watering hole outside camp, the enemy knew about it; so when we needed water, we had to send a platoon to fight its way down and back. Food ran low, but when the airborne tried dropping fresh supplies, the planes stayed so high that the wind blew the parachutes outside the perimeter. We asked them to stop, because all they were doing was feeding the enemy. We were soon down to rice and salt. Sometimes Sergeant Hung would crawl out through the wire and come back with a certain kind of root he'd dig up in the jungle. It looked like a big turnip and could be eaten raw, so we'd sit with our rice and pass the root back and forth, taking bites (Schwarzkopf and Petre 1992).

Gen. Schwarzkopf's account should give pause to anyone who thinks that in time of war, an engineer or infantry headquarters battalion would be safe from direct enemy attack and thus appropriate for assignment of women under the Secretary of Defense's 1994 guidance. The only time a direct combat battalion headquarters is immune from combat or enemy attack is during declared peacetime, but forward-deployed "peacekeeping" units are always vulnerable to attack when our troops are situated on hostile borders. Until a peace treaty between North and South Korea is signed or American troops are withdrawn from the Republic of Korea's soil, however, the U.S. Army should never assume that American troops in the 2nd Infantry Division are not vulnerable to ground combat. Women should not be assigned to these units.

To sum, in violation of the spirit and intent of Secretary Aspin's assignment policy for women in the military, women have been placed in units that have essential ground combat functions. Many advocates have reasoned that the very fact that women have taken these assignments for regular duty or that women have functioned as trainers to ground combatants is proof that women are capable and ready to serve as ground combatants. Because the contexts in which women have been placed do not resemble the phenomenon of direct ground combat, policymakers should reject the arguments to end the combat exclusion policy as specious. The argument that women can be assigned to the headquarters element of a combat battalion is a fallacy of accident: The headquarters element may not see combat, but all individuals assigned to the headquarters are needed on the battlefield at one time or another. The argument that women trainers have demonstrated by their teaching proficiency an ability to succeed in combat is a simple *non sequitur*. Finally, the faith-based argument—that we should simply believe that women can succeed as ground combatants because there is no evidence to the contrary—should be dismissed as *ad ignorantiam*. A preponderance of evidence supports the need to strengthen, not repeal, ground combat exclusion policies for women.

Direct Ground Combat as It Really Happens

Theoretically, the Army "trains as it fights." Realistically, combat training in the Army, with its complex web of legal and political requirements to sanitize the experience for the sake of international and local civic relationships, is never a matter of "training as we fight." In peacetime, our soldiers do not carry live ammunition on guard duty or while moving to and from training ranges. In wartime, battles will not be planned so that humvees and howitzers avoid destruction of environmentally protected habitat—as they are required to do during combat training. Despite the Gulf War and the countless minor deployments of the past decade, American soldiers have not experienced prolonged ground combat since the Vietnam War. Before considering the physical, psychological, sociological, legal, and moral reasons that should be the basis for continued exclusion of women, we must dwell even further on the gritty reality that we would impose on women if the restrictions were lifted.

Battle Focused Training—the in-depth battle training guide for battalion and company soldiers—does not explicitly define ground combat except by cataloging hundreds of physically grueling tasks, maneuvers, and operations in minute detail (Department of the Army 1990b). One can only assemble a definition for direct ground combat by stringing together the tasks in a unified sequence. The short list would include tactical road marches; tactical movements; attacks and counterattacks by fire; assaults; breaching or defending an obstacle; performing engineer reconnaissance; conducting river crossings; defending convoys against ground attack; securing and defending positions; laying and operating machine guns; operating grenade launchers; operating tube-launched, optically tracked, wire-guided (TOW) missile launchers; maintaining machine guns, launchers, turrets, and vehicles; repairing track on armored carriers and tanks; attacking fortified positions; defending against NBC attacks; breaching minefields; and laying minefields (Department of the Army 1990b).

For better or worse, the Army's battle-focused training manuals rarely allude to the grim reality of ground combat (Department of the Army 1990b, 1990c). These manuals merely prescribe the specific skills, tasks, and operations that soldiers must master to survive in combat. These tasks sound cold, clinical, and devoid of trauma, horror, or physical strain—and they can be, in a training context, when the training team is physically qualified, mentally prepared for the operation, and opposing a mere simulated enemy with simulated ammunition. In the absence of war, men who have no prior experience of combat or exposure to more realistic accounts of combat easily could be deceived into thinking that ground combat is as much fun or as threatening as deer or duck hunting. Men and women alike would be deceived—and thus ill-prepared—if their only understanding of ground combat were drawn from task-oriented training manuals such as *Field Manual 25-101* (Department of the Army 1990c) or from the training exposures they receive in basic training or during ROTC summer camp.

Leadership manuals, on the other hand, do provide realistic descriptions of ground combat (Department of the Army 1987). Leadership manuals are the most important references for leaders to be reminded of the life-threatening, terrifying nature of ground combat (Department of the Army 1983). To convey the gravity of war to leaders, the Army most often depends on classic historical accounts of actual battles to drive home the physical horror, the psychological chaos, and the soul-wrenching ethical dilemmas of combat. The account of Private First Class Dexter Kerstetter—a cook's helper whose heroism is recounted in *Common Sense Training* to emphasize the necessity for all soldiers to be optimally trained as combatants—accomplishes the task in a way that battle-focused training manuals never could:

CITATION: Medal of Honor. He was with his unit in a dawn attack against hill positions approachable only along a narrow ridge paralleled on each side by steep cliffs which were heavily defended by enemy mortars, machine guns, and rifles in well-camouflaged spider holes and tunnels leading to caves. When the leading element was halted by intense fire that inflicted five casualties, Private Kerstetter passed through the American line with his squad. Placing himself well in advance of his men, he grimly worked his way up to the narrow steep hogback, meeting the brunt of enemy action. With well-aimed shots and rifle-grenade fire, he forced the Japs [sic] to take cover. He left the trail and moving down a cliff that offered only precarious footholds, dropped among four Japs [sic] at the entrance to a cave, fired his rifle from his hip and killed them all. Climbing back to the trail, he advanced against heavy enemy machine-gun, rifle and mortar fire to silence a heavy machine-gun by killing its crew of four with rifle fire and grenades. He expended his remaining ammunition and grenades on a group of approximately 20 Japs [*sic*], scattering them, and returning to his squad for more ammunition and first aid for his left hand, which had been blistered by the heat from his rifle. Resupplied, he guided a fresh platoon into a position from which a concerted attack could be launched, killing three hostile soldiers on the way. In all, he dispatched 16 Japs [*sic*] that day. The hill was taken and held against the enemy's counterattacks, which continued for 3 days. Private Kerstetter's dauntless and gallant heroism was largely responsible for the capture of this key enemy position, and his fearless attack in the face of great odds was an inspiration to his comrades in their dangerous task (Collins 1978).

Private Kerstetter's heroism should remind us of an unalterable fact: Cooks aren't just support staff in the Army who can limit their training to the culinary arts. Cooks must be as strong and proficient as infantrymen because in a *protracted* war, they are likely to fight in direct ground combat, up-close and personal. In every combat service support unit to which I have been assigned, female cooks believe they have no responsibility to fight. When they are pressured to do combat training in the field or even required to practice field sanitation instead of returning to garrison for baths every 48 hours, they adopt resistance tactics such as "unplanned pregnancies." The Air Force may indoctrinate its personnel to believe that wars can be won in a day without dropping a pint of American blood. The Navy may relish its capacity to float "Love Boats" with all the requisite drugs to prevent pregnancy and sexually transmitted diseases for their invincible and insulated combat aviators and long-range missile technicians. By contrast, the Army and the Marines can never escape the fundamental reality of their work. Ground combat is filthy, brutal, bloody, killing work that cannot be sanitized, gentrified, cleansed of the bloody gore, or feminized into a nonviolent ethos.

The story of Sergeant York—the Tennessee mountain boy whose faith caused him to question the morality of war during World War I—also is recounted in many leadership manuals. *Military Leadership* (Department of the Army 1990a)—the guide that provides the moral, technical, and tactical principles of combat leadership—highlights the following passage to illustrate the timeless quality of ground fighting:

> The essence of Alvin York's life was compressed into four hours of October 8, 1918, in the mud and blood of the Argonne Forest [in France]. . . . At 6:10 a.m., York's company was ordered to . . . seize a German-held rail point.

Hidden in woods overlooking a valley, a German machine-gun battalion opened up on the company, killed most of its forward ranks.

York, the only surviving noncom, was left in command. He called for the others to come forward. They advanced and succeeded in overcoming the first machine gun nest and taking its crew prisoner. York told someone to see to getting the prisoners to the rear; then he moved out in advance of his tiny command to see what lay ahead of them. He had gone forward only a few yards when a line of 35 machine guns opened up and pinned him down.

The Tennessean found himself trapped and under fire within 25 yards of the enemy's machine gun pits. . . . He began firing into the nearest enemy position, aware that the Germans would have to expose themselves to get an aimed shot at him. And every time a German head showed over the parapet, York drilled a bullet into it!

After he had shot down more than a dozen enemy gunners in this fashion, he was charged by six German soldiers who came at him with fixed bayonets. York . . . drew a bead on the sixth man, and then on the fifth. He worked his way down the line, and practically before he knew it, the first man in line was charging the eagle-eyed American sharpshooter all by himself. York dropped him with a dead center shot.

York again turned his attention on the machine gun pits. Every time he fired, another enemy soldier fell. . . . In between shots York called for the Germans to surrender. At first it may have seemed funny to the well-entrenched enemy; but the joke had become rather hollow by the time the Tennessean had killed his twenty-second victim. Shortly afterward a German officer advanced under a white flag and offered to surrender if York would stop shooting at his men. York demanded—and received—the surrender of the remaining Germans. Having taken a total of 132 prisoners, and knocked 35 machine guns out of action, York finally returned to his regiment's lines. He left the prisoners . . . and headed back to his own outfit.

Endless stories of guerrilla, trench, urban, jungle, mountain, and desert warfare drive home the fundamental principle that good combat training must diligently prepare the soldier for the grueling reality of a protracted battle. Combat training must incorporate the examples, illustrations, and stories of real combat situations to reinforce the unending need for the most rigorous tactical training, toughest physical conditioning, and most strenuous character formation that are essential to survival in ground combat.

Direct Ground Combat as It Is Imagined

Because words can never adequately describe combat, military trainers and recruiters often show movies to honestly communicate the primary combat mission. When I enlisted in 1983, my recruiter encouraged me to see *Deer Hunter, Private Benjamin,* and *An Officer and a Gentleman* to understand the "hardships" I would endure as a female recruit and officer candidate. Today, the cinematography of *Saving Private Ryan, The Thin Red Line, Courage Under Fire,* and *GI Jane* conveys the reality of modern combat and the fantasies of would-be heroes. The former two movies can only instruct the soldier about the absolute requirement for rigorous physical, tactical, and moral training as a prerequisite for survival. In the latter two, the gender-constructed fantasies create a participation mystique at best, particularly for those who cannot live up to the screen dream. At worst, they foster delusions for those who would try to recreate the cinematic illusions in our contemporary military culture.

The most persistent myth to propel the argument for allowing women in ground combat is the mistaken belief that our high-tech military equipment will spare American combatants from the ravages of war because such gadgetry makes physical inferiority irrelevant to combat success. The Air Force version of this myth is that foxholes and firefights are obsolete: There won't be any foxholes in the next war. From now on, the Air Force will send bombers out, all the targets will be hit, the pilots will fly home the same day for supper, and the war will be over!

This common misperception is what I call the *Star Trek* fallacy: the myth that ground combat has become so high-tech, so lightweight that any 110-pound woman in shapely tights with hair flowing to her waist can take on whole battalions of enemy forces at arm's length. With a nifty flick of her laser pen, the enemy, in the heat of battle, will drop to the wayside with nary a spurt of blood or gash in the gut. The heroine of the *Star Trek* fallacy, of course, stands tall as a conqueror when the peace is won, her bosomy silhouette untouched by the ravages of war.

On sheer technological grounds, this myth has been debunked at the National Training Center and other evaluation sites. At these test sites, Army troops zip around in nifty computerized tanks, transmitting battle-tracking data with computerized laptop computers. When they are tested by objective evaluators, however, our troops actually lose their ground battles to ragtag enemy forces that use traditional tactics against our high-tech soldiers.

Someday, computers may win wars without the expense of American combat troops. To date, however, military computers in ground combat equipment do not function dependably enough even to allow soldiers to train properly. The Institute for Defense Analyses (IDA) reports that high-tech simulators fail to transmit graphics of the battlespace and battle-tracking overlays 75 percent of the time. During IDA's observations, text messages reached their destination on the battlefield an average of 23 percent of the time. In the IDA's final report, a battalion commander described this problem: "Just because we would hit send, that didn't mean they would get it. . . . So we kept sending and sending" (Armed Forces Newswire Service 1997).

I was privileged to participate in the digitized Army's training program while I was in Korea, during the warfighting exercises in 1995. For 11 months during 1996–1997, I was assigned to the 4th Infantry Advanced War Fighting Experimental Division as it tested computerized battle equipment and twenty-first century fighting strategies. In both situations, the greatest fears of Vietnam combat veterans were realized, albeit in simulated peace-time conditions. When computers went dead, the digitized Army was incapable of functioning; soldiers dallied until systems were a "go." This deficiency is gender-neutral. High-tech equipment and high-flying precision bomber pilots won't win a war in the 21st century with a flick of a laser pen—whether the combatants are of mixed gender or exclusively men.

Most military trainers would agree that science fiction has a role to play in military training. *Star Trek* provides marvelous entertainment and brilliant leadership philosophy for the student of military science. I am only a recent fan, having discovered that many of the Army's field training scenarios tailored for the Generation X soldier are situated in places such as Cardasia. The use of science fiction localities and enemy characterizations frees the military of the danger of demonizing world leaders who are today's designated threats to our national security. Since the end of the Cold War—and as the Iran-Iraq war demonstrated—we know that our enemy today could be our friend tomorrow. In this context, using fictional characters and notional localities to practice combat drills makes sense.

To inculcate the highest leadership values, using the *Star Trek* milieu to make field training palatable to the young soldier makes sense. Women benefit from the leadership lessons in every episode of this tele-legend. Women warriors are treated with respect. Federation warriors carry out humanitarian missions as much as they fight off evil enemies. The professional ethics of Federation officers are unsurpassable. These are all important moral messages and leadership models for our military to inculcate.

We must distinguish fact from fantasy, however, especially when we are planning for earthly combat ventures. Too many implicit assumptions drawn from science fiction fantasies are driving contemporary military personnel policies. The *Star Trek* fallacy, for example, wrongfully depicts ground war and combat as bloodless, gutless, brainy, brawnless, and, worst of all, disembodied. In the fantasy, women command and fight alongside male combatants because there is nothing physical about the task, other than the utterance of high-speed technological instructions and the aiming of that three-ounce laser pen.

In sum, advocates who push to assign women to ground combat roles base their argument on imagined understandings of the nature of ground combat. All discussion of strategy, tactics, equipment, and personnel requirements for the successful prosecution of ground combat must have, as central reference points, illustrations and stories from real combat scenarios. We make the gravest mistake—we commit the *Star Trek* fallacy—when we push for personnel policies that are based on the unknown potential of future combat technology. We can only formulate our strategies and our personnel policies on the basis of the reality that is, not on the fantasy that may one day come true but for now remains a fantasy.

As a feminist, I believe that women deserve much more sober and honest information about the military situations into which our legislators could place them by changing the combat exclusion policy. As a soldier, on the other hand, I do not discount the value of technological developments that one day could make the use of military force a bloodless affair. I know that Force XXI should never be reduced to mere "stubby pencil" technology again. No matter how sophisticated American technology becomes, however, the true nature of war will never change. Regardless of how banal the metaphor sounds to the uninitiated, war was, is, and always will be a living hell. Thus, we need computers and laser technology, but we need the best brawn, too. When our computers are destroyed on the battlefield with electromagnetic pulses, the equipment burns down but the fight goes on. Our Army deserves the best equipment that money can buy to win battles. Even more, however, our combatants deserve the best-qualified soldiers to stand beside them when they have to put their bodies and their lives on the line.

❏ HISTORICAL ARGUMENT AGAINST ASSIGNMENT OF WOMEN IN COMBAT

Lorry Fenner correctly argues that the debate about women's roles in the military should be historically contextualized (Fenner 1998). The participation of women in the profession of military arms cannot be decided in a historical vacuum. The underlying premise of her argument, however—that women should be in ground combat or not serve at all—commits the fallacy of false alternatives (Fenner 1998). We can use the talents of women in the military but limit their participation to assignments that would preclude or, to the greatest extent possible, avoid ground combat exposure. By reviewing the record to date, I believe we should draw the following historical inference: not that women's military participation is an all-or-nothing proposition but that women can make valuable but limited contributions to the military profession.

In-depth analysis of women's war experiences and contributions to war efforts are available elsewhere (see, e.g., Presidential Commission 1993). Similarly, feminist scholars have uncovered stories of rare women such as Margaret Cochran Corbin, who continued an artillery battle after her husband was killed during a battle in the Revolutionary War, or the rare small band of women who organized to capture a military courier (GenderGap 1998). In the Mexican War, two identified women and a "large number of women and children" in an Iowan battalion of Mormon volunteers fought in Santa Fe, New Mexico; Texas; and California. (The Department of Defense reports 78,789 male combatants in that war.) The GenderGap account includes an estimate of 400 women who cross-dressed so they could serve as combatants during the Civil War (GenderGap 1998), compared with 2, 213,582 men who fought (U.S. Department of Defense and U.S. Coast Guard 1997).

The Army attempted to increase its ranks of women during WWII but had difficulty maintaining a force of 60,000 women on a voluntary basis (GenderGap 1998); DoD statistics confirm more than 16 million men fought in WWII. At the conclusion of World War II, the Army formed the Women Army Corps (WAC). Of the women who served in combat support roles, 45,000 remained with the WAC program; the remaining 15,000 chose to return to civilian life, despite the Army's pressure tactics to retain them (GenderGap 1998). After the Gulf War, the Department of Defense, under pressure from feminist advocates, opened 90,000 near-combat slots to women. At the peak of the Army's recruiting crisis in 1999, the Army lost first-enlistment recruits at an annual rate of 47 percent (U.S. House Armed Services Committee 1999). The shortage of 10,000 military recruits should never have occurred if the "glass ceiling" myth were true: namely, that women's participation in military life was restricted by recruitment ceilings and limited assignment and promotion opportunities.

Feminist literature often uses documented cases of female POWs to justify the placement of women in ground combat. Once again, the number of women POWs is insignificant, as the WWII Los Banos statistics reveal. Of the 2,147 prisoners, 11 were Navy nurses (GenderGap 1998). The experience of a female POW, furthermore, typically is not comparable to that of the male combat POW. For example, all of the nurses who were taken prisoner in the Philippines were allowed to set up nursing stations. Feminist historians record that these nurses did not experience the beatings and torture that male combatants in POW camps routinely experienced:

> The nurses remaining on Corregidor were taken prisoner on May 7, 1942, one day after General Wainwright surrendered his 11,500 troops in the Philippines. The nurses knew that Japanese soldiers had killed British nurse prisoners in the previous year and many expected to be executed. However, while some of the men on the Corregidor were killed or tortured by their captors, most of the troops and all the women were spared the immediate horrors inflicted on the U.S. troops captured on Bataan, where nearly 25,000 POWs died on the infamous Death March, with another 22,000 dying during the first two months they were held in Camp O'Donnell (GenderGap 1998).

Women Combatants in Western Nations and the Middle East

In the 20th century, dozens of stories are recounted of women resisters and spies who were tortured to death alongside their male colleagues. The Presidential Commission on Women in Combat acknowledged estimates of 100,000 women combatants in the Yugoslavian Army in WWII. The outcome, by all historical accounts, was clear: Yugoslavia was unequivocally defeated on two fronts in that war, surrendering to Hitler's German Army within one month of repudiating the Tripartite Axis agreement (Braakhuis 1997–99). Obviously, women's participation was not the cause of defeat, but this example illustrates the negligible difference that women combatants make when nations desperately resort to their participation.

Often, the conscription practices of foreign nations are noted to prove that women are capable of participation in ground combat. Israel, as a nation, conscripted men and women alike. During its War of Independence, women were pushed into combat positions. Although Israel won the war, the government imposed combat exclusion policies on women because the problems associated with women's participation in ground combat units by far outweighed the benefits. I personally traveled through Israel in 1977, when women toted rifles in the military and boasted of their service as officers in the armed services. The record shows—and my experience confirmed—that women had no expectation of serving on the front lines.

Despite that limitation, junior enlisted women pushed to avoid the required military service as often as our junior enlisted women adopt resistance strategies to avoid field duty.

Two Other Examples: Burundi and Eritrea

Burundi's government requires universal mandatory military service. Aside from the protracted internecine combat that has resulted from forced universal service, women are fleeing the country, marrying before their education is complete, and committing other acts of desperation to avoid participation in the fratricide that universal service perpetuates in that nation (Kadende-Kaiser 2000). Similarly, advocacy journalists write stories about women's participation in the Eritrean military—a necessity because of ceaseless civil strife within that nation. To what extent do we wish to borrow the cultural norms of a nation whose limitless propensity to lapse into civil war perpetually threatens its fragile infrastructure—which, in turn, is rebuilt again and again by nongovernmental organization (NGO) agencies?

Overall, in comparing the wartime enlistment rates by gender, we must note that the numbers of women who felt spiritually or morally compelled to take up arms as combatants were as statistically insignificant in prior American wars as in the present day. With the rare identification of individual women such as Deborah Samson or Sara Borginis, scholars have only been able to guess that a few hundred women cross-dressed to serve in any particular war. Even if we could prove that a few hundred women disguised themselves to take up arms, compared to the hundreds of thousands—and, in some cases, millions—of men who carried the burden of ground combat, we must honestly characterize these women's stories as exceedingly rare or anomalous.

American women's lack of desire to participate in ground combat or universal conscription is confirmed in women's overwhelming vote against the Equal Rights Amendment in the mid-1970s because opponents falsely correlated the right of equality among American citizens with the responsibility to take up arms as ground combatants. The attitude of American women has not changed since. Since *Rostker v. Goldberg,* 448 U.S. 1306 (1980), there has been no ACLU or NOW movement to demand universal conscription for women—presumably because these organizations would lose their base of support if they pursued such litigation for equal treatment under the law. Finally, the unwillingness of women to voluntarily meet military recruiting and retention shortages after 90,000 near-combat positions were opened to women during the 1990s, coupled with women's high attrition rates, should stifle all speculation that the only thing keeping women away from such training is an institutional glass ceiling.

❏ PHYSIOLOGICAL REASONS TO EXCLUDE WOMEN FROM DIRECT GROUND COMBAT ASSIGNMENTS

The Army's Physical Training Manual provides the litany of physiological differences between men and women that are the basis for substantially lower physical training standards for women (Department of the Army 1992). Feminist groups that seek advancement opportunities for women have never contested these standards. Consider the following differences:

- The average 18-year-old man is 70.2 inches tall and weighs 144.8 pounds, whereas the average 18-year-old woman is 64.6 inches tall and weighs 126.6 pounds.
- Men have 50 percent greater total muscle mass, based on weight, than women.
- A woman who is the same size as her male counterpart generally is only 80 percent as strong. Therefore, men usually have advantage in strength, speed, and power over women.
- Women carry about 10 percent more body fat than men of the same age. Because the center of gravity is lower in women than in men, women must overcome more resistance in activities that require movement of the lower body.
- Women have less bone mass than men, but their pelvic structure is wider. This difference gives men an advantage in running efficiency.
- The average woman's heart is 25 percent smaller than the average man's. The man's heart can pump more blood with each beat, thus creating a slower resting heart rate (five to eight beats per minute slower) in males.
- Women become fatigued faster than men because their heart rates are five to eight beats faster per minute.
- The lung capacity of men is 25–30 percent greater than that of women.
- Women respond to heat stress differently from men. Women sweat less, lose less heat through evaporation, and reach higher body temperatures before sweating starts.

These physiological handicaps are the basis for "gender-norming"— that is, for holding women to a lower standard of physical performance than men. Even with the most recent physical testing standards, the gap in expectations for men and women is drastic. The explication of physiological gender differences is summarized with the following emphatic conclusion (Department of the Army 1992):

> Women must be treated differently from males, although they can still achieve high levels of physical performance. Gender differences can be alleviated when exercise is conducted by ability groups. When unit runs are conducted, the gender difference cannot be ignored.

In 1998 and 1999, the Army publicized new standards that were supposed to minimize gender scoring disparities. Table 1, a snapshot of the Army's new physical fitness standards as extracted from the new guidelines, reveals the gender gap in ability and expectations for male and female soldiers. In the chart from which Table 1 is extracted, the gender difference is deliberately obscured by setting women's standards far apart from the men's, unlike the side-by-side format used on the Army's scorecard (McHugh 1999).

The Supreme Court adjudicated gender discrimination cases such as *United States v. Virginia et al.* by applying tests that require "heightened scrutiny" of broad policies that are based on stereotypes or generalizations about the female gender. In the cases involving VMI and The Citadel, the Supreme Court struck down policies that systematically exclude women

Table 1. Army Physical Fitness Test Standards

	17–21 years		22–26 years		27–31 years	
	Men	Women	Men	Women	Men	Women
Push-Ups						
Maximum Score	71	42	75	46	77	50
Passing Score	42	19	40	17	39	17
Entry Level	35	13	35	11	30	10
Sit-Ups						
Maximum Score	78	78	80	80	82	82
Passing Score	53	53	50	50	45	45
Entry Level	47	47	43	43	36	36
2-Mile Run						
Maximum Score	13:00	15:36	13:00	15:36	13:18	15:48
Passing Score	15:54	18:54	16:36	19:36	17:00	20:30
Entry Level	16:36	19:42	17:30	20:36	17:54	21:42

from access on the basis of stereotypical assessments of women's abilities such as the physical training standards in Table 1. By contrast, feminists are not challenging the physiological basis for the Army's policy generalizations about women's physical limitations for scoring purposes because the evidence reveals that most women would be immediately disqualified if they were held to the same standards as men. In other words, demanding equal treatment or equal standards of performance in the Army would not be in women's best interests because the preferential standards in Table 1 provide women with a handicapped score that give them a competitive edge for promotion purposes.

These new standards have been touted as an amelioration of the gender gap in standards. In fact, however, the gap is just as wide as before, but some of the standards for men have been lowered to reduce men's resentment about preferential treatment for women. The irony, however, is that women's advocates choose to ignore stereotypical generalizations when such assumptions give women a competitive edge over men, thus calling into question whether disputing the legal validity of stereotypical generalizations as the basis of any military personnel policy is ever appropriate.

In congressional testimony and in subsequent GAO reports, advocates have argued that the Army's physical fitness test does not measure a soldier's ability to perform a specific job, such as combat infantry; instead, the scores measure the individual's general cardiovascular fitness (General Accounting Office 1998b). This distinction permits the Army to gender-norm physical training standards on the basis of the effort required to achieve cardiovascular fitness rather than the effort required to perform combat-related tasks. With the shift in emphasis, the specious argument can be made that the lower standards for women are equitable to men's higher physical performance standards. As Table 1 emphasizes, women don't have to do as much work to achieve cardiovascular fitness as men do. Therefore, the Army need not demand as much from women to achieve equal cardiovascular fitness. Cardiovascular fitness is not the *sine qua non* for battle-ready fitness, however, or for combat fitness. A 90-year-old man who walks three miles daily and lifts light weights may have extraordinary cardiovascular fitness. No one would argue that such a man would have the physical strength, the speed, or the endurance to serve as a ground combatant.

The U.S. Postmaster General prescribes standards for package mailing that could easily be adopted by the Army's Chief of Staff. Scotch or masking tape has the essential characteristics of tape: the ability to close and seal a document. An envelope or a featherweight package sealed with scotch or masking tape will be accepted for mailing. Scotch or masking tape lacks the quality of strength, however; therefore, these types of tape are rejected as sealing materials for heavy packages. Only when tape of proper tensile strength is used will the Post Office accept a package for mailing. Thus, the package and all parties to the transaction are protected from unnecessary damage or harm. If material objects are worth this kind of protection, don't we owe it to our combatants, their families, and our national security to only accept combatants who have essential characteristic of a combatant—such as the necessary strength to accomplish the tasks for which they are being recruited?

In the meantime, the 1998 GAO report confirms the Army's data to justify gender-norming of physical training standards, although the GAO cites data from the National Academy of Sciences:

> In addition to being generally smaller, female soldiers have only 50 to 70 percent of a male's strength, with the greatest disparity in the area of upper body strength. Women have smaller lung capacities and hearts than men. Women also carry about 10 percentage points more body fat than men. As a result of these and other differences, women exerting the same effort as men in running, push-ups, and other cardiovascular and muscular endurance tests are generally at a disadvantage. Therefore, a single fitness standard applicable to both men and women would be unfair to women because meeting that standard would require a much higher level of effort from a woman than it would from a man (General Accounting Office 1998a).

Undoubtedly, Table 1 provides solid physiological reasons for gender-norming—that is, curving—the Army's physical training standards. These physiological data also provide the first and strongest argument for excluding women from ground combat. That is, women may do less to achieve cardiovascular fitness, but physiologically they cannot do as much as men can do, either to improve cardiovascular fitness or to *get the job done*. The documented physiological weakness that undergirds the Army's policy of demanding less physical training from women also should be used to systematically exclude women from ground combat assignments. Women want to have it both ways—easier performance standards as well as easy access to the privileges conferred on those who serve in the Army's ground combat units. Only if and when the cart is put behind the horse, and women prove they can do the physically grueling work of ground combat, should they ask for the opportunity to be ground combatants.

The plea to accept equal effort rather than equal performance as equitable combat standards for both genders is built on another *non sequitur* argument: The physical training test as it presently exists does not measure a soldier's physical ability to do specific jobs in the military; therefore, you can't use it to determine whether a soldier is qualified to do specific combat-related jobs. The fact is, the present test is at least a preliminary screen for *both* cardiovascular fitness and physical ability. The curved scores represent cardiovascular fitness. The raw scores clearly indicate a soldier's strength, speed, and endurance. If a soldier can't do more than 13 pushups, does anyone believe that soldier has the physical strength to lug a backpack through a 12-mile road march? Could such a cardiovascularly fit soldier push up tent poles in a cluster of large tents or push a humvee out of the mud, as soldiers often have to do? If a soldier can't do 15 push-ups or a single pull-up (not tested since the Army integrated the genders), will that soldier have the strength to rappel off a helicopter to rescue wounded combatants? If a soldier can't keep pace in a running group, will that soldier keep pace on a 12-mile road march? Will that soldier run to the foxhole? Can that soldier carry a buddy as they flee from a bullet-strafing enemy? If soldiers, even noncombat-ants such as male chaplains—let alone women—expect to be less than a liability to the fighting team, they must be strong enough to carry equipment and even human beings. Consider this account of an unnamed Vietnam chaplain who was assisting with casualty evacuations (a combat service support role):

> A chaplain had been assisting with casualty evacuation. Heavy fire made close approach of "dust-off" choppers impossible, so casualties were carried about a quarter of a mile across flooded rice paddies. Stretchers were not available, and medics were in short supply.
>
> The sergeant had been hit by rifle fire through the flesh of both legs. Walking was impossible. The chaplain picked him up in a "dead man's carry" and set out across the mud. According to the sergeant, the chaplain started to slip and stumble, and was about to drop him into the muck. He (the chaplain) stopped, leaned his head back, and said, "God, I've gone was far as I can go. From here on it's up to you."
>
> In the sergeant's words, "So help me, sir, that chaplain walked across the water!" (Ackermann 1989).

No doubt this chaplain was abetted by the Almighty and the acute adrenaline rushes such rescue missions trigger. Let there be no doubt, however: The chaplain, although a noncombatant, kept himself in superior physical condition to be useful to the mission. If women are to be consid-ered for ground combat, or even remain in combat service support roles, we must reject the specious argument that equal cardiovascular effort results in equal fitness. We must reject cardiovascular wellness as the standard for combat fitness and return to raw scoring methods that measure a soldier's combat-ready fitness—that is, the soldier's ability to accomplish the ground combat mission. Women must be held to the same raw *physical ability* standards as men.

Not one advocate for women in ground combat has ever raised a complaint about gender-norming or demanded to expunge from the Army's training manuals the physiological information that quantifies women's physical limitations. Nor have they demanded to raise women's physical training standards to equal that of men, even after congressional hearings at which women officers and sergeants obtusely argued that "equal effort" is the same as "equal outcome" or "equal performance." The new promotion point worksheet for enlisted soldiers clearly demonstrates the preferential impact of gender-based physical fitness scores (*Army Times* 2000). The charts provide irrefutable proof that "equal effort" results in preferential treatment of women when promotions are at stake. To receive 50 promotion points out of a possible score of 150, a 17-year-old man must do 71 push-ups, 78 sit-ups, and run 2 miles in 13 minutes. A 17-year-old woman receives 50 promotion points for completing 42 push-ups, 78 sit-ups, and a 2-mile run in 15:36. Until women can prove they have equal strength and stamina to men by holding themselves to the same physical standards as men at all levels of training, there is simply no point in arguing that women are equal to the task of ground combat.

Gender Differences: Physical Wellness

The significant difference in physical condition between men and women service members should be considered before we decide to lift the ground combat exclusion for women. There is a myth—cited in many congressional testimonials and in the writings of retired General Jeanne Holm—that women lose less time from work than men do, even after pregnancy and maternity leave is factored into documented lost time (Holm 1992). Recent and long-term studies in all branches of the service are steadily and persistently debunking this myth. Studies are proving that women have greater physical, medical, and psychological needs in the field. Therefore, their support requirements are greater.

Consider combat aviation positions, which have been open to women since 1993. When male and female pilots completed a comprehensive anonymous questionnaire for the Naval School of Health Sciences, women self-reported that they were twice as likely as male pilots to be medically grounded for a period of more than 30 days (Voge 1996b). This figure did not include time lost for pregnancy or maternity leave. Nor did it consider the effect of menstruation on women's capabilities. Menstrual concerns are a sore subject of discussion for women soldiers, raising outright hostility and denial of problems when the subject is openly addressed. Yet 41 percent of all female aircrew members admitted to taking some form of medication for menstrual distress while in flight status—which, investigators noted, should raise safety-of-flight concerns (Voge 1996a). In Voge's comprehensive study, only 9 percent of the women admitted to any form of menstrual distress; fewer than 1 percent took themselves off flight status as a form of personal responsibility.

Incontinence and menstruation are physical conditions that dispro-portionately affect women's ability to function in Army field conditions. One-third of 450 female soldiers indicated that they experienced urinary incontinence during exercise and field training activities (Sherman, Davis, and Wong 1997). The authors noted that 13.3 percent of the respondents restricted fluids significantly during field exercises, leaving them vulnerable to dehydration-related injuries. A study of men and women in the Texas Gulf Coast region revealed that women with histories of urinary tract infections were five times as likely as men to develop nontransitional cell carcinoma of the bladder (Orihuela et al. 1997). When women go to the field as support soldiers, they minimally have access to porta-potties, which makes the experience of menstruation minimally hygienic and private. There are no showers or private bathing conditions. Ground combat soldiers do not train, let alone fight, in these "ideal" health conditions. They dig cat holes to bury their feces. They "leak" against trees. They have bath deprivation contests. It is not uncommon for male combatants to outdo each other with stories of weeks, even months, of bath deprivation. Fertile women, who serve in situations that are much safer than ground combat or ground combat training scenarios—that is, training situations that are minimally sanitary—still suffer adverse health consequences when they live with lax hygienic conditions.

This fact is accidentally corroborated in studies of Gulf War veterans. American women did not serve as ground combatants in the Gulf War, and there was no excess of unexplained hospitalization among the general population of active-duty men and women veterans of the Gulf War. Yet women who served in the Gulf were at increased risk of hospitalization for inflammatory diseases of the ovary, fallopian tube, pelvic cellular tissue, and peritoneum, as well as infertility (Gray et al. 1996). This same study of 547,076 veterans of the Gulf War and 618,335 other veterans from the same era who did not serve in the Gulf confirms that post–Gulf War trends for women's hospitalizations were consistent with hospitalization trends among Navy women (Hoiberg 1980). Personnel at Tripler Army Medical Center reported that half of the female Gulf War veterans they treated had gynecologic problems while serving in the Gulf, and 43 percent admitted gynecological problems after their return in 1991 (Wittich 1996).

Endometriosis, a debilitating gynecological condition, affects 6.2 percent of Army women, resulting in a mean sick time of 15 days per hospital admission per active-duty patient regardless of age or race (Boling and Abbassi 1988). Sexually transmitted diseases are epidemic among American teenagers and among today's soldiers. One study of female ROTC cadets revealed that 85 percent of the women experienced sexual activity by the mean age of 17.7 years (Stafford et al. 1996). Furthermore, 12 percent of the cadets reported a previous diagnosis of a sexually transmitted disease, and almost 7.8 percent had human papilloma virus (HPV) infections when they were tested at the ROTC training site.

Despite regulatory guidance against fraternization and adultery, sexual activity among co-workers is prevalent and contributes to health issues for men and women. Abel (1998) studied sexual risk behaviors among ship- and shore-based Navy women because of the morbidity and mortality associated with sexually transmitted diseases (STDs) and HIV. This study determined that more than 41 percent of the women were having sex with more than one partner, and 45 percent of the women reported that their partners did not use condoms. Using these statistics, and assuming that 200 women are assigned to a brigade, about 90 women are vulnerable to pregnancy and sexually transmitted diseases. At least 180 men also are vulnerable to life-threatening STDs. Furthermore, we cannot assume that soldiers who are engaging in "low-risk" sexual activity—condom sex with one partner—are safe from pregnancy or STDs. A small minority of soldiers is chaste. Abstinence is not valued in our society; it is ridiculed. Sexuality counseling and prevention classes, which are standard fare for trainees, are not eradicating high-risk behaviors. Abel, Adams, and Stevenson (1994) conducted a study of military women that determined that self-esteem was not a factor in the epidemic spread of chlamydia among military women; these findings were confirmed in a second study (Abel, Adams, and Stevenson 1996). In a Madigan Army Hospital study, 61 percent of pregnant junior enlisted soldiers reported that their pregnancies were unplanned. Unplanned pregnancy rates for junior enlisted soldiers exceed the national average by as much as 11 percent (Clark, Holt, and Miser 1998).

One study chastised the Army for not providing gynecological resources during the Gulf War to treat female soldiers before and during deployments (Markenson, Raez, and Colavita 1992). The study concluded that a large portion of the hospital's gynecological resources during this conflict were employed to treat preventable conditions. Wittich (1993) recommended deployment of U.S. Army medical personnel to Honduras for six-month tours to take care of the gynecological needs of female soldiers and indigent Hondurans. This proposal sounds reasonable until the severe shortage of obstetricians for stateside soldiers and family members is taken into account. The Army settles enormous malpractice claims for military spouses' bad pregnancy outcomes. Until this situation can be adequately turned around, why deploy gynecologists to take care of a small number of women who acquire STDs in situations of indiscipline (i.e., illegal conduct)? Why take on gynecological care for a civilian population for which the Army has no legal responsibility?

Studies of deployed Army and Navy men and women are revealing significantly higher rates of sick call for women than for men. Shipboard women visited clinics at rates of 189 per week per 1,000 personnel. Men visited sick call clinics at rates of 117 per week per 1,000 personnel. Upper respiratory complaints and requests for contraceptive pills were the most common reasons for women to visit clinics. Similarly, a pharmacoepidemiological analysis of prescribed medications for troops who were deployed to Somalia indicated a great gender disparity (Grabenstein et al. 1995). Although women represented 6.8 percent of the troops deployed, they constituted 31.5 percent of prescription recipients and received 29.4 percent of the prescriptions. Women were 6.5 times as likely to receive prescriptions as men. Excluding contraceptives, women were 3.4 times as likely to obtain prescriptions.

Britain's Royal Navy discovered that women are three times more likely to consult doctors than male sailors, and women were four times as likely to consult with the RN group practitioner as male sailors (Scott-Moncrieff 1994).

Musculoskeletal-related disabilities are significantly higher among U.S. Army women than among men. A study of 41,750 Army disability cases revealed that women experienced higher overall disability as well as musculoskeletal disability risks and that there were specific jobs in which women experienced higher rates of musculoskeletal disability (Feuerstein, Berkowitz, and Peck 1997).

Initial entry training situations are providing abundant evidence that women's physiological disadvantages also make them vulnerable to higher rates of injury. Amoroso, Bell, and Jones (1997) noted provocative gender differences in the injury rates of female and male army parachutists. Although women jump under less-hazardous conditions—in stat-line, nontactical, daytime environments—they are more likely to experience injury. Amoroso's descriptive retrospective study used 10 years of parachute injury data as reported to the Army by its safety and manpower centers. Women's injuries were more likely to be lower-extremity fractures. These findings were corroborated in a study of Australian Royal Air Force recruits. Researchers found that women were particularly prone to "overuse" injuries, which rose from 0.2 percent in 1985 to 8.8 percent in 1990 (Ross and Woodward 1994).

Similarly, a study of military cadets revealed that women had 2.5 times the rate of injuries as men and 3.9 times the rate of injuries resulting in hospitalization (Bijur et al. 1997). This study revealed that women were excused from physical activities at significantly higher rates than men were as a consequence of their injuries. The authors advised that greater pretraining conditioning could reduce the injury rate substantially; that conclusion, however, would seem to confirm that the entry-level fitness standards for women are too low. A second study of injuries among candidates in officer training programs showed that women and older cadets sustained significantly more injuries than male or younger candidates (Heir 1998). A study of Marine recruits determined that 11.5 percent of female recruits experience stress fractures, compared to 7 percent of the men (Winfield et al. 1997). Risk factors that contribute to stress fractures in female Marine trainees include undertraining prior to accession, younger age categories, women with fewer menstrual periods, and women with narrow pelvises. The authors of this study conclude that increased subtalar joint range of motion was *not* a risk factor for women.

Kang and Bullman (1996) studied mortality among U.S. veterans of the Gulf War to determine if these veterans have higher-than-normal mortality. The study confirmed the statistically significant higher mortality rates among Gulf War veterans in general. The authors noted that women were more greatly affected than men. Female veterans of the Gulf War had higher rates of death from external causes, as well as from accidents.

Pregnancy Necessitates Extended Absence and Medical Care

Finally, although pregnancy is not considered an illness or physical disability, a pregnant woman soldier cannot even work in the motor pool, let alone in deployed or ground combat circumstances. Pregnancy-related risks are obscured by most proponents of women in combat. Early studies have been denounced as inaccurate, but the evidence is persistent. Hoiberg (1984) found that pregnancy accounted for nearly one-third of all female servicemembers' hospitalizations. A 1997 study of Navy women's health care inadvertently underscored the correlation between high pregnancy rates and wartime versus peacetime ship deployments. The study found that in 1990, 2.7 of 100 women became pregnant per month; in 1995 (peacetime), the pregnancy rate of that same ship was 1.5 per 100 women (Hughey and Patel 1997). If these ships were deployed for six months, the ship's pregnancy rate was actually 18.2 percent during the year leading up to the Gulf War and dropped only to 9 percent in a less stressful, peacetime deployment. The study's method of reporting understates the impact of pregnancy because it does not take into consideration the fact that the same pool of 100 women account for the monthly 2.7 or 1.5 pregnancies during a six-month deployment.

Pregnant women are evacuated from ships, but replacements are not rotated in to take over their responsibilities. In the same way that naïve consumers are lured into credit card plans with low monthly rates that produce annual interest rates of 18–22 percent, quantified rates such as 2.7 or 1.5 pregnancies per month can lure policymakers into thinking that the shipboard or deployment pregnancy rate is statistically insignificant, when the rate is quite devastating to military readiness.

There is no question, however, that women should be relieved of deployment assignments when they become pregnant. Every study has shown that military working conditions create risks for the mother and her child. A study of 3,603 pregnant enlisted Navy women revealed that women over the age of 30 were at increased risk for cesarean delivery (Irwin et al. 1996). During the military deployment to Somalia, some female soldiers inadvertently used mefloquine before discovering their pregnancies. A registry was established to follow the outcomes of their pregnancies. Among the 72 pregnant soldiers, there were 17 elective abortions, 12 spontaneous abortions, 1 molar pregnancy, and 23 live births. One infant died within 4 months of viral pneumonitis. The outcome for 19 soldiers was unknown. Researchers concluded that there was an "unexpected high rate of spontaneous abortions although mefloquine does not cause gross congenital malformations in children" (Smoak et al. 1997). Questions were raised, however, about the correlation between elective abortions and congenital defects in the unborn. British studies of workplace hazards for pregnant military women have echoed findings in American studies. Croft (1995) identifies "30 major workplace hazards to pregnant or breast-feeding service women," providing guidance for avoidance of these contaminants to reduce risk.

The University of Pennsylvania studied pregnancy outcomes of 140 women who were stationed aboard the USS E.S. Land or the USS Hunley.

Researchers noted that the women received excellent prenatal care; never-theless, pregnant sailors stationed onboard submarine tenders were at high risk for some adverse pregnancy outcomes (Spandorfer, Graham, and Forouzan 1996).

Just before the Iraqi invasion of Kuwait, Ramirez et al. (1990) studied the relationship between occupational physical activity and the risk of preterm birth among U.S. Army active-duty soldiers between 1981 and 1984, using 604 cases (preterm deliveries—less than or equal to 37 weeks gesta-tion) and 6,070 controls (term and postterm deliveries). Women who had the highest physical activity levels had increased odds of preterm delivery—ranging from 1.69 to 1.75. A cohort study of 842 black and 1,026 enlisted Army women resulted in a cumulative probability of preterm delivery of 13.5 percent for black women soldiers. White pregnant soldiers had a 10.5 percent cumulative probability of preterm delivery (Adams et al. 1993).

Pregnant active-duty servicewomen, despite their considerably light-ened work responsibilities and ready access to health care, have higher rates of primary cesarean, transfer for preterm complications, pregnancy-induced hypertensive syndromes, and intrauterine growth retardation (Magann and Nolan 1991). The study compared 331 pregnant soldiers to 1,218 pregnant military spouses and found that active military service continues to be associated with poor pregnancy outcomes. In a study of 1,825 black and white enlisted women who delivered between 1987 and 1990 at the four largest stateside Army hospitals, investigators concluded that this population of otherwise healthy enlisted women experienced severe antenatal morbid-ity, as measured by their hospitalizations. Women who had multiple gesta-tions and women whose pregnancies ended before 20 weeks of gestation were excluded from this study. Of the 1,825 women studied, 702 required antenatal hospitalization (Adams et al. 1994). The risk factors are so persist-ent that researchers have recommended not only "mandatory education for military leaders regarding sensitivity to women's reproductive issues" but also "specialized briefings for women inductees on the realities and risks of pregnancy in the military" to reduce negative pregnancy outcomes (Tam 1998).

Recent studies are correlating low-level radiation as a by-product of military activity with high incidences of childhood cancer and leukemia in children born after fetal exposure to the radiation (Stewart 1999). Stewart recommends reevaluation of the effects of low-level radiation as the result of military uses of radiation. Similarly, an Israeli study recommends prudent avoidance of unneeded exposures to military radar, particularly during preg-nancy, because radio frequency (RF) exposures are correlated with increased spontaneous abortion and increased childhood cancers (Goldsmith 1997). Geeze (1998) concludes that pregnant aviators may inadvertently subject their fetuses to decreased cognitive capacity, frank mental retardation, and childhood leukemia from cosmic radiation—an occupational hazard for all commercial and military flight crews. *In utero* exposure to excessive (i.e., hazardous) noise levels, was correlated with hearing loss in newborns (Pierson 1996). All ground combat experience is coupled with deafening noise levels.

Deployed Women Require Greater Medical Resources

Hines (1992) studied the ambulatory health needs of women deployed to the Persian Gulf with a heavy armor division. Hines concluded that women deployed in this setting do not pose a significant health care burden attributable solely to their gynecologic needs, although Hines recommended gynecologic consultants, along with equipment and resources needed to manage pregnancy complications, pelvic pain, and abnormal cervical cytology.

Surely, the better option is to restrict women from deploying with a ground combat armor division. First, setting up an obstetrical/gynecological clinic in a combat theatre is impractical. Second, studies show that otherwise healthy women who are living in close proximity to political violence (war) have increased risk of pregnancy complications (Zapata et al. 1992). Third, active-duty status, even in optimal circumstances, is now identified as a high-risk factor for pregnant Army women (Magann and Nolan 1991).

As this review shows, women's greater vulnerability to disease and injury is documented in study after study. Other scattered research projects confirm the wellness gender gap. Record review of 5,467 periodontal patients in a military practice revealed that women show a greater tendency toward abscess formation while undergoing periodontal treatment (Gray, Flanary, and Newell 1994). Gray also found that Caucasian women were three times as likely as male patients to develop tooth abscesses. Women who were tested at a gender-separated recruit camp had no reported rubella infections. When they were relocated with males, the infection rate became comparable (Pollard and Edwards 1975). The cost of treatment for head trauma victims among service personnel totaled $43 million in 1992 for approximately 5,568 noncombat head injuries to soldiers (Ommaya, Dannenberg, and Salazar 1996). In this study of these hospital cases, military active-duty male soldiers were 1.6 times more likely to experience head trauma than the civilian population, whereas women were 2.5 times more likely to experience head trauma than the civilian population.

If each one of these wellness factors is considered separately, the impact on unit readiness might be ameliorated. Taken together—and combined with the National Academy of Science's conclusion that women have 50 percent of the strength that men have—no one can argue that lifting the ground combat exclusion policy for women would be beneficial to women's physical wellness. Similarly, the medical wellness data for women do not support the argument that lifting the ground combat exclusion for women will contribute to the national defense. Such a change of policy can only be detrimental to women's physical well being—and equally detrimental to the state of military readiness.

❏ PSYCHOLOGICAL REASONS TO EXCLUDE WOMEN FROM DIRECT GROUND COMBAT ASSIGNMENTS

Ground combat is up-close and personal, as foregoing narratives of ground combat memories attest. In addition, all ground combat training is up-close and personal. Military training requires that soldiers train the way they fight. If women were to become ground combatants, they would have to participate in all kinds of body-contact training—from strip-down naked chemical detoxification exercises to fireman's carry rescue drills and hand-to-hand combat. deYoung (2001) addresses the cost of the Army's sexual harassment program, including prevention training, investigative hearings, and trial proceedings for alleged perpetrators of harassment and assault. Although mixed-gender physical body contact is limited to early morning exercise sessions, mixed-gender sleeping tents, and mixed-gender all-ranks social bars, and the Army has aggressive prevention training sessions, more than 50 percent of active-duty women perceive that the Army does nothing to stop the problem of harassment or assault (deYoung 2001).

Advocates for revocation of the ground combat exclusion for women base their theoretical support of women ground combatants on imaginary renderings of women as celluloid Amazon warriors. *GI Jane* movie myths are postmodern constructions, founded on the assumption that gender identity is a voluntary construction—something that can be manipulated and reshaped at will. No matter how many movies are marketed to reshape the female psyche into *GI Jane* or *Xena* war heroes, however, real-life examples of women who have been able to withstand even simulated ground-combat horrors without being damaged to the point of permanent disability are extremely rare.

I interviewed a retired woman first sergeant who was top rate in the signal corps and a former drill instructor. She was selected for an Army experiment to determine whether women could handle Special Forces training. Despite encouragement from the sergeants who ran the program, as well their extreme efforts to keep her in the program, she reported that her body and spirit gave out in a few weeks.

The Army tried to bring women into the Special Forces long before *GI Jane* and *JAG* movie and television fantasies fueled public speculation about women's suitability for such roles. There are no women graduates of the Army Special Forces Program, however, because there are no women capable of the brutal physical and psychological training.

More recently, the Canadian government bowed to political pressure by permitting women to complete combat infantry training alongside men. The Canadian Army had 137 women serving in combat assignments in 1998. Of 100 women who attempted infantry training, only one woman completed the course. Despite expensive recruiting and sensitivity campaigns to recruit such small numbers of women, women have an attrition rate of 42 percent, compared with a 10 percent attrition rate for male soldiers who are assigned to combat positions (Murray 1998). Reasons for attrition include women's experience of being called names such as "slut," "whore," "bitch," and worse, as well as the rigorous physical demands of combat training (Pugliese 1998).

American women have had the most fortuitous peacetime opportunity to demonstrate their desire and passion for public service as professional soldiers since the Gulf War. Not only were public advocates strongly encouraging military service; the Army also spent a fortune—twice the usual cost per recruit—to bring women onto the active-duty force. Even when large bonuses were announced (such as the $60,000 college scholarship fund), the Army has experienced annual recruiting shortages of 10,000 per year. Moreover, female recruits persistently have left the military before their service contracts were honored, at the rate of 45 percent (U.S. House Armed Services Committee 1999). Clearly, the peacetime attrition statistics for the past decade—when women were promoted at higher rates than men under standards less rigorous than the male standard—irrefutably demonstrate that the Army cannot attract and retain good women to the fighting force. Why should we plan for failure in our ground combat operations by forcefully assigning women to ground combat operations through the lifting of the ground combat exclusion policy when women persistently demonstrate the lack of psychological hardiness for sustained military service?

As it is, the U.S. Army could not treat women with more gentility without eroding gender relations to the point of no return. In the most protective learning laboratories, mixed-gender training scenarios result in outrageously expensive sexual harassment courts martial and disciplinary proceedings. Officially, the closest physical contact Army men can have with women is body touching during nonviolent physical exercise, or to pin on awards. Traditional male bonding rituals and macho contests are grounds for court martial if, after the fact, a woman interprets the experience as an assault. Existing legal precedents on sexual harassment and assault make criminal proceedings inevitable and costly every time a woman interprets physical contact as harassment or assault. Posttraumatic stress disorder (PTSD) claims by female soldiers and veterans confirm the greater psychological damage experienced by women when men and women on the same team have physical contact, and researchers have noted that sexual stress was almost four times as influential in the development of PTSD as duty-related stress (Fontana and Rosenheck 1998). When two men similarly challenge each other, the psychological damage is recovered on the spot: The loser in physical horseplay of any kind pays a bet or buys a round of drinks.

What will happen when men and women are supposed to body-wrestle; perform bayonet attacks and chokeholds; simulate strangulation; strip for a simulated NBC exercise; or rifle-butt, body-tackle, or guerrilla-attack each other? Large numbers of men will be charged with sexual harassment or assault, if present prosecution trends in the U.S. and the Canadian armies are indicative of women's propensity to interpret physical contact as harassing or assault-like behavior. Large numbers of women are being treated for PTSD; women's participation in ground combat training will increase their PTSD rates astronomically, however, if present statistics are indicative of women's psychological reaction to close physical contact with men who are not their chosen sexual partners.

Already, gender differences in the experience and the interpretation of body contact, horseplay, and macho strength contests is clear. With statistically insignificant exceptions, women do not toughen up; they do not grin and bear the taunts, the body tackles, the "wood-shedding" (a boxing and physical strength contest) that secretly is used on indomitable but undisciplined soldiers in last-ditch efforts to form warrior discipline and obedience in the rebel. We all may agree that such training tactics are primitive and undesirable. So is war, however, as a response to another nation's political or economic transgressions. Yet nations do go to war on occasion, and hardened men do settle their authority issues, on occasion, by "wood-shedding."

The difference between a warrior and a victim is that the former learns from the experience, whereas the latter is disabled by it. I know of no instance besides the celluloid *GI Jane* in which a woman emerged from a wood-shedding experience as a confirmed warrior. By contrast, I know of no experience in which an enlisted male soldier emerged from a sergeant's wood-shedding to file charges—and thus claim for himself a public identity as victim, rather than a warrior.

We should not underestimate the extent to which military women seek help for physical or psychological trauma because of their experiences as soldiers. Sajatovic, Vernon, and Semple (1997) report that primary psychosis is more severe or refractory among female veterans than among male veterans. Given the statistical propensity of women to internalize victimization identities, are we going to privilege female ground combatants with rights to incriminate their combat buddies when they "feel" abused during training or horseplay? Should we? If women are demanding the right to fight as ground combatants, at some point, like men, they must submit to the physical harshness, the bruises, the attacks, the brutality of the training experience itself. As ridiculous as the film *GI Jane* was—in the sense that it does not realistically depict women's typical responses to physicality by their fellow soldiers—the message of the film is right on target. *GI Jane* asserts correctly that women combatants must accept the fact that the blood, guts, and glory of warriors are given and received in training and combat contexts.

If the ground combat exclusion is lifted, Army women aviators will be able to fly combat helicopters not only as trainers and test pilots but also in the heat of combat. Women aviators routinely defend their right to fly combat planes in combat situations, based on their intellectual and technical equality—resorting to the *Star Trek* fallacy that physical or emotional strength is not required to fly combat planes. Flying airplanes is only a small part of the combat aviator's job, however. In war, the pilot must be able to survive a crash and, most likely, enemy captivity.

In peacetime or wartime, the evidence suggests the need to expand the combat exclusion policies and restrict the role of women to training and support aviation roles. An expose of Air Force Academy prisoner of war training, for example, revealed that female cadets were completely traumatized by male cadet simulations of enemy rape attacks (Foster 1995). They could not fight off their attackers; they were physically and psychologically overwhelmed by the experience. Rather than admit defeat on the issue of women's suitability for combat, the Air Force curtailed all hand-to-hand training simulations. To this day, films are used to train women to fight off sexual assaults. This training, no doubt, should effectively prepare women to fight off the enemy—as long as the real combat enemy has the tensile strength of a videotape character.

The wartime autobiography of Major Rhonda Cornum, the most celebrated female Gulf War POW, should sober the imagination of anyone who believes women can muster the same adrenaline as men to survive enemy capture. By her own account, Maj. Cornum and the other woman POW received preferential treatment while they were in captivity. Five of Cornum's subordinates died in her Army helicopter crash. Maj. Cornum, who ridiculed the man who died protecting her, walked away from the crash with two broken arms. In Cornum's first Iraqi interrogation as a POW, she admitted her chopper was shot down during a search and rescue mission. She instructs her reader that the Iraqi guards were less rough with her after her admission—which was, she admitted, a violation of the soldier's code of conduct. In her second interrogation, Maj. Cornum manufactured details about her rescue mission to throw her captors off guard, rationalizing that this tactic would prevent further slaps, hits, and permanent injuries from her captors (Cornum 1993).

Maj. Cornum acknowledged that she violated the military Code of Conduct by revealing information about her unit and fictionalizing other details. There was hardly a need for her to worry about torture in prolonged captivity. She also admitted in her book that she knew the war was over before her first interrogation started (Cornum 1993). As the senior ranking officer in her captive group, Cornum had the legal and moral responsibility to set the standards for her troops. The standard she set was: Sell out if you think it will prevent physical violence or mutilation. Cornum acknowledged the heroism of Captain Anderson, the Air Force pilot and POW whom Cornum's medical team attempted to rescue (Cornum 1993). According to Maj. Cornum, Capt. Anderson, who followed her into the interrogation room, refused to reveal any information except his name, rank, and serial number, for which he was repeatedly beaten by the Iraqis (Cornum 1993).

Immediately, our sympathies are with Maj. Cornum when we are reminded of her two broken arms and her eventual admission that she was sexually assaulted by one of her guards. If we contrast Maj. Cornum's betrayal of her unit, however, with the response of Vice Admiral James B. Stockdale (Ret.)—who as a crippled POW faced captors in far more dangerous circumstances—the gender difference cannot be ignored. Admiral Stockdale's captivity lasted eight years. He describes his experience and the lessons learned:

> This is stoicism. It's not the last word, but it's a viewpoint that comes in handy in many circumstances, and it surely did for me. Particularly this line:

"Lameness is an impediment to the body but not to the will." That was significant for me because I wasn't able to stand up and support myself on my badly broken leg for the first couple of years I was in solitary confinement.

What attributes serve you well in the extortion environment? We learned there, above all else, that the best defense is to keep your conscience clean. . . . A little white lie is where extortion and ultimately blackmail start. In 1965, I was crippled and I was alone. . . . The one thing I came to realize was that if you don't lose your integrity you can't be had and you can't be hurt. Compromises multiply and build up when you're working against a skilled extortionist or a good manipulator. You can't be had if you don't take that first shortcut, or "meet them halfway," as they say, or look for that tacit deal, or make that first compromise.

Men get on quickly with the business of assimilating knowledge of character traits of their fellow prisoners. . . . Does he have moral integrity? In the privacy of the torture room, will he go to the wall in silence, or will he do what is so commonplace in the business world nowadays and try to make a deal? . . . The intensity of life in jail clearly illuminated for us prisoners of war the truth that for the greatest number of us, for our maximum happiness, maximum self-respect, maximum protection of one another, each of us had to submerge our individual survival instincts into an ideal of universal solidarity. "No deals" and "Unity over self" became our mottoes (Wakin 1979).

Compared to Stockdale's account of his experience with captivity, the Cornum POW account is an example not of bravery but of weakness at best and cowardice at worst. By Cornum's own admission, as a field-grade officer, she did not have the psychological grit or the physical strength to endure prolonged captivity. In her first interrogation, she put herself above the group and above her country. By contrast, Admiral Stockdale's analysis of the moral, psychological, and physical traits required not only for personal survival but also for the well-being of other captives and for the protection of military intelligence are essential qualities in a combatant. Yet because we are desperate for examples of women who can prove the wisdom of the current trend to slot women in ground combat assignments, we do not examine Cornum's own description of her captivity for meanings that might conflict with the outcome of achieving women's equality through combat heroism. Instead of gleaning truth from Cornum's account, the nation glossed over her experience and cited Maj. Cornum repeatedly for bravery as the first woman POW in the Gulf War, simply because she experienced captivity.

Before we decide to retain women in combat pilot, ground combatant slots, we must note the vast difference in importance that women pilots, technicians, and ground combatants will have to the enemy's intelligence-gathering organizations. Female pilots, intelligence analysts, and ground combatants do have significant technical, operational, and strategic information that must be safeguarded, at the expense of personal survival or injury. If women can be as easily intimidated into giving up tactical information as Maj. Cornum was, why should the nation compromise tactical security by putting women into situations where they have enormous amounts of battle intelligence but neither the physical nor the psychological strength to withstand enemy interrogation?

Maj. Cornum's experience should be used not as the justification for putting women into ground combat but for limiting the military roles of women. In the following section, I review the tort claims of combat pilots such as Paula Coughlin and others who claimed powerlessness to stop sexual horseplay at pilot conventions or during Air Force Academy simulated rape training. These women flew their aircraft for extended periods of time before they revealed their prolonged debilitating psychological trauma. Similarly, female Army recruits put the combat mission at risk because a large percentage of women are impaired even during peacetime training conditions. A comprehensive study of the sexual histories of new recruits concluded that about 50 percent of Army women recruits had prior sexual trauma (Martin et al. 1998). This study concluded that childhood sexual abuse may be more widespread among female soldiers than among civilian women. These women are at high risk for permanent disability induced by tactical training situations that result in PTSD reactions. These examples suggest, that as a nation, we err when we place women in positions that are beyond their psychological capability.

We could continue to make full use of female pilots as trainers and transporters and as Army trainers in noncombat environments. We should avoid women's high risk of PTSD, however, and we must take precautions to prevent the leaking of sensitive or secret information. We should withdraw women from aerial and ground combat units that could result in their captivity during wartime operations, resulting in an excessive security risk to an ongoing war effort.

❏ LEGAL REASONS TO EXCLUDE WOMEN FROM DIRECT GROUND COMBAT ASSIGNMENTS

There are expensive legal ramifications to lifting the ground combat exclusion in the context of our highly litigious, rights-oriented society. The four legal concerns are the application of sexual harassment and sexual assault doctrines to coed ground combat situations; compromise to the Law of Land Warfare, as it pertains to war crimes such as sexual assault; erosion of unit cohesion and morale wrought by preferential treatment in litigation granted to women under Title VII; and government liability to children who experience adverse health outcomes consequent to their *in utero* combat experience or negative psychological outcomes related to postnatal combat-separation from their birth mothers.

Sexual Harassment Litigation

The Tailhook scandal, which was brought to public attention by female aviator Lieutenant Paula Coughlin, illuminates the double bind in which sexual harassment and assault laws place the military and women. In Lt. Coughlin's case against the Hilton Hotel, the testimony of other women aviators strongly indicates that she eagerly participated in sexually raucous horseplay with her fellow aviators, to the point of signing a trophy memento (Legal Intelligencer 1994). For two nights, Coughlin's participation was inarguably voluntary. At some later point, her attitudes apparently changed. Whether by coercion or by choice, Lt. Coughlin walked down the Hilton's hallway, "the gauntlet," during which she claims that her peers grabbed her breasts and her underwear. She won $7 million in damages from the Hilton because the hotel did not exercise proprietary authority to stop the raucous proceedings, plus $400,000 from the Tailhook Association, which sponsored the convention. A psychiatrist testified that this single experience, which was the result of Lt. Coughlin's choice to attend a convention that was renowned for its unseemly rituals, induced major depression, posttraumatic stress, and a peptic ulcer that resulted in Lt. Coughlin's inability to cope (Legal Intelligencer 1994). Lt. Coughlin's credibility was attacked in the trial because she continued to fly helicopters and she renewed her military contract before she ever filed a complaint, even though she claimed she was suicidal from the time of the attack until after she left the military.

Congressional policymakers must consider these documented cases of noncombat trauma when they decide whether women combat pilots or ground combatants are psychologically suited for the rigors of ground combat or prolonged captivity by the enemy. The military spends about one-half million dollars training helicopter pilots, as well as millions of dollars to build each helicopter. Lt. Coughlin made the legal claim that as a trained combat pilot, she was completely disabled by one physical episode, regardless of its disputable nature. If her disability was real, she was a menace to her flight crew every time she flew after that one physical encounter. If her disability was not real, Coughlin's legal exploitation of sexual harassment laws to make a quick fortune cost the Hilton Hotel $7 million. Worse, at least $0.5 million of the Navy's training funds was wasted, in addition to the cost of the very expensive federal investigation of the Tailhook scandal.

I have reviewed the psychological and physical disadvantages of women combat pilots and soldiers, offered a detailed analysis of the psychological impact of mere training experiences in hand-to-hand combat or POW scenarios, and cited consistent data on psychological trauma that women soldiers experienced prior to their military service. These data should alarm the budgetary analyst as well as the policymaker, but they also should demonstrate that women need the protection of Title VII because they cannot hold their own in mixed-gender situations that involve physical contact. As long as women need Title VII and Title IX to protect them from American men, they will need the combat exclusion policy to protect them from male enemies, foreign and domestic.

Title VII Sexual Harassment/Assault Doctrine Compromises Military Readiness and the Law of Land Warfare

Assuming that women need Title VII policies to prevent harassment or to remedy discrimination, harassment, or assault by employers in the civilian sector or in the military, the application of Title VII doctrine has destroyed military readiness and morale in most Army support units. If the combat exclusion were lifted for women under present Title VII sexual harassment policies, we can be certain of one thing: Military readiness effectively would be destroyed. Furthermore, policies that prohibit soldiers from committing wartime rape and other atrocities since the Nuremberg trials would be effectively nullified if the legal assumptions that undergird Title VII continue to be applied to working relationships between men and women who wear the uniform.

First, the application of Title VII policies has resulted in preferential treatment of women in every way: recruiting, physical training, professional competence, and personal conduct standards. As I demonstrate in my discussion of physiology, physical training standards for women are significantly lower for women at the accessioning point, and these differences remain throughout all schooling and professional assignments. When women were restricted from combat and near-combat assignments, the differential could be ignored by male soldiers as a standard that was based on cardiovascular fitness, not a standard that would predict performance in combat situations. Now that women have been placed in heavy vehicle maintenance units, as well as support and combat units that require heavy lifting, rugged field duty, road marches with heavy rucksacks, and physically draining labor, the preferential treatment is a cause of nonreadiness and the destruction of unit cohesion.

In a December 1999 radio interview (KSFO-AM, San Francisco) with Geoff Metcalf, I was asked about gender issues in the Military. A male caller expressed his frustration that he was required to do the heavy lifting of wheels and other equipment for female soldiers in his company. When he refused and asked his supervisor to hold the female soldier equally accountable for heavy lifting, he was ordered to do the woman's work or suffer the consequences: punishment for sexual harassment. Supervisory fear is rooted in a daily reality of military life: When male supervisors and co-workers demand that women "hold their own," they are slapped with "hostile work environment" complaints that could result in court-martial proceedings. Similarly, when commanders ask how to curtail high rates of single-parent pregnancies in units that require heavy field duties, female officers and senior sergeants openly intimidate commanders to suspend the query under threat of sexual harassment complaints—a certain career terminator since Tailhook. Once again, any serious discussion of women's limitations, including personal choice to escape twelve or more months of field duties through pregnancy and maternity leave, is easily conflated into sexual harassment under the "hostile work environment" doctrine.

The most offensive misuse of Title VII doctrines, however, occurs when female soldiers conflate their sexual escapades—their consensual sexual activities—into sexual harassment or rape to avoid accountability for their participation in adultery, fraternization, or pandering of sexual goods for favors from their peers and superiors. Unfortunately, constructive force doctrines have been used by the military and by feminist legal advocates to argue that women are incapable of giving consent to consensual sex whenever their sexual partner or business client outranks them or is more physically imposing than they are.

Unequal Interpretation of the Feres Doctrine

There is a way to circumvent the possibility of massive liability claims against the Army by women combatants who do not have the psychological hardiness to withstand the sexual, social, physical, and psychological stresses of combat or combat training. The Army could expand the scope of the Feres doctrine and require that all women in the combat arms profession waive their rights to pursue grievances or to claim damages under Title VII statutes, as men are required to sacrifice their tort rights by virtue of wearing the uniform. Simply stated, if women continue to argue for assignments as ground combatants or even as combat service support soldiers, they will have to relinquish their right to file sexual harassment and sexual assault charges. They must relinquish the protection of Title VII and assume the combatant's status as battlefield equal. To accommodate demands for full equality, we must assume that women combatants are capable of "holding their own" among their peers and while they are under enemy control. Is there a women's rights group, a single woman, or a lawfully practicing attorney who believes, however, that women do not need such preferential protection under the law as provided by Title VII? If there is, why have they not pursued legal remedies to end the preferential treatment of women who have used the judicial process to gain power and prestige in the military as no male soldier has succeeded in doing to recover for injuries to life and limb? To the extent that women deem themselves incapable of handling body contact—and thus require protections provided by Title VII and Title IX—we must admit that women, as a protected class, are not up to the risks of trauma associated with ground combat.

Lawsuits Related to Maternal Deprivation and Birth Defects Attributable to Combat Duties

If the United States were to commit women combatants to a protracted ground war, inevitably, large numbers of children who suffered disabilities or other health complications because of their neonatal combat experiences would be eligible to sue the government for damages. Their mothers may have voluntarily committed themselves to a combat theatre, but children conceived in such circumstances and subjected to highly adverse pregnancy outcomes can blame two guilty parties for their disability: their mothers and the U.S. Army.

There are no studies correlating birth defects with male combatant exposure to toxic chemicals. Although many Gulf War veterans have sued the Army, however, alleging that the war was responsible for the birth defects with which their children were born, they have not been able to prove any connection between their war duty and their children's health.

Ample evidence has been accumulated in the past decade, however, that correlates women's adverse pregnancy outcomes with their active-duty service. Although Army women cannot sue if their children have birth defects or are stillborn, they are entitled to compensation through the Department of Veterans Affairs for psychological treatment that is related to adverse pregnancy outcomes stemming from active-duty service. Their spouses can sue the government for wrongful birth, however, and their children, with the assistance of aggressive attorneys, can fight for medical compensation. Recent Supreme Court decisions contain commentary that suggest that the Feres Doctrine is ripe for reversal. In a 1999 appeal from the Third Circuit, the Court denied the appellant a rehearing on the validity of the Feres doctrine, but the decision cited six cases of "counterintuitive" results and noted that members of the Court "repeatedly have expressed misgivings" (*Richards v. United States,* No. 98-7235). Child advocates who sue the government for wrongful birth because of *in utero* combat trauma will make compelling cases with which the public can sympathize until the doctrine is overturned.

Furthermore, society will unnecessarily pay one way or another for all of the social and medical support services for children who are disabled *in utero* during maternal combat deployment. The Supreme Court is ruling consistently for all kinds of accessibility resources, from nurses in the classroom to installation of elevators and provision of technical and medical equipment that will facilitate the mainstreaming of the handicapped. If the Supreme Court chooses not to hold the federal government liable for *in utero* combat trauma, state governments will still be responsible for funding the support services needed by children who are born with birth defects and chronic illnesses caused by war trauma.

No responsible corporation would take the unnecessary risk of placing pregnant workers in environments that are known health hazards to unborn children. The medical cost of treating premature babies alone, whom Proctor and Gamble has called "million dollar babies," has caused most private employers and insurance companies to take extraordinary measures to protect women from negative pregnancy outcomes. Why would the Army unnecessarily risk the well-being of unborn children by putting women in toxic work situations? True, if the mother miscarries or aborts the child, she cannot file a claim against the Army; her husband could, however.

Similarly, the psychological damage of long-term separation between mother and child is well documented. Research concerning children's traumatic response to their mother's wartime deployment also has begun; strangely, however, it is being discounted. While children are small, they have no rights to sue. With a guardian *ad litem*, or when their psychological disability can be established, they will have the ability to sue the government for depriving them of their primary maternal guardians. The further we move from a welfare state to a returned emphasis on responsible parenting, the closer we move toward a legitimate claim that children whose mothers are deployed or killed in combat were deprived by the state of their sole protectors and guardians.

People often argue that children suffer from paternal deprivation as much as they suffer from maternal deprivation. Military deployments seem to provide emotional offsets for children that enable them to insulate themselves from the emotional effects of paternal separation. Not so with maternal separation. The legal liability for inflicting unnecessary maternal separation arising from combat, particularly in the event of maternal death, would fall on the U.S. government.

The courts have ruled consistently that women alone have the absolute constitutional right to determine whether to bear children. I argue that the corollary responsibility to parent the children also falls on the mother. In peacetime, women are fighting legal battles to leave their children behind during field training and deployments. As we move along the continuum of rights advocacy, children will be winning the next set of legal battles. If women serve as ground combatants in the next protracted war, the children who are damaged by maternal separation or maternal death may have the right to sue both mother *and* the military. These children could claim damages for violating their right to be cared for by the mother who exercised her constitutional right to birth the child but not her constitutional responsibility to care for the child.

❑ ETHICAL REASONS TO EXCLUDE WOMEN FROM DIRECT GROUND COMBAT ASSIGNMENTS

Pragmatic feminist reasons for maintaining the American combat exclusion for women range from avoiding the unnecessary and excessive physiological and psychological burdens wrought by women's combat training to avoiding the host of legal complications that would follow such a policy change. In addition, at least seven ethical considerations must be resolved before the ground combat exclusion for women can be safely lifted. At this juncture in history, lifting the combat exclusion policy is not in the best interests of women or the American public.

First, the ethical framework from which feminists have pushed the assignment of women to combat roles in the military is diametrically opposed to the ethos required in combat fighting units. The feminist doctrine that undergirds the struggle to put women in ground combat slots is based on personalist or egoist ethical frameworks. Women should be free to choose occupations, lifestyles, and commitments, based on personal desires and ambitions, with no commitment to self-sacrifice for the sake of a larger national or global mission. American civil society has strong tolerance for a pluralistic morality that spans personalist, utilitarian, communitarian, and deontological worldviews. Military culture, on the other hand, requires strong conformity to a character ethic that requires repeated self-sacrifice, emphasis on the greater good rather than personal gain, and an absolute primacy of duty over choice or personal preference.

In the civilian world, shaping one's life, educational plans, or career path according to one's desires, dreams, or fancies—without regard to the impact of one's decision on one's peers, family, community, or employer—is acceptable, however selfish. Market forces eventually weed out less-qualified but ambitious seekers of power and position. When unqualified persons are not rooted out of operations that demand expertise and skill, the employer suffers; usually, however, the consequence does not involve loss of life or limb. One exception is worthy of comparison: Americans would not want unqualified physicians to treat us, and thus risk our lives or physical well-being. One does not have a right to practice medicine; the privilege is conferred only on persons who are professionally qualified to practice. Professional associations reserve the right to disqualify those who are not capable of practicing medicine in a way that meets the minimal ethical obligation: no harm done. Similarly, Americans should not be forced by self-centered, nonqualified women to use the services of women as combatants; in doing so, we would put other lives and our national defense at risk.

Second, the feminist strategy to push women into combat for the sake of greater career advancement contradicts the military ethos, which requires selfless sacrifice, duty, and honor and places country ahead of personal interests. The feminist elite is willing to impose grave hardship on a large underclass of women who serve at the bottom of the rank structure for selfish gain.

The vast majority of American women are not remotely interested in military service or combat duty as a path to fulfillment. Historically, they have preferred to deny themselves greater legal guarantees under the Equal Rights Amendment rather than participate in compulsory military service. Yet a small number of college-educated women volunteers (officers) who can obtain career advantages for themselves without making the sacrifice that ground combat training entails are pushing hundreds of thousands of poorer, less-educated women into near-combat and combat positions to increase the odds of their own promotion. At most 14 percent of women who wear the uniform think that women should be required to serve in combat (Miller 1998). No more than 24 percent of any rank structure would volunteer for combat duty, but they want the abstract right for women to choose combat for the sake of career advancement.

The evidence overwhelmingly shows that women who want ground combat slots opened to women demand this mission for the class of women not as an act of self-sacrifice or selfless service but for the exclusive purpose of achieving personal fulfillment or advancing their career prospects. This motivation for putting women in ground combat slots is wrong because women combatants *qua* combatants do not contribute to the strength of our national defense. Nor do we bring the best talent available to the mission; nor do we proffer the skills or endurance power that will enhance survivability or combat success in ground combat operations.

The third ethical dilemma related to the lifting of the ground combat exclusion for women is the range of legal and physical strategies that women can adopt to opt out of the mission at their convenience, creating a perpetual state of preferential treatment of female conscripts. By constitutional fiat, men can be conscripted whenever a national emergency exists. Men are required to register for selective service to ensure that an abundant pool of healthy combat capable soldiers can be mustered for national defense. When men are called to duty, they cannot choose their occupational specialty, their assignments, or their promotion opportunities. If a male soldier is disappointed because he is assigned to logistics or support operations—thus depriving him of the likelihood of being promoted to general for lack of ground combat experience—he cannot march into Congress to demand better promotion opportunities.

For every woman who is assigned to such dead-end logistics positions, there are tens of thousands of men who have suffered similar indignities for the good of the service. A soldier's duty is to serve where he is assigned, for the good of the service. If he is released from active duty after 3, 10, 15, or 20 years of service—although he would have preferred 30 years on active duty—he cannot sue the government to demand retention because the Army's personnel plans did not conform to his "dream sheet." Over the decades, women have sued to remain on active duty as pregnant single soldiers, despite the heavy imposition pregnancy places on military readiness. They have sued to be released from active duty when they preferred motherhood to heavy combat assignments, despite the consequent waste of high-cost training. Congressional watchdogs and women's groups have leveraged rank for women, based not on individual women's accomplishments but as a *quid pro quo* to end relentless prosecution of high-profile sexual misconduct cases. Successful integration of women into the Armed Forces will be eternally compromised as long as women can demand that the Army turn its ethos of selfless service inside out to accommodate the selfish career goals of the few who are least qualified to demand such treatment.

The fourth moral concern is that feminist arguments for placing women in ground combat rely on questionable uses of technology without due regard for noncombatants who live in the midst of our "targets of opportunity." In the Gulf War, as well as strategic bombing strikes on Serbia, Sudan, Afghanistan, and Iraq, war calculus overemphasized technological superiority and tactical proficiency to the exclusion of many social, religious, and moral considerations that might have changed the planning, staffing, and execution of each campaign. The public perception of total battlefield success may cause us, for some time, to refrain from analyzing our military strategies for moral failures that necessarily result from the disproportionate use of firepower that effects extensive collateral damage in the battle zone. The Highway of Death in Kuwait; the strafing of the Iraqi desert with depleted uranium shells; the indictment of NATO pilots who are being accused of war crimes because they allegedly blew up civilians in one of their high-tech "pinprick" bombings: These are just three examples of the overuse of technology in military operations. There are times in every battle when ground combatants must be used to absolutely minimize the risk of harm to civilians and noncombatants that high-technology weaponry too often inflicts.

Since Vietnam, military analysts and feminist advocates alike have allowed themselves to be blinded by the benefits of technology to the point of obscuring the criminal harm that also can result from its use. As one nation in a worldwide community of nations, we must scrutinize the excesses of each war campaign not only to assess public perception of the outcome. We also must assess the impact of our technology and war-making strategies on those who are not engaged in the fight: women, children, elderly and disabled noncombatants. We have the moral responsibility to demonstrate to the international community that we are, indeed, not a nation that uses its overwhelming arsenal to achieve political policy without regard to the lives of innocent noncombatants in "rogue" nations. Instead, we strive to commit our superior force solely for the betterment of international security and well-being.

Feminists who have at the heart of their concern the career advancement of the statistically insignificant number of women who could hold their own as ground combatants must weigh the moral responsibility of our nation to protect the well-being of noncombatants. To increase the participation of women in American combat operations that would not depend on women's physical strength for effective participation, we must consider the evidence that our nation's use of overwhelming technology obliterates the distinction between the combat support soldier and the ground combatant. Greater emphasis on remote-control computerized operations also obliterates the distinction between those who are legitimate military targets—combatants— and those who are particularly vulnerable to war crimes and morally questionable outcomes such as collateral damage (noncombatants).

Fifth, the contemporary practice of invoking constructive force doctrines to absolve women soldiers of responsibility for their participation in consensual sexual misconduct compromises the Law of Land Warfare doctrines. In the conduct of any war, the U.S. military is bound not only by the Law of Land Warfare but by a rich and strict moral code that governs the profession of arms. This moral code governs the conduct of war, the training of combatants, and the treatment of soldier and civilian alike. If women are to serve as combatants, they must take full responsibility for their participation in criminal or immoral activity. Legal reliance on constructive force laws to defend women against culpability in adultery/sexual misconduct results in undermining the Law of Land Warfare requirements to disobey illegal, unethical orders. Since women have been pushed into ground combat assignments, situations of fraternization, consensual adultery, and other consensual sexual misconduct episodes have skyrocketed. The American culture of victim feminism has attempted to hold women's gains in the military by using strategies to absolve women of their consensual participation in sexual misconduct by relying on constructive force doctrines.

As constructive force doctrine is presently interpreted, women of junior rank cannot be held criminally responsible for their participation in consensual sex with superior officers because the senior ranking sergeant or officer has coercive power over the female subordinate. This doctrine was built into the Uniform Code of Military Justice (UCMJ) prior to the expansion of women's assignment opportunities, when the military assumed that female soldiers needed greater protection than male combatants. Women can't have it both ways, however. Constructive force doctrines are a repudiation of every soldier's responsibility to practice moral courage. The shameless wholesale appropriation of this doctrine by feminist attorneys and congressional advocates to save the careers of women who participated in immoral and illegal activities not only compromises the morale of the unit to which the offenders belong. The double standard—that is, the nonstandard for women in sexual misconduct cases—compromises the requirements of the Geneva Convention and the Law of Land Warfare for American soldiers.

Until the recent application of constructive force doctrine to sexual misconduct cases, all soldiers, male or female, were required to disobey every implied or explicit order that is illegal, unethical, or immoral. Now, because women in military units who by their example and legal defense get away with criminal behaviors by arguing that they were "just obeying orders," the legal defense of male soldiers who participate in war crimes such as rape or mass murder because they were "just obeying orders" is strengthened. As in every other instance, the legal standards for men have to be lowered as long as women are not held to any standard.

The sixth ethical concern relates to women's reproductive choice. If the combat restriction is lifted, women's right to choose pregnancy or delayed parenthood will be compromised. When women choose to abandon their children for the sake of military or other careers, the right to reproductive choice is compromised for all women. Planned abandonment of children by career women reinforces the legal notion that women are not capable of living up to the primary parenting responsibilities that accompany reproductive choice. Because women have the constitutionally protected right to choose when or whether to give birth, they also have primary responsibility for parenting the offspring they bear. In the post-welfare society, 11 percent of military women are still bearing out-of-wedlock children. Military doctors frequently mention Depo Provera as an involuntary medical remedy to prevent this type of irresponsibility in units where such lifestyle choices are predictable responses to field duty and deployment.

Similarly, the evidence that correlates high rates of spontaneous abortions, birth defects, and childhood leukemia among children conceived in military zones suggests that women who choose to participate in ground combat also are choosing or are complicit in the resultant birth defects or life-threatening diseases in their children. If women voluntarily choose to participate in war efforts that compromise the health of their unborn children, they are morally responsible for the harm that comes to their children because their constitutional right to choose motherhood is accompanied by the primary responsibility to safeguard the fetuses they carry.

A government that forces women to serve in combat zones has a moral responsibility to provide for military children who are born with birth defects and other anomalous conditions. Yet under the Feres Doctrine, our government refuses to accept this liability. The government refuses to provide abortions for women who do not want to bear children. Interestingly, however, all government studies show that women who took mefloquine in their first trimester of pregnancy suffered unusually high rates of spontaneous abortions. Will our government, in its zeal to deny liability for harm to children conceived in war zones, reverse its position from forced childbearing to forced abortions to prevent lifetime financial obligations to children born with defects? Either way, putting individual women in situations in which they must choose between one harm (abortion) and another (birth defects in their unborn children) is not in women's best interests.

Seventh, the feminist argument to lift the ground combat restriction against women as a means to increase the full complement of civil rights to which women are entitled in American democracy could accomplish the reverse. By accepting warrior myths that confer special status and privileges on persons who have mastered the combat arms profession, we deny the unique nature of American democracy: its commitment to protect the weak from the tyranny of the strong. President Franklin Roosevelt proved that one need not be a warrior to exercise superb international leadership in time of war or peace.

No American war has required greater than 13.1 percent of American men to fight; the percentage decreased to slightly more than 1 percent in the Gulf War (U.S. Civil War Center 1999). American women have been elected to every national office short of the presidency without assuming the warrior mantle. Although the military is experiencing temporary personnel shortages, it does not wish to return to universal conscription as standard procedure for filling its ranks, insisting that the ranks can easily be filled entirely with the best-qualified volunteers. Excessively valorizing military service in a nation that requires about 1 percent of its population to practice the profession of arms makes no sense. Overvalorizing military service and ignoring the massive shortages our nation is experiencing in other helping professions such as teaching and nursing makes less sense. Finally, risking the loss of human and civil rights of those who cannot serve because of their physical limitations by assigning "first-class citizen rights" to those who are capable of brute force makes no sense. We have properly moved beyond the legal era when warrior service was the *sine qua non* to obtain other privileges, political status, or economic benefits that a just democracy bestows on all citizens: health care, education, job training, and political access.

In short, demanding military service as a prerequisite to special benefits and leadership positions in American society can only, in due course, undermine the rights of disabled, physically weak, elderly, and other noncombatants in society by privileging warrior status for preferential treatment, pay, advancement, and political power.

❏ CONCLUSION

All discussion about the extent of women's participation in the military should revolve around the warrior ethos, not around abstract, imagined constructions of gender/citizen/class/race/national/warrior identities. In deciding who should serve as a ground combatant, the criteria should be based on qualifications that are necessary or required to get the job done. Congressional decisions to lift or loosen ground combat exclusion policies should not prioritize abstract political theories about the rights and responsibilities of citizens over economic, social, political, and physical realities that demonstrate the imprudence or impracticality of placing women in ground combat assignments.

In this analysis, I have drawn on military doctrine and on historical and experiential accounts that describe the practical and realistic nature of the ground combat experience during training and time of war. The ethos of military culture incorporates complex ideas that are summed up in four ideas: duty, honor, country, and selfless service. The indispensable core values of Army leaders are courage, candor, commitment, and competence. In post-Gulf War training, the competencies of a soldier can be distilled into three words: be, know, and do. From Gen. Schwarzkopf's description of the enemy attack on his battalion headquarters to the movie characterization of the nerdy signal corps clerk-turned-patrolling infantryman in *Saving Private Ryan*, the stories I have quoted point to the unalterable requirements of every person who serves in or supports a ground combat unit. Whether the soldier peels potatoes, decrypts code, changes flywheels, or commands the battalion, each must have the physical and psychological capacity to engage the enemy in an up-close and personal way. Each must be prepared to fight the ground war as infantrymen rather than support staff. The fact that no soldier on the modern battlefield is immune from ground combat does not strengthen the case to lift the ground combat exclusion. To the contrary, in light of the extensive evidence I have cited, it should give us pause to consider further restricting women's roles.

As a feminist, I can understand how women came to believe that ground combat duty is the *sine qua non* for decorated valorous service. The impetus in this campaign to lift the ground combat exclusion, however, is based on false perceptions and distorted logic that runs thus: If women combat service support soldiers perceive themselves as inferior and male combatants perceive themselves as superior, women will be deprived of their rightful promotion opportunities. Therefore, women must be ground combatants to compete for their fair share of high-level promotions in the military—and perhaps for the highest office in the land.

There is no correlation between feelings of superiority/inferiority and promotion rates for women. In fact, GAO studies show that women are promoted at higher rates than men, even though they are officially excluded from ground combat assignments (General Accounting Office 1997, 1998a). Regardless, I argue—as a feminist—that women err when they allow their feelings of inferiority to color the debate about the assignment of women to support or ground combat roles. The error is compounded when women obscure their motivations for obtaining ground combat status. The self-interest of the strategy to push women into combat for the sake of high-level promotions is masked with the seemingly moral justification that the "burden" of ground combat falls disproportionately on men. According to this argument, to qualify for full citizenship, women ought to volunteer for ground combat to assume their fare share of the burden of national defense.

The artifice of civic responsibility as the basis for ground combat assignment is elaborated with contrived arguments about the volunteer Army's inability to recruit qualified men to carry out the ground combat mission. According to this argument, we must place women in ground combat because there simply are not enough qualified men who can or will do the job. History has repeatedly shown that women have not been willing to meet the recruiting demands of the active-duty military, in war or in peace—not in World War II and certainly not in 1999, when the Army offered extraordinary financial incentives to meet recruiting shortages. Women who have taken up the slack and volunteered for combat support roles, furthermore, experience much higher rates of physical and psychological disability, hospitalized medical care, and attrition before their first enlistments are completed than their male counterparts—not to mention gender-specific issues arising from pregnancy and complications thereof.

Finally, the ethical price for lifting the ground combat exclusion is costly not only to women but also to their children. The litigation issues that would result from lifting the ground combat exclusion are cost-prohibitive, even if the Supreme Court were to rule against women in every case. Children who are deprived of maternal care, in a legal era that prioritizes women's right to choose motherhood, are likely to sue their mothers and their government when they are deprived of that care because of callous military personnel policies. Children who are born with defects to warrior mothers would have the right to litigate for compensation—as would families, cities, and states that would be slapped with the burden of raising war babies born with disabilities. The argument that high technology makes women's participation in ground combat more feasible—because ground combat casualties are unlikely once we switch to high-tech strategies—is ethically problematic. Overuse of technology to minimize casualties in armed conflict will result in criminal harm to noncombatants who must live in close proximity to active military combat and to the world community, which has a moral vested interest in minimizing collateral damage from remote-controlled, high-technology warfare.

There may be a point in human history when war will be as extinct as a social phenomenon as the dinosaur is an extinct species. In the interim, the nature of military conflict may be such that women can participate as equals in every aspect of ground combat. Attempts to lift the ground combat exclusion for women have not been grounded in ethical strategies. Advocates for women in ground combat rely on Supreme Court rulings that outlaw job exclusion that is based on gender stereotyping about women's abilities. Advocates cite these rulings to demand the job, yet women's advocates rely on stereotypes to keep women in jobs for which they are not physically qualified. Thus, we want women to have equal opportunity but not equal accountability. We want women to have combat assignments without holding women to the same standards of competence, character, or performance as male combatants.

We would never send an undertrained welterweight boxer into a ring with a world champion heavyweight boxer. The immorality of such a crass publicity stunt would be obvious to everyone. Therefore, it should be obvious that the promoters of women in combat are engaged in an illusory public relations campaign that has resulted only in physical harm and damage to the women who have been ill-matched for the fight. Until women are willing to give up the privilege of stereotyped but legally defined lower standards of physical fitness, performance, and personal conduct, they should be excluded from the heavyweight ring, and the ground combat exclusion policy should be retained.

Our nation and women would be better served if we begin to rethink the notion that combat service should confer special privileges, rights, and entitlements. Women, elderly persons, physically disabled persons, and children should not be relegated to second-class citizenship because they are not fit for ground combat assignments. Instead, we must uphold advances made in the courts and confer privileges, rights, benefits, and entitlements as appropriate, with the expectation that all citizens will bestow their own gifts of service according to the national need and according to their unique abilities.

A time may come when the average woman can perform hard physical duties and handle physical and emotional trauma with the same resiliency as men. That moment has not arrived. In this moment in history, female soldiers suffer tremendously with every step taken to lift the combat exclusion. Therefore, I respectfully conclude that the ground combat exclusion for women should not be lifted.

ACKNOWLEDGMENTS

I wish to thank Rita Simon for this opportunity to reflect on this issue as it impacts all of my Army colleagues and friends and their families. I also wish to thank Cynthia Phillips and LTC Joseph P. Regan (ret.) for reading this manuscript. Finally, I thank Lorry Fenner for her research and her contribution to this necessary public discourse about women's participation in military service.

REFERENCES

Abel, E. 1998. Sexual risk behaviors among ship- and shore-based Navy women. *Military Medicine* 163 (4): 250–56.

Abel, E., E. Adams, and R. Stevenson. 1994. Self-esteem, problem solving, and sexual risk behavior among women with and without Chlamydia. *Clinical Nursing Research* 3 (4): 353–70.

———. 1996. Sexual risk behavior among female army recruits. *Military Medicine* 161 (8): 491–94.

Ackermann, Henry F. 1989. *He Was Always There: The U.S. Army Chaplain Ministry in the Vietnam Conflict*. Washington, D.C.: Office of the Chief of Chaplains, Department of the Army.

Adams, M. M., F. E. Harlass, A. P. Sarno, J. A. Read, and J. S. Rawlings. 1994. Antenatal hospitalization among enlisted servicewomen, 1987–1990. *Obstetrics and Gynecology* 84 (1): 35–39. Study sponsored by the Division of Reproductive Health, National Center for Chronic Disease Prevention and Health Promotion, Atlanta.

Adams, M. M., J. A. Read, J. S. Rawlings, F. B. Harlass, A. P. Sarno, and P. H. Rhodes. 1993. Pre-term delivery among black and white enlisted women in the United States Army. *Obstetrics and Gynecology* 81 (1): 65–71. Study sponsored by the Division of Reproductive Health, National Center for Chronic Disease Prevention and Health Promotion, Atlanta.

Amoroso, P. T., N. S. Bell, and B. H. Jones. 1997. Injury among female and male parachutists. *Aviation Space Environmental Medicine* 68 (11): 1006–11.

Armed Forces Newswire Service. 1997. Report says army has yet to prove digital is the way to go. October 17.

Army Times. 2000. Newslines. Careers. The new promotion point worksheet, March 20, p. 15.

Bijur, P. E., M. Horodyski, W. Egerton, M. Kurzon, S. Lifrak, and S. Friedman. 1997. Comparison of injury during cadet basic training by gender. *Archives of Pediatrics and Adolescent Medicine* 151 (5): 156–61.

Boling, R. O., and R. Abbassi. 1988. Disability from endometriosis in the United States Army. *Journal of Reproductive Medicine* 33 (1): 49–52.

Braakhuis, Wilfried. 1997–99. Axis offensive 1941: American involvement. In *The world at war.* Available at <http://www.euronet.nl/users/wilfried/ww2/1941. htm>.

Clark, J. B., V. L. Holt, and F. Miser. 1998. Unintended pregnancy among female soldiers presenting for prenatal care at Madigan Army Medical Center. *Military Medicine* 163 (7): 444–48.

Collins, Arthur S., Jr., LTG. 1978. Training management. In *Common Sense Training: A Working Philosophy for Leaders.* Novato, Calif.: Presidio Press.

Cornum, Rhonda (as told to Peter Copeland). 1993. *She Went to War: The Rhonda Cornum Story.* Novato, Calif.: Presidio Press.

Croft, A. M. 1995. The employability of pregnant and breastfeeding servicewomen. *Journal of the Royal Army Medical Corps* (JV6) 141 (3): 134–41.

Denver Post. 1995. Academy cadet files suit over simulated rape. *Denver Post* (28 May), p. C3.

Department of the Army. 1983. *Field Manual 22-100: Military Leadership.* Washington, D.C.: Headquarters, Department of the Army.

———. 1987. *Field Manual 22-103: Leadership and Command at Senior Levels.* Washington, D.C.: Headquarters, Department of the Army.

———. 1990a. *Field Manual 22-100: Military Leadership.* Washington, D.C.: Headquarters, Department of the Army.

———. 1990b. *Field Manual 25-101: Battle Focused Training.* Washington, D.C.: Headquarters, Department of the Army.

———. 1990c. *Field Manual 63-20: Forward Support Battalion.* Washington, D.C.: Headquarters, Department of the Army.

———. 1992. *Field Manual 21-20: Physical Readiness Training.* Washington, D.C.: Headquarters, Department of the Army.

———. 1996. *Field Manual 17-95: Cavalry Operations.* Washington, D.C.: Headquarters, Department of the Army.

deYoung, Marie E. 1999. *This Woman's Army: The Dynamics of Sex and Violence in the Military.* Central Point, Ore.: Hellgate Press.

———. 2000. As we turn: Army women in the twenty-first century. In *A Look Backward and Forward at American Professional Women and Their Families,* edited by Rita J. Simon. Lanham, Md.: University Press of America.

———. 2001. Sexuality: Histories, behaviors and lifestyles that impact military readiness. In *Women in the Military,* edited by Rita J. Simon. Piscataway, N.J.: Transaction Publishers.

Fenner, Lorry. 1998. Either you need these women or you do not: Informing the debate on military service and citizenship. *Gender Issues* 16 (3).

Feuerstein, M., S. M. Berkowitz, and C. A. Peck, Jr. 1997. Musculoskeletal-rated disability in the U.S. Army personnel: prevalence, gender, and military occupational specialties. *Journal of Occupational Environmental Medicine* 39 (1): 68–78.

Fong, Tillie. 1995. Rape program too realsitic, cadets say. *Rocky Mountain News* (7 April), p. 52A.

Fontana, A., and R. Rosenheck. 1998. Duty-related and sexual stress in the etiology of PTSD among women veterans who seek treatment. *Psychiatric Services* 48 (5): 658–62.

Foster, Dick. 1995. Air Force admits cadet abused. Discharged student says academy's survival training made her ill. *Rocky Mountain News,* August 11.

Geeze, D. S. 1998. Pregnancy and in-flight cosmic radiation. *Aviation Space Environmental Medicine* 69 (11): 1061–64.

GenderGap. 1998. American Women in the Military. Available at <http://www.gendergap.com/military/Warriors.HTM>.

General Accounting Office (GAO). 1997. NSIAD-99-2: *Gender Issues: Information to Assess Service Members' Perceptions of Gender Inequities is Incomplete.* Available at <http://frwebgate.access.gpo.gov/>.

———. 1998a. *GAO/NSIAD-98-157: Gender Issues: Analysis of Promotion and Career Opportunities Data.* Available at <http://frwebgate.access.gpo.gov>.

———. 1998b. *GAO/NSIAD-99-9: Gender Issues: Improved Guidance and Oversight Are Needed to Ensure Validity and Equity of Fitness Standards.* Available at <http://frwebgate.access.gpo.gov/>.

Goldsmith, J. R. 1997. Epidemiologic evidence relevant to radar (microwave) effects. *Environmental Health Perspectives* 105 (supplement 6): 1579–87.

Grabenstein, J. D., C. L. Filby, R. A. Vauter, T. R. Harris, and J. P. Wilson. 1995. Prescribed medication use among troops deploying to Somalia: pharmacoepidemiologic analysis. *Military Medicine* 160 (11): 571–77.

Gray, Gregory C., Bruce D. Coate, Christy M. Anderson, Han K. Kang, S. William Berg, F. Stephen Wignall, James D. Knoke, and Elizabeth Barrett-Connor. 1996. The postwar hospitalization experience of U.S. veterans of the Persian Gulf War. *New England Journal of Medicine* 335: 1505–13.

Gray, J. L., D. B. Flanary, and D. H. Newell. 1994. The prevalence of periodontal abscess. *Journal of the Indiana Dental Association* 73 (4): 18–20, 22–23; quiz 24.

Harrell, Margaret C., and Laura L. Miller. 1997. *New Opportunities for Military Women: Effects upon Readiness, Cohesion, and Morale.* Santa Monica, Calif.: Rand.

Heir, T. 1998. Musculoskeletal injuries in officer training: One-year follow-up. *Military Medicine* 163 (4): 229–33.

Hines J. F. 1992. Ambulatory health care needs of women deployed with a heavy armor division during the Persian Gulf War. *Military Medicine* 157 (5): 219–21.

Hoiberg, A, 1980. Sex and occupational differences in hospitalization rates among Navy enlisted personnel. *Journal of Occupational Medicine* 22 (10): 685–90.

———. 1984. Health Status of women in the U.S. military. *Health Psychology* (3): 273–87.

Holm, Maj. Gen. Jeanne, USAF (Ret.). 1992. *Women in the Military: An Unfinished Revolution,* rev. Novato, Calif.: Presidio Press.

hooks, bell. 1984. *Feminist Theory: From Margin to Center.* Boston: South End Press.

Hughey, M. J., and T. G. Patel. 1997. Changes in women's health care aboard one ship. *Military Medicine* 162 (10): 671–74.

Irwin D. E., D. A. Savitz, W. A. Bowes, Jr., and K. A. Andre. 1996. Race, age, and cesarean delivery in a military population. *Obstetrics and Gynecology* 88 (4 Pt): 530–33.

Kadende-Kaiser, Rose. 2000. The impact of mandatory military service on women's choices for higher education in Burundi. National Association for Women in Higher Education conference proceedings, January 6–8, 2000, New Orleans, LA.

Kang H. K., and Tim A. Bullman. 1996. Mortality among U.S. veterans of the Persian Gulf War. *New England Journal of Medicine* 335 (20): 1498–1504.

Legal Intelligencer. 1994. Navy pilot testifies in Tailhook case. *Legal Intelligencer,* October 18.

Magann, E. F., and T.E. Nolan. 1991. Pregnancy outcome in an active-duty population. *Obstetrics and Gynecology* 78 (3 Pt 1): 391–93.

Markenson, G., E. Raez, and M. Colavita. 1992. Female health care during Operation Desert Storm: The Eighth Evacuation Hospital experience. *Military Medicine* 157(11): 610–13.

Martin, L., L. N. Rosen, D. B. Durand, R. H. Stretch, and K. H. Knudson. 1998. Prevalence and timing of sexual assaults in a sample of male and female U.S. Army soldiers. *Military Medicine* 163 (4): 213–16.

McHugh, Jane. 1999. The new PT test . . . will it drive down your score? *Army Times.* February 15.

Miller, Laura L. 1998. Feminism and the exclusion of army women from combat. *Gender Issues* 16 (3).

Murray, Maureen. 1998. Women army grunts set sights on combat. *Toronto Star.* April 26.

Ommaya, A. K., A. L. Dannenberg, and A. M. Salazar. 1996. Causation, incidence, and costs of traumatic brain injury in the U.S. military system. *Journal of Trauma* 40 (2): 211–17.

Orihuela, E., D. C. West, M. Pow-Sang, and M. M. Warren. 1997. Increased incidence of non-transitional cell carcinoma of the bladder in women of the Texas Gulf Coast Region. *South Medicine Journal* 1990 (8): 801–05.

Pierson, L. L. 1996. Hazards of noise exposure on fetal hearing. *Seminars in Perinatology* 20 (1): 21–29.

Pollard, R. B., and E. A. Edwards. 1975. Epidemiologic survey of rubella in a military recruit population. *American Journal of Epidemiology* 101 (5): 431–37.

Presidential Commission on the Assignment of Women in the Armed Forces. 1993. *Report to the President: Women in Combat.* Washington, D.C.: Brassey.

Pugliese, David. 1998. Women in combat jobs abused: Report: studies paint gloomy picture of harassment. *Ottawa Citizen.* June 18.

Ramirez, G., R. M. Grimes, J. F. Annegers, B. R. Davis, and C. H. Slater. 1990. Occupational physical activity and other risk factors for preterm birth among U.S. Army primigravidas. *American Journal of Public Health* 80 (6): 728–30.

Ross, J., and A. Woodward. 1994. Risk factors for injury during basic military training. Is there a social element to injury pathogenesis? *Journal of Occupational Medicine* 36 (10): 1120–26.

Sajatovic, Martha, Lance Vernon, and William Semple. 1997. Clinical characteristics and health resource use of men and women veterans with serious mental illness. *Psychiatric-Services* 48 (11): 1461–63.

Schwarzkopf, Norman, and Peter Petre. 1992. *It Doesn't Take a Hero.* New York: Bantam.

Scott-Moncrieff, N. F. 1994. Comparative female to male consultation rates in NHS primary care: extrapolation to the Royal Navy. *Journal of the Royal Naval Medical Service* 80 (2): 85–89.

Secretary of Defense. 1994. Memorandum from the Secretary of Defense: Direct ground combat definition and assignment rule. Washington, D.C.: Navy Public Affairs Library.

Sherman, R. A., G. D. Davis, and M. F. Wong. 1997. Behavioral treatment of exercise-induced urinary incontinence among female soldiers. *Military Medicine* 162 (10): 690–94.

Smoak, B. L., J. V. Writer, L. W. Keep, J. Cowan, and J. L. Chantelois. 1997. The effects of inadvertent exposure of mefloquine chemoprophylaxis on pregnancy outcomes and infants of U.S. Army servicewomen. *Journal of Infectious Diseases* 176 (3): 831–33.

Spandorfer, S. D., E. Graham, and I. Forouzan. 1996. Pregnancy outcome in active duty seagoing women. *Military Medicine* 161 (4): 214–16.

Stacey, Judith, and Barrie Thorne. 1998. The missing feminist revolution in sociology. In *Feminist Foundations: Toward Transforming Sociology,* edited by Kristen A. Myers, Cynthia D. Anderson, and Barbara J. Risman. Thousand Oaks, Calif.: Sage Publications.

Stafford, E. M., R. S. Stewart, Jr., G. R. Teague, R. R. Gomez, B. A. Crothers, T. J. Michel, T. H. Patience, and D. C. Moore. 1996. Detection of human papillomavirus in cervical biopsies of summer camp ROTC cadets with abnormal papanicolaou smears. *Journal of Pediatric and Adolescent Gynecology* 3: 119–24.

Stewart, A. 1999. Detecting the health risks of radiation. *Medicine, Conflict and Survival*. 15 (2): 138–48.

Tam, L. W. 1998. Psychological aspects of pregnancy in the military: A review. *Military Medicine* 163 (6): 408–12.

U.S. Civil War Center. 1999. Statistical summary of America's major wars. *Civil War Information*. Available at <http://www.cwc.lsu.edu/cwc/other/stats/warcost.htm>.

U.S. Department of Defense and U.S. Coast Guard. 1997. Casualties in principal wars of the U.S. In *World Almanac and Book of Facts*. Available at <http://web.lexis-nexis.com/>.

U.S. House Armed Services Committee. 1994a. *Women in Combat*. Testimony by Lieutenant General Theodore G. Stroup, Jr. to Subcommittee on Military Forces and Personnel. October 6.

———. 1994b. *Women Assignment Policy*. Prepared statement by LTG George Christmas to Subcommittee on Military Forces and Personnel. October 7.

———. 1999. Testimony by National Security Study Group to Subcommittee on Military Personnel. November 4.

Voge, V. M. 1996a. Self-reported menstrual concerns of the U.S. Air Force and the U.S. Army rated women aircrew. *Military Medicine* 161 (10): 614–15.

———. 1996b. General characteristics of the U.S. Air Force and the U.S. Army rated female and male aircrew. *Military Medicine* 161 (11): 654–57.

Wakin, Malham M. 1979. *War, Morality, and the Military Profession*. Boulder, Colo.: Westview Press.

Winfield, A. C., J. Moore, M. Braker, and C. W. Johnson. 1997. Risk factors associated with stress reactions in female Marines. *Military Medicine* 162 (10): 698–702.

Wittich, A. C. 1993. The military gynecologist in low-intensity conflict environment. *Military Medicine* 158 (4): 275–77.

———. 1996. Gynecologic evaluation of the first female soldiers enrolled in the Gulf War comprehensive clinical evaluation program at Tripler Army Medical Center. *Military Medicine* 161 (11): 635–37.

Zapata, B. C., A. Rebolledo, E. Atalah, B. Newman, and M. C. King. 1992. The influence of social and political violence on the risk of pregnancy complications. *American Journal of Public Health* 82 (5): 685–90.

PART THREE

Reflections

Response to deYoung

Lorry M. Fenner

Marie deYoung and I agree on at least three things. First, no one who is unqualified, untrained, or poorly led should be put into combat. Second, it would be a wonderful thing if nations found a way to resolve their differences other than war. And third, military and combat service should not be a qualification for first-class American citizenship.

On the other hand, deYoung and I differ in many other significant respects; I address only a few here. deYoung proposes that not for a long time, if ever, will women be qualified or trained well enough to participate in combat. I counter that we should choose appropriate standards, train those who can meet these standards for the task, and provide them with competent leaders. deYoung's position is that women are "handicapped"—psychologically, physically, and morally—and therefore can never be more than military "misfits." And whereas deYoung proposes that the connection between military service and citizenship is a myth or an ideological and "abstract" desire of "advocacy feminists," the evidence indicates that it is a reality.

The nation-state system is based on the government's ability to protect its sovereignty and the lives and prosperity of its people. The armed forces of a nation are a core institution, and armed defense (combat) is this institution's defining feature.[1]

Finally, deYoung and I disagree entirely on the definition of a "feminist." Although I consider myself a feminist, I do not recognize myself in her type of feminism or the one(s) she attacks. I do not agree that all women are physically, psychologically, and morally weaker than all men, nor am I part of a conspiracy based on ignorance to destroy national defense.

deYoung's paper is a prime exhibit of what I argued against. Her arguments are a "moving target"—dispersed, ephemeral, and contradictory. She neglects any consideration of the nature of warfare except to assure us that ground combat is hell (although she sometimes doubts that air warfare or naval warfare are) and that science fiction is not reality. She does not consider the force structure needed to implement our national security and military strategies. She barely acknowledges that we have a problem recruiting qualified male volunteers, and she ignores demographic trends. And she easily dismisses the important debate about our political ideology that has very real and material effects, in favor of an implied cultural ideology that would restrict married women to motherhood or single, childless women to teaching and nursing. In this cultural argument, she proposes (but does not support) that feminists and advocates for gay Americans have conspired, with the complicity of Army leaders, to create a "crisis" for the Army's culture and "military ethos" in championing individual rights at the expense of national security. She ignores the reality that readiness challenges have been caused not by personnel policies but by changes in the world. deYoung ignores the security dilemmas of the post–Cold War era in which our forces, rightly or wrongly, have been reduced and spread thin around the globe, conducting a wide range of missions beyond classic set-piece battles.

The biggest challenge is keeping my response to an acceptable length. Countering all of the errors of fact, analysis, and logic in deYoung's essay would require a very long paper—even longer to show the questionable use of sources and expose all the red herrings she advances. Readers will see many of these errors themselves, and I can only encourage them to critically examine her sources. Of the several sources I checked, she seems to have either misinterpreted their findings, attributed findings to them that do not follow from the research, or taken leaps from the researchers' credible findings to support her incredible contentions. I also encourage readers to look to my bibliography for the arguments of noted and respected scholars—not questionable and limited Internet research or unsupported assumptions.[2]

One representative example of the misuse and misinterpretation of sources involves my 1998 *Gender Issues* article. deYoung accuses me of presenting a false dichotomy—that we should accept women in all military roles or none at all. In fact, in "Either You Need These Women Or You Do Not," I present the post–World War II debate in which Senator Margaret Chase Smith argued that if the Services were going to use women in an emergency (which they had done and planned to do), women should train for such emergencies in peacetime and be allowed to aspire to careers. deYoung inadvertently demonstrates my actual contention—that the logical extension of arguments against expanding opportunities for military women is that women would not serve in the military at all. She argues that all soldiers must be fungible to allow for "cross-leveling"—that is, that all soldiers must be qualified to be infantrymen—and she accuses all career women of intentionally (and immorally) abandoning their children.[3]

One other example of misuse is highlighted by the Stuart and Halverston (1997) study of psychological symptoms of deployed and nondeployed soldiers. Their actual findings include the conclusion that "gender difference had little to no effect on reported symptom measures among deployed soldier samples." They also found that their controls were not adequate and recommended further study of male and female soldiers.

In my essay I address most of the physical and psychological arguments against military women. Here too, some of deYoung's sources are questionable and others are poorly interpreted, but the primary problem is that she bases her argument almost entirely on generalizations from personal experience (already a decade old) and anecdotes. If she and I merely compared our military experiences, without amplifying those experiences with more objective evidence, we would simply be at an impasse because they have differed so much. I challenge anyone who has found credible sources that confirm the physical and psychological weakness of all women to bring this objective information forward. Certainly our lawmakers, military leaders, and courts could not contest such obvious evidence if it were real, and policy decisions of such import should be made only in the face of hard data. The fact that no such compelling evidence has come to light over the more than 50 years of this controversy should indicate to researchers the low likelihood of finding it.[4]

I also address the nature of war. In this regard, deYoung does not admit even that the 1994 definition of ground combat bears little resemblance to missions our soldiers carry out today, nor does she acknowledge that "the front" has become increasingly difficult to define since World War II. I agree that current exclusion policies are unworkable and that women in noncombat or combat support positions are not protected from harm; they never have been. No matter how we try to define combat, the reality remains complex and confusing. Certainly, women volunteers must be told the full extent of the dangers and unknowns they face in any military occupation, from nursing to teaching to cooking to the chaplaincy—as should male volunteers. I argue that we would best be rid of a blanket (largely fiction in practice) exclusion that is based on gender rather than ability.

Although historical examples and popular culture sources can be helpful, we also see constant evidence of their misuse. I know of no responsible historian or debater who would support the contention that Yugoslavia fell to the Nazis because that nation employed military women. Instead, most would contend that the Yugoslav resistance, including women members, tied down valuable German forces in the Balkans, thereby contributing to the Nazi defeat. We do know that the Soviet Union defeated the Nazi forces with the help of almost one million military women.[5] I also know no one who would support an argument that Americans will devolve to tribal warfare, as in Burundi and Eritrea, if we allow qualified women into more military specialties.[6]

Beyond the questionable historical and contemporary sources, de-Young uses touching narratives that, as I suggest, are ideal for eliciting an emotional response. Nevertheless, they cannot replace adequate analogies. In truth, few men are Medal of Honor winners; warfare has changed significantly since World War I and even World War II; and snipers do not require brute strength as much as they need intelligence, good eyesight, and a steady hand. During the Tet Offensive, American military women served under fire in South Vietnam with then-Capt. (later Gen.) Norman Schwarzkopf. Although they were not trained for combat, they served well and bravely in their roles, alongside male soldiers who were trained for combat. Interestingly, after DESERT STORM, Gen. Schwarzkopf publicly supported military women. In addition, to really examine the POW experience rather than the asymmetric comparison of Vietnam-era Navy pilot James Stockdale and Gulf War doctor Rhonda Cornum, readers should consult Elliott Gruner's excellent study of POWs, which includes men and women.[7] And rather than dismissing some World War II nurses' experiences because they were not the same as many soldiers', perhaps we should consider the whole range of women's captivity and treatment in war. Stories of suffering and moral courage are not limited to men.[8]

At the other end of reduction, I know of no responsible debater or self-respecting feminist who would portray a buxom, long-haired, lycra-clad woman with a "laser pen" as emblematic of future warfare. We should not reduce this part of the debate to absurd, adolescent male fantasies. deYoung offers no support for the statement, "too many implicit assumptions drawn from science-fiction fantasies are driving contemporary military personnel policies." Beyond discussing the leadership lessons that can be learned from *Star Trek* and dismissing digitization and Information Age technology on the basis of her personal experience of some failures in the early uses of computers on the battlefield, however, deYoung does not address the extensive advances that all of the Services have made. Nor does she address the technology that our adversaries use against us. I do agree, however—as would all responsible military thinkers and trainers—that all of us should be trained to operate independently of the technology, so that we can function if it should fail. Still, we cannot wish away the scientific advances (which in earlier times were still science fiction fantasies) in all areas of warfare or dismiss the real changes in military forces and equipment in favor of a romanticized foxhole. If we had simply denied the possibilities of firearms, submarines, airplanes, and electronics after their first failures, where would we be relative to our adversaries today?[9]

In addition to these arguments—which fail in every regard—deYoung proposes several legal/financial and ethical arguments that move us no further in the debate. Rhetoric and unfounded, unsupported assumptions cannot be allowed to substitute for objective information and conscientious debate. Here deYoung simply rehashes her earlier faulty physical, psycho-logical, and historical arguments—as if, because she has mentioned them previously, they had become fact. She grossly misinterprets (or misrepre-sents) *Feres*, mistakenly applies Titles VII and IX, and takes mind-boggling leaps in suggesting that International Humanitarian Law (IHL) will be compromised and claims by damaged children will bankrupt our treasury if women continue to expand their military service.[10] In addition, deYoung's seven "ethical" arguments really are only three, which actually hinge on conservative cultural ideology, leaps of logic, and more red herrings. If her argument really is that she would like to reinscribe the cultural ideology of an earlier era, rather than hide behind these tortured arguments on law and ethics, she should simply take the position that women should confine themselves to the roles of mother, teacher, and nurse.

Because I did not discuss this area in my essay, I dedicate some space here to addressing a few of the fallacies in the law and ethics sections of deYoung's. First, contrary to what she implies, *Feres* applies to military men *and women*. This case was decided on the basis of jurisdiction and how best to support injured military members. In the 1950s, the courts decided that the federal government provided more care and compensation for injured soldiers and their families than state courts and systems could. There was no reason for soldiers to go to the expense, time, and trouble of trying to sue in civil court for monetary damages. Although the Feres doctrine protects military doctors and commanders from frivolous lawsuits, it does not mean that commanders and doctors cannot be charged with negligence and malfeasance under the UCMJ when applicable. They are held account-able, and soldiers can obtain justice when they are abused or assaulted.

Male soldiers have used the remedy of military and civilian courts to obtain redress.[11]

Also contrary to deYoung's argument, Titles VII and IX were not instituted to prevent or redress sexual assault but as civil rights measures to prevent and respond to real discrimination. The former was written for and invoked primarily in cases of racial discrimination; the latter addresses inequality of athletic opportunities in academic institutions.[12] Would deYoung also have minority men renounce protections they receive under Title VII? Would she term the existence of such protection "racial privilege"? Neither law applies to "male enemies, foreign or domestic." deYoung does not provide any evidence for her assertion that "the application of Title VII doctrine has destroyed military readiness and morale in most Army support units." Finally, these two U.S. laws bear no relationship to IHL, laws relating to crimes against humanity, UCMJ assault violations, the Laws of Armed Conflict, or the Hague or Geneva Conventions—all of which protect men *and* women of all races, military and civilian. Most important, deYoung does not say (or know) that *the military is exempt from both Title VII and Title IX.* All military members—regardless of race, gender, or religion—forego these rights when they take their oaths of enlistment; they are covered by other protections from abuse instead.[13]

Therefore, Title VII has not given "preferential treatment" to military women in recruiting or training or in standards of competence or conduct. Women indeed may be required to meet different standards of basic physical fitness, but they are not afforded different or "lower" job standards.[14] No evidence is provided that women escape standards or duty requirements by threatening sexual harassment complaints. Saying it does not make it so, and anecdotes do not suffice for evidence. The possibility that it could happen should not be used to bar all women from service, any more than the possibility of false racial discrimination complaints should be used to bar racial minorities. The problem is not the class of people but the policies, the treatment of individuals, and the appropriate application of leadership. Male officers and NCOs should not claim "victim" status and use this status as a cop-out for not doing their jobs.

There also is no evidence that women are more litigious than men (nor that they have a "statistical propensity . . . to internalize victimization identities"). deYoung imagines that women "do not have the psychological hardiness to withstand sexual, social, physical, and psychological stresses of combat and combat training" and therefore will bring suit when they misinterpret horseplay or legitimate training. Again, legal protections for military members against frivolous lawsuits are in place; for argument's sake, however, if deYoung's proposal were logically extended and one substituted "minority men" for women, she apparently would deny their right to seek redress if real discrimination or racial harassment occurred—a proposal that could support open season on minorities and women.

deYoung's "bodily contact" in training is not rape or sexual assault. When it becomes either, it should be treated as a crime, not play. Most women know the difference. The scene in *GI Jane* to which deYoung refers was not "wood-shedding"; clearly, to all involved, it was not for toughening up the undisciplined but an illegal assault and a power trip.

In real life, protection under the law does not cover women at the expense of men. Finally, deYoung does not seem to realize that "combatants" and POWs have more protection under IHL and the Laws of Armed Conflict that noncombatants.[15]

Incredibly, deYoung argues—without providing evidence of even one case—that military women have used this "legal" preferential treatment and men's fear of false accusations to gain power and prestige. At the same time, she claims that "no male soldier has ever succeeded" in obtaining redress for injuries to life and limb. The reality is that if a man is raped or sexually assaulted by his commander or colleagues, he is protected under the law; if he feels he has been abused by individuals or the institution, he can seek redress (and many have done so); if a military doctor negligently or intentionally maims a male soldier, that doctor can be punished, and the member and family will be provided for; and if a soldier's male colleagues intentionally (or unintentionally) harm him, they can be charged, tried, and punished.[16] Military women deserve no less consideration and protection.

Just one more example of how deYoung gets these legal issues and cases wrong is the case of "simulated rape training." This exercise actually was Survival, Evasion, Resistance, and Escape (SERE) (and POW) training in which Air Force Academy cadet trainers were "simulating" rape as torture and punishment against male and female cadets. This exercise was not an official part of the training but an abuse of power by unsupervised cadet trainers. In this case, trainees (who are not allowed to fight back and injure an instructor) did not know if the rape was to be only "simulated." Although this "training" was stopped, SERE and POW training continue; a traditional, more advanced program is given to all aircrew personnel (male and female) by officer and NCO expert trainers. Women do not have to see a film to know that there is a high probability that they will be raped, and just as deYoung claims that live ammunition might not be used in training, neither should cadets rape each other in the USAFA environment.[17] The *young man* who originally brought the complaint and later left the Academy, along with the young woman who was interviewed on television, knew that.[18]

Still, as training is supposed to show (and I think we can all agree), war and combat do pose "excessive physiological and psychological burdens" on *everyone* in the war zone—men and women, military and civilian. Again, however, deYoung leaps when she imagines—despite thinking that most women cannot pass the qualification standards—"large numbers" of military women, "large numbers" of pregnancies under combat conditions, "large numbers of children" born under these conditions, and large numbers of disabled children. At the same time, she also claims that there are no studies that correlate birth defects with male combat (or even employment) exposure. By similar thinking, she ignores the related effects on children whose fathers died or were disabled in combat or paternally transmitted Agent Orange disabilities (the jury is still out on Gulf War Syndrome and the anthrax vaccine's effects on male reproduction). Instead, "wanting it both ways," she proposes that *Feres* will not be applied and will be overturned, whereas previously she has implied that it will remain in force and that it places a burden only on men. Even if the doctrine is misguided and eventually overturned, the rest of her premises are built on extreme possibilities in every case.

All male and female soldiers can get medical and psychological trauma support; their dependents (many more belonging to male soldiers than to female soldiers) are afforded access to many government services as well. Although state governments (and the federal government) bear the expense for service-related disabilities, most of this assistance (to date) has been provided to men. Incidentally, those same state governments pay the costs for health care services for people who smoke (many more military men than military women), abuse alcohol, suffer parental abuse, suffer from exposure to toxic chemicals in civilian jobs, or live in toxic environments. If we apply rigorous and relevant job standards, as I have advocated, we are extremely unlikely to employ late-term pregnant military women in a combat zone. Nor do I have so little faith in the integrity of the majority of servicewomen that I think many will rush to conceive to avoid exposure to danger. Though that can happen, I do not expect a higher rate than for male malingerers—those who smash a hand or shoot a foot to make themselves ineligible for combat or military service.[19]

deYoung makes more unsubstantiated claims in two additional areas—that the children of military mothers suffer more from separations than the children of military fathers and that from a *limited* right to choose abortion, women have an unlimited right to give birth and a commensurate constitutional responsibility to care for the child.[20] The connection is completely unsupported; again, however, for the sake of argument, why would not similar rights and responsibilities accrue to fathers? In fact, courts have upheld the responsibilities and rights of fathers, and I know of no case in which someone has sued for the combat death of their father, even under conscription. This argument is another piece of the cultural belief that insists that women bear not just primary childcare responsibility but all responsibility for offspring.

From the legal arena deYoung moves to the ethical and commits similar errors of evidence and logic. For the sake of brevity, three of the ethical arguments focus on women's feminist goals and strategies for career advancement that are personalist, egoist, and selfish for career advancement, competing against and distinct from a (presumably exclusively male) military ethos of self-sacrifice, duty, honor, and country. deYoung asserts that military men have always just done their duty, without career aspirations, egos, or competition for plum assignments and promotions they thought they deserved. Further, she implies that no men ever accepted promotions or positions on the basis of political connections, nepotism, or other non–merit-based considerations.

In reality, members who serve in combat arms and aviation and on combat vessels are promoted at higher rates than those in support positions—and they probably should be because combat is the core function of the military. I am aware of no feminist, scholar, or military woman, however, who supports pushing unqualified others into combat for personal gain. Most argue for voluntary service for those who are qualified, and even in the case of involuntary service would place only qualified personnel in combat positions. Putting young men in danger simply because they are male—and therefore "qualified"—would be just as unethical, after all.

We all agree, apparently, that not being in combat positions does not protect women from harm. In any case, female officers have not argued that they should be given combat command over unqualified and nonvolunteer junior enlisted women or men. Such a position would certainly not help their careers (if that were their motive). Few female officers are very political, and fewer claim to be feminists; many do seek equal opportunity to contribute, along with the privileges that others earn from these same types of contributions. Of course, one doesn't have the right to any profession, but in our democracy we hope that all have the opportunity to compete fairly for education and training and to be judged against real standards, rather than to be barred because of group membership or stereotypes.

Just as deYoung paints all military women (and feminists) as self-serv-
ing and immoral careerists, she mistakenly supposes that all military men
are altruistic and void of egos and career goals. In addition, she ignores the
reality of a masculinist approach, based on preferred cultural norms, that
would exclude women from the military even if they are qualified and can
contribute to national security. Would sending our forces into combat
understrength or with less-qualified personnel be ethical simply because
some people do not want even qualified women to contribute?

This issue is not a question of female immorality and ethics, even if
there were such things. Male volunteers do get to choose from available
career fields, just as women do—except that the latter, of course, cannot
volunteer for combat posts. Conscripts are not put into jobs they want if they
are unqualified.[21] Male soldiers do complain when they don't get the jobs
they want—whether those jobs entail combat (for promotions) or positions
that provide good training for civilian jobs. Men have brought legal cases and
appealed to Congress when they felt slighted by the Services. They have
sued over lack of promotions and being "downsized" (or RIF'd), and some
have lobbied for early release from their military commitments.[22] Men complain if they do not think they are getting an opportunity to contribute to their
fullest capacity.

deYoung provides absolutely no evidence for the insulting proposition
that most women "leverage rank . . . not based on accomplishments but as
quid pro quo to end relentless prosecution of high-profile sexual misconduct
cases." The fact is that there are men and women of every sort in the
military—those who do their jobs and leave, those who aspire to careers,
and those who complain. We should remember, however, that just as a
higher percentage of women have left the service for family reasons, there
are more single male parents in the service, and a higher percentage and
number of men have left for disciplinary reasons.[23] These few examples
should at least call deYoung's ethical approach into question.

Another fallacy masquerading as morality is deYoung's contention that
feminists are immoral to argue in favor of high-tech weapons, so that
physically weaker women can participate in combat, because these weapons cause more civilian casualties. This argument fails in every respect.
Feminists do not argue for high-tech weapons, and female officers do not
use technology as the basis for their argument that qualified women should
be allowed to compete for combat positions. They do base their arguments
on abstract notions about democracy that I find so important and that
deYoung discounts out of hand. Moreover, all evidence points contrary to
deYoung's contention that these high-tech and precision weapons cause

more civilian casualties than industrial-era "dumb" weapons. deYoung also seems to be blind to the damage that ground forces do to people, infrastructures, agriculture, and the environment, as well as strategies and operational doctrines of attacking centers of gravity to end conflicts as soon as possible. Incidentally, no NATO member has been indicted by the International War Crimes Tribunal, as deYoung claims.

deYoung's tortured logic continues through her review of what she calls constructive force doctrine and women's reproductive choices. The former does not compromise the Laws of Armed Conflict, and the latter does not compromise all women's choices. The rules for military conduct correctly place the burden of proper conduct on senior personnel in all cases. This obligation is especially true for persons in positions of power and trust, but the rules do not automatically relieve more junior personnel of accountability. First, deYoung should remember that consensual sexual conduct and promiscuity are not crimes in the military,[24] although abuse of authority and behavior that is injurious to good order and discipline can be punished under the UCMJ. Although I agree that all members must be held accountable for their actions, in most cases the courts have recognized the higher culpability of persons in positions of authority even where gender was not an issue. Lt. William Calley, not his men, went to prison for the massacre at My Lai.[25]

In any case, the UCMJ and international law still require soldiers to disobey illegal orders against third-party victims—although not necessarily against themselves. In the latter case, constructive force has been used in only one case that I know of: the Aberdeen scandal. In that case, the women did not bring rape charges. The Army brought the case—and not to exonerate the women but to punish men who had abused their authority, not female NCOs or officers who were protecting their "careers" but with trainees.[26] Men have the same access to protection against abusive supervisors and trainers. The use of this principle in one domestic, internal military case does not strengthen the legal defense of male soldiers who commit war crimes in the international arena.

Similarly, deYoung's argument that women's reproductive choices will be compromised by the few women who would choose and be qualified for combat and who might also choose and be able, on demand, to get pregnant and bear a child exposes her real contention that women outside the home are immoral and unethical (i.e., "women choose to abandon their children for the sake of military or other careers"). In this discussion of parental responsibility and morality, deYoung also conveniently ignores the children that American servicemen have fathered and abandoned all over the world. In any case, this argument indicates that deYoung thinks that there should be no women in the military at all. She does not address the resulting failure of the AVF and the possibility of conscription.

I cannot in these few pages address every fallacy of deYoung's presentation and argument. Addressing, yet again, moving targets of group stereotypes as opposed to individuals' abilities, the nature and future of warfare, and the obligations and privileges of citizenship—not to mention the imagined legal and ethical dilemmas that deYoung presents—is frustrating and exhausting. I do think these latter two areas would provide fruitful ground for a real debate by legal experts and ethicists. I hope I have at least alerted readers to enough discrepancies that they will check sources and closely examine the logic in these important debates.

In sum, I believe that the military can construct and enforce real and appropriate job and conduct standards. We can get beyond the symptoms of problems that some present as "gender" or "women's issues" to identify the real challenges that we should spend our time addressing. We can ask our best members to be true leaders in all of these areas and to work to resolve the real problems. We can make all our members responsible for meeting standards of behavior and performance. We can continue to field an effective military force—the best in the world—for all of our various types of missions. Although we will make errors and encounter new problems, we do not face an abstract crisis in military culture or ethos. I do not believe that there has been a conspiracy to ruin the military through destructive personnel policies. I do believe that we will continue to face the challenges of fielding a military that truly reflects the democracy and civil society it serves—a political experiment at which we have succeeded for more than 200 years.

More than—and because of—all this, I continue to believe that the heart of democratic ideology, as well as the real practice of democracy, calls on us to question and discard cultural ideologies that are not based on measures of merit and would bar individuals from opportunities to compete and contribute because of their membership in any particular or stereotyped group. I do not believe that democracy and civil rights can exist only in the abstract. I continue to believe that democracy and diversity are not mutually exclusive to or incompatible with military effectiveness—that democracies can protect their people and their prosperity without foregoing their foundational principles. In fact, I believe that democratic armies are stronger and more often victorious than those peopled by soldiers living under political or cultural tyranny. And I will always believe that we can continue to do better at fulfilling the promise of democracy for all of our people in one of our most important core institutions—and thereby improve the domestic and international security, prosperity, and happiness of all of our citizens.

NOTES

1. See Kerber, *No Constitutional Right to Be Ladies;* Elshtain, *Women and War;* Stiehm, *Bring Me Men and Women;* Enloe, *Does Khaki Become You?*

2. GenderGap1998 is a women's history website constructed by a well-meaning "system administrator." deYoung's source for World War II history is a very nice website from the Netherlands. I suggest that Gerhard Weinberg's *A World at Arms* and Gerald Linderman's *The World Within War: America's Combat Experience in World War II* (Cambridge, Mass.: Harvard University Press, 1999) are better World War II histories. deYoung's sources on military women and PTSD resulting from sexual assault—A. Fontana and R. Rosenheck, "Duty-Related and Sexual Stress in Etiology of PTSD among Women Veterans Who Seek Treatment," *Psychiatric Services* 48, no. 5 (May 1998): 658–62, and R. H. Stretch et al., "Effects of Premilitary and Military Trauma on the Development of Posttraumatic Stress Disorder Symptoms in Male and Female Active Duty Soldiers," *Military Medicine* 163, no. 7 (July 1998): 466–70—actually consist of research on women veterans who are already self-reporting for PTSD and sexual trauma; many were more than 75 years old—making historical context very important (although deYoung ignores it). The implication that a huge number of servicewomen suffer from stealthy PTSD that could erupt at any time and make them totally ineffective and dangerous in any capacity is not supported by these studies. Stretch et al. actually find that a higher percentage of men suffer from service-related stress; more women suffer from preservice stress. Solving the problem of sexual abuse would go a long way toward reducing women's PTSD. Men suffer from "nonsexual trauma" in military service—showing the opposite of what deYoung proposes. There is no support for the claim that "women's high risk of PTSD" predisposes them to give away sensitive or secret information (World War II Resistance history shows just the opposite). In addition, consider J. W. Sentell, M. Lacroix, J. V. Sentell, and K. Finstuen, "Predictive Patterns of Suicidal Behavior," *Military Medicine* 162, no. 3 (March 1997): 168–71. Suicide is the third-leading cause of death in the military; although military rates are lower than civilian rates, and "military female rates tend to be lower yet than military male rates."

3. See Enloe, *Does Khaki Become You?,* on fungibility. The Army does not use this policy across the board. Obviously, not all military personnel are substitutable except at the lowest levels—consider doctors, lawyers, radio operators, pilots, and chaplains, to name just a few. deYoung uses a study that purportedly shows that it is not combat jobs or even heavy labor jobs that hurt women in terms of childbearing but that all active-duty women suffer compared to civilian women in any job. She also argues that women can do jobs other than combat support, but she does not suggest what these jobs might be, beyond teaching and nursing. This argument conflicts with her fungibility argument, does not support deployment rotations, and does not address the danger or heavy work that nurses face. Elsewhere in her paper, deYoung obviously wants all women to provide relief for civilian teaching and nursing shortages, rather than joining the military in any capacity.

4. If the percentage of pregnant women in the services were extrapolated from deYoung's experience, we would be closer to 100 percent of women rather than the 10 percent that service data reflect. Of interest might be other data such as deYoung uses. In 1943, John O'Donnell of the *New York Daily News* reported that 500 WAACs had been evacuated from North Africa for pregnancy; actually, only three had been. All were married, and all but the one whose husband was in the Service there had been pregnant before they went. In addition, there were not even 500 Army women in North Africa at the time. Pregnancy number exaggerations have been attributed to military women for a long time (see Lorry Fenner, "Ideology and Amnesia: The Public Debate on Women and the American Military, 1940–1973," Ph.D. diss., University of Michigan, 1995).

In another study that deYoung cites to show that women are less "well" than men, women reported to doctors more often than men. The statistical difference shrinks when contraception and required yearly pap smears are excluded. Even so, there is contrasting evidence available that women prevent more-serious illness by going to doctors earlier and more often than men. Doctors agree that bad hygiene causes disease and illness, which hurts readiness and combat effectiveness. Therefore, men's adolescent "bath deprivation contests" are counterproductive, and leaders should stop them. On the other hand, women have lived in field conditions, gone camping, and opened frontiers over the course of history. Finally, males also have higher infant mortality rates and lower life expectancies. I think the real measure we should use is who misses duty for illness. All the evidence shows that even when pregnancy is included, military women miss less work than men.

Another source with which deYoung means to show that military women are less "well" is a Gulf Coast study of civilians of undetermined age. This study really is useless with respect to generally healthy, young military personnel who are prescreened for many illnesses before enlistment.

deYoung's selective research omits many other studies, of which I mention only a few. R. M. Bray, J. A. Fairbank, and M. E. Marsden, "Stress and Substance Use among Military Women and Men," *American Journal of Drug and Alcohol Abuse* 25, no. 2 (May 1999): 239–56, show that "the relation between substance use and stress varied by gender. Military women reported substantially lower rates of heavy drinking than men. . . . These findings suggest that more effective stress management strategies may need to be implemented for military men to reduce the link between stress and heavy alcohol use, illicit drug use, and smoking." R. E. King, S. E. McGlohn, and P. D. Retzlaff, "Female United States Air Force Pilot Personality: The New Right Stuff," *Military Medicine* 162, no. 10 (October 1997): 695–97, show that female pilots score higher on desirable personality characteristics than male pilots and civilian women. Even with this finding—and the fact that women can pull G's better—I still would not suggest that men should be barred from high-performance aircraft. J. P. Maloney et al., "Evaluation and Comparison of Health Care Work Environment Scale in Military Settings," *Military Medicine* 161, no. 5 (May 1996): 284–89, found "no significant gender difference" in perceptions of work environment.

The physical studies that deYoung interprets are even more telling. P. T. Amoroso, N. S. Bell, and B. H. Jones, "Injury Among Female and Male Parachutists," *Aviation Space Environmental Medicine* 68, no. 11 (November 1997): 1006–11, found that training methods and equipment geared toward men might not be effective for women, resulting in more injuries. This study called for more research with additional controls and examination of "reporting bias." H. M. Kipen et al., "Prevalence of Chronic Fatigue and Chemical Sensitivies in Gulf Registry Veterans," *Archives of Environmental Health* 54, no. 5 (September-October 1999): 313–18, found "no effects of gender, race, branch, duty status (active or reserve), or rank . . . " in a study of Gulf War veterans and specific illnesses. Michael Feuerstein, Stephen Berkowitz, and Charles Peck, Jr., "Musculoskeletal-Related Disability in U.S. Army Personnel: Prevalence, Gender, and Military Occupational Specialties," *Journal of Occupational and Environmental Medicine* 39, no. 1 (January 1997), specifically point out that their findings on musculoskeletal disability "do not imply a causal link" between the military jobs women do and their greater propensity for injury. The findings specifically call for more study because women experienced greater discrimination and a "second shift" at home that most likely were related to their injuries. In a study of British Army officer cadets, G. E. Harwood, M. P. Rayson, and A. M. Nevill, "Fitness, Performance, and Risk of Injury in British Army Officer Cadets," *Military Medicine* 164, no. 6 (June 1999): 428–34, found that "the females demonstrated greater improvements than the males . . . " and "no gender difference was found in injury rates." L. K. Trent and S. L. Hurtado, "Longitudinal Trends and Gender Differences in Physical Fitness and Lifestyle Factors in Career U.S. Navy Personnel (1993–1994)," *Military Medicine* 163, no. 6 (June 1998): 398–407, found that "women's scores were significantly better than men's on a number of factors." M. S. Taylor, "Cold Weather Injuries During Peacetime Military Training," *Military Medicine* 157, no. 11 (November 1992): 602–04, found "no risk associated with gender or rank." And Gregory C. Gray et al., "The Postwar Hospitalization Experience of U.S. Veterans of the Persian Gulf War," *New England Journal of Medicine* 335 (1996): 1505–13, is not primarily about women. It compares women with men and states that many hospitalizations are not the result of the Gulf War. The conclusions were that in the two years after the war, there was "no excess of unexplained hospitalization for those remaining on active duty."

The point is that studies show a multitude of conflicting findings; one must be careful in using them or combining them for purposes for which they were not intended.

5. The Presidential Commission Report has no reference to Yugoslavia's World War II forces. I also examined the web source deYoung cited, without success; the Commission's report does discuss female Soviet combat volunteers, however. deYoung contends that, historically, American women have failed to volunteer in large enough numbers for military service. Her evidence is completely out of context. Of course, this is a *non sequitur* in a discussion about whether qualified women volunteers should be admitted to more specialties today and in the future. Still, the women who served in World War II were volunteers, in contrast to the men who served (most of whom were draftees). Women had to fight cultural stereotypes of the kind deYoung supports (more virulent in the 1940s) to volunteer. Women's opportunities also were circumscribed: Restrictions included age, marital status, and parental status, which further reduced the numbers who could apply (see Fenner, "Ideology and Amnesia," as well as Mattie Treadwell, *U.S. Army in World War II: The Women's Army Corps* (Washington, D.C.: Office of Chief of Military History, 1954)—the official Army WAAC/WAC history).

The implication that this all means that there is no glass ceiling also is surprising. Just one example: Olveta Culp Hobby, Director of the WAC—who had authority over almost 200,000 women—was given only the rank of colonel, whereas male officers with far fewer support troops under their authority received general's stars. deYoung criticizes women who will not or could not volunteer and those who want to volunteer. She criticizes women who try to get out of combat training and deployments and those who are fighting to be able to participate fully. She also demands that women must prove themselves capable, but she would bar them from even getting a tryout.

6. No doubt many Africans are fleeing their war-torn and starving countries; men and women alike seek to avoid military service. With regard to deYoung's use of the Israeli example, again she generalizes from her experience. My conversations with former Israeli Air Force officer and aircrew member Ilana Kass (now at the National War College and a consultant to the Joint Chiefs of Staff) reflect a much different reality. Israelis know that their entire nation is the "front line" in any future war.

7. Elliott Gruner, *Prisoners of Culture: Representing the Vietnam POW* (New Brunswick, N.J.: Rutgers University Press, 1993). Gruner is an Army Officer and a former U.S. Air Force Academy and West Point instructor. deYoung reads Cornum's biography much differently than I do. In addition, deYoung seems not to know of the historical changes in the Code of Conduct as a result of the Vietnam War. POW and Code of Conduct training now emphasize that captives should know their limits and prevent captors from reaching them. Cornum is not a traitor, and she did not ridicule her colleagues. I think the 101st would be surprised by that claim. She was a doctor who did not attend survival school, as the rest of the men had. She was dragged by her hair from beneath her burning helicopter with two broken arms, a smashed knee, toxic finger injury, and shrapnel wounds in her shoulder and head. The fact that she was alive and at all capable was amazing. She cared about her comrades in arms. She gave up information on her unit because the Iraqis had the helicopter with its markings and the unit patch on her flight suit. She had no idea, although the war was close to over, how long she would be held. To then make the leap that "if women can be so easily intimidated into giving up tactical information as Major Cornum was . . . " is completely off base.

8. See Shelly Saywell, *Women in War* (New York: Penguin Books, 1986). See also many secondary sources and autobiographies of our Army and Navy nurses in

World War II under fire and as prisoners. See also sources about women in the Holocaust.

9. Science fiction includes much gore and violence. Female characters in *Starship Troopers, The Terminator* series, and the *Alien* series, to name only a few, do not resemble deYoung's sterile fantasies.

10. Most of these laws evolved into their present state after the women of other nations served in actual combat in World War II—which would make moot any suggestion that women serving in combat would destroy this body of law relating to female combatants. See Geoffrey Best, *War and Law Since 1945* (Oxford: Clarendon Press, 1997) and *Humanity in Warfare* (New York: Columbia University Press, 1980).

11. For just one example of the military holding commanders responsible, see Bradley Graham, "Marines Charge Captain in N.C. Death," *Washington Post,* 16 October 1999, 1.

12. If anything, Title IX has gone a long way in addressing the physical conditioning and team cohesion acculturation that young women were lacking on enlistment in earlier decades.

13. I discussed these issues with three attorneys who are familiar with military law, including Robin Wink, USAFA graduate and former USAF lawyer (now with the Justice Department); I withhold the others' names because they remain on active duty. In addition, I discussed the issue with several academic specialists on history, law, and the military, including Elizabeth Hillman of Yale and Rutgers Universities.

14. deYoung moves from "difference" to women's "handicaps" very glibly. Her presentation of physical fitness standards is skewed; her tables do not include requirements for personnel over the age of 31 (which would of course show "lower" standards for older men). I would agree that the strongest woman will probably never be as strong as the strongest man—but neither are other men. In any case, members only have to meet the required standard of fitness or performance; they need not be the strongest. deYoung's analysis implies that no military women can exceed the minimum male fitness standards in pushups, situps, and a run at any age. Many do so on a routine basis. deYoung wants to associate VMI with active-duty forces; that school's top graduate for 2000—a woman—far exceeded even male fitness standards and excelled academically and militarily. The military women deYoung criticizes may not publicly argue against differences in standards; they just perform. Military women should not be compared to 90-year-old men, and men and women are not different kinds of packing tape. The point is that the post office would accept any tape with the appropriate tensile strength. And whereas we might not put a welterweight in the ring with a heavyweight, we might certainly put a smaller world-class martial arts expert in the ring with a champion heavyweight boxer.

15. Best, *War and Law Since 1945,* and *Humanity in Warfare.* See also the USAFA's *Journal of Legal Studies* 6 (1995/1996).

16. Men sometimes do bring complaints, of course. In just one recent example, a male Marine brought a case against a civilian female supervisor. See

Steve Vogel, "Harassment Claim Targets a Quantico Boss," *Washington Post*, 20 February 2000, C1.

17. Like her innumerable strawpersons, deYoung "wants it both ways" when she ridicules nurses' experiences as POWs in World War II because they were not brutalized as much as male soldiers. In context, they had harrowing and physically demanding experiences that required courage and stamina to survive. Moreover, deYoung makes no reference to the Geneva Convention rules (which may not be followed) for different treatment of medical personnel and officers. Maj. (Dr.) Cornum would have been held under these rules.

18. Other complaints of physical abuse have been brought by male military members or their families; recall the infamous "blood wing" pinnings on prime-time television and the Air Force basic training death of Micah Schindler.

19. West Point graduate and retired Army Colonel and University of Michigan history instructor Thomas Collier mentioned his experience in Vietnam in an e-mail to me in March 2000: "Goldbricking was an old Army term long before women started doing it. . . . Men got VD to avoid training and deployment. I can recall helicopter evacs off S&D in Vietnam of guys who got the clap, guys who didn't take their malaria pills, guys who didn't take care of their feet. Different technique, same goal." Statistics also show that most young men are little interested in joining the military or going into combat these days. Otherwise we would not be having a recruiting shortage of young men.

With regard to exposure to hazardous conditions in the workplace, federal laws require workers—including women in their childbearing years—to be fully informed of hazards so they can choose whether to work in dangerous jobs. History shows that civilian employers have intentionally misinformed men and women—and those employees have suffered harm. See U.S. Nuclear Regulatory Commission, Office of Nuclear Regulatory Research, Regulatory Guides 8.13 (December 1987) and 8.29 (February 1996). See also Rick Maze, "Lawmakers: Agent Orange Study Elevates Distrust," *Air Force Times*, 3 April 2000, 16, and Rajiv Chandrasekaran, "War's Toxic Legacy Lingers in Vietnam: Cancers, Birth Defect Attributed to U.S. Use of Agent Orange," *Washington Post*, 18 April 2000, A23. My e-mail exchanges with the Deputy Director of the Gulf War Syndrome Study Office of the Secretary of Defense's Staff, Roger Kaplan (also a former Army officer), verified my impressions that male soldiers' offspring have been affected by toxic agents.

20. Because the government does not even provide military women overseas with abortions, suggesting that the government will soon *require* them to have abortions is a far leap.

21. In the Korean Conflict and other wars, untrained minority men were placed into combat positions in emergencies and when it suited the military to do so.

22. Just a couple of men who left early include Academy graduates Chad Hennings (USAF pilot) and Napoleon McCallum (USN)—both to play professional sports.

23. If deYoung does not trust retired Air Force Major General Jeanne Holm's experience, extensive research, and credible sources, she should consider the testimony of the commander of the USS *Eisenhower*, Captain H. Denby Starling, who reported to newspapers in February 2000 (*Virginian-Pilot, Newport News, Navy Times*) that he welcomes female sailors on his ship and even would like more—for exactly these reasons. In addition, according to G. W. Talcott et al., "Prevalence and Predictors of Discharge in USAF Basic Military Training," *Military Medicine* 164, no. 4 (April 1999): 269–74, "Overall, discharges by gender were equal, but reasons for discharge varied by gender. . . . Results suggest that women and ethnic minorities are not biased in favor of discharge. . . . "

Finally, retired Army LTC Robert Carrington, a former infantryman and person-nel specialist for the Secretary of the Army, informed me in an interview that although women do attrit in basic training (through which they gain no benefits, as deYoung mistakenly asserts) and first assignments at a higher rate than men, because of their higher retention in subsequent tours they actually leave the Army at a lower overall rate than men. Carrington further pointed out that Army attrition rates have always been high for men and women alike but that the pundits only worry about these high rates when recruiting is down (Pentagon interview, March 2000, and e-mails on 28 February 2000). Also see Betty Maxfield, "Army Demographics FY99," Headquarters Department of the Army, Office of Deputy Chief of Staff for Personnel, Human Resources Directorate, Demographics Unit, Washington, D.C.

24. deYoung clearly thinks that the problem for all is a lack of chastity. This is not a woman's problem; a culture of loose sex and widely available penicillin generally was associated with military men long before about 15 percent of the force was women.

25. In another sobering case, a female Air Force lieutenant colonel commit-ted suicide rather than face charges for a consensual but adulterous case of fraternization with an enlisted man. She took this drastic measure so her family would not be deprived of her military benefits. This female officer was not the man's trainer and he was not a trainee; the man was not charged with misconduct.

26. Department of Defense Instruction 5505.8 (DODI 5505.8) defines "sexual misconduct" and criminal sexual activity. The latter involves "force, coercion, or intimidation; abuse of position or rank; fraternization. . . . " Instructors at Aberdeen violated every part of this old rule; it was not invented by feminists or in the midst of the recent scandal at that Post. In addition, throughout her argument, deYoung makes little distinction between career officers and noncommissioned officers as opposed to first-term or one-term members. She ignores this distinction, which makes a huge difference in military men's and women's attitudes and behavior.

Response to Fenner

Marie E. deYoung

I was pleasantly surprised to find that Dr. Lorry Fenner had volunteered to write the argument that would compellingly assert that women
should be allowed to serve in the U.S. military as ground combatants.
Fenner has access to the best research data, the most up-to-date studies, and
a position at the United States War College. I hoped that her position would
move the dialogue about women in the military beyond the present
ideological cross-talk that dominates the public discussion, whether in the
congressional chamber or on the national talk show. I suspect that Dr.
Fenner did not have the heart to make her position stick; with her superior
research and analytical skills, she could have persuaded the public, legislative bodies, and the Supreme Court. She did not persuade me, however,
and her paper will not persuade the people who have the responsibility to
maintain military readiness.

First, I believe that we were asked to advocate for or against women's
assignment to ground combat roles. Fenner's overarching rhetorical response
is to avoid direct discussion of the nature and reality of ground combat. She
scoffs at brutal descriptions, violent scenarios, and the concrete implications
for women who would be exposed to this reality with the accusation that
"visceral" imagery or narratives are illogical appeals to emotionalism. This
tactic is brilliant, but it is not helpful to the public debate or to women who
will suffer or benefit from any policy changes that might flow from her
position. In analyzing the nature of a job, task, mission, or profession, one

must always discuss the concrete nature of that task, the circumstances that will endure, the requirements to successfully complete the task. In mentoring potential candidates for a particular profession, one always exposes the candidate to the harsh circumstances, the stresses, the unique hurdles that they must overcome to achieve success in that profession. This argument would hold for the butcher, the pastry chef, the physician, the police officer, the opera singer, or the teacher. It should hold for the ground combatant as well.

Second, although Dr. Fenner and I agree that the most important obstacle to successful integration of women in the armed forces is the existing dual standard for physical fitness, she does not help her position by evading the present reality. We have no dispute about the facts: The standards of physical fitness for women are unequivocally lower than the standards for men. This differential erodes morale and contributes to women's training failure, as at least one study has shown (GAO 1997). We agree that in noncombat jobs, women can work around lower performance standards by using equipment such as dollies or wagons to move heavy equipment. The ground combatant's job description, however, includes a required ability to lift and carry heavy objects and human beings; to engage in hand-to-hand combat; to carry heavy loads; to endure captivity, rape, and torture. Only physically qualified and emotionally rigorous individuals need apply. No one has a right to hold a job for which he or she is not qualified. No one has a right to serve in any profession for which he or she is not qualified. Could you imagine hiring a monotone to sing the lead in *La Traviata* to give her the opportunity, the thrill of being a coloratura soprano? Hiring a nonqualified singer is no less foolish than hiring a nonqualified soldier to be a ground combatant, although it may be less dangerous to life and limb (if not to one's sanity). The debate about women's work in the military can never escape discussion of the context, the visceral reality, that work entails.

Third, contrary to Dr. Fenner's standard for public discourse, the historical argument about the nature of citizenship is not historical but an appeal to emotion. An attempted correlation is made between past denial of citizenship or full voting rights for women and women's exclusion from the selective service system or from the obligation to bear arms. In American society, however, women made advancements in many social justice causes, including suffrage, strictly through nonviolent, democratic processes, not through violent revolution or by taking up arms. Women achieved freedom for slaves, temperance goals, and progress in women's rights during the 19th century as a result of their political strategies and campaigns, not because a few dozen women chose to cross-dress and "pass" as men.

Fenner's allusion to the 1928 Supreme Court case involving Rosika Schwimmer, a famous conscientious objector who was denied citizenship because of her pacifism, does not support the argument of universal service either. Male pacifists were similarly denied citizenship until 1946. These cases were fought successfully to limit the right of our government to impose military service on our citizens. The context of that story suggests that the woman, as a potential citizen, intentionally suffered personal consequences to move the country toward the path of nonviolence, the path of disarmament—not toward universal conscription. Regardless of whether any women have been denied their full rights as citizens in the past because they refused to bear arms, women now have full rights as American citizens. Their rights are contingent not on military service but on the fact of their birth as Americans—as they should be. Thus, we have powerful women in Congress who are pacifists, as well as some who have worn the uniform. American women have been elected to every office but vice president and president. One wheelchair-bound man and one male draft dodger already have served as president. Lifting the ground combat exclusion will not enhance women's chances of being elected president. Honing their presidential skills, competencies, and abilities will improve the odds. Combat service will not be the deciding factor. As Julia Nixon recently stated, when the right woman runs, America will elect her.

Fourth, the political argument about a universal obligation of citizens to bear arms is an outdated appeal to emotion. Economically and sociologically, the nation cannot afford the price of imposing universal service. It is not cost-effective. Compulsory universal service is the strategy of desperate nations whose overinvestment in perpetual war-making eventually destroys them. Universal service would be necessary only if the United States chose to engage in a total war. We have had the luxury of selecting service members on the basis of the needs of the military. Even in World War II, the United States never experienced a state of total war, as totalitarian and fascist regimes did. About 10 percent of our population served during the war. Furthermore, creating policy on the basis of a total war scenario makes no sense in the nuclear age, when the world can least afford to cultivate or encourage that political scenario.

Fifth, the argument that admission to ground combat assignments would improve women's status and end arbitrary discrimination practices is based on an appeal to emotion. Fenner bemoans the 1979 Supreme Court ruling that limited women's participation in the military and preserved veterans' preferences. She creates a false example of discrimination when she claims that "there was no ceiling on men's service." Military men have been and will continue to be subject to ceilings, based on the good of the service and their physical limitations—just as women are. Men with poor vision cannot be pilots. Men with low intelligence scores cannot serve in military intelligence or in the officer corps. My friend Thomas Hale will soon publish a book of letters he wrote as a volunteer ambulance driver during World War II, during which his team liberated part of the Bergen Belsen death camps. Tom was excluded from active-duty service because he was 5'1"—not tall enough to serve in battle. He, and thousands like him, found alternate ways to serve in the struggle for democracy. Similarly, throughout my career I served with male Army logisticians who had never seen combat. As much as they would like to wear a general's star, they accept their assignments as valuable contributions to the nation's defense.

Sixth, Fenner's characterization of people who disagree with her positions as irrational or conservative political anti-feminist extremists is disheartening. There are many rational, liberal feminists like myself who have come to realize that thrusting women into near-combat and ground combat units will not further the cause of the women's equality. Policy analysts of military readiness issues ought to refrain from the extremist rhetoric of the extreme right and the extreme feminist left. To be lumped with Falwell, Schlafly, and Donnelly because one espouses an opposing viewpoint is not any more instructive than to hear opponents of women in the military accuse leaders such as Fenner of shallow political correctness rather than substantive policymaking.

In addition, Fenner is not afraid to use irrational coded feminist appeals to evade hard questions regarding the appropriateness of lifting the ground combat exclusion for women. Thus, in her discussion of coverture—defined as women's substitution of domestic duties for civic obligations—she tends to insert a repeated comment that is not germane to the debate on women in combat: Until recently, coverture laws included male spousal control of a woman's body. Equating a woman's choice to be a homemaker with male domination, male sexual aggression, or usurpation of any women's rights is simply unfair to the women who choose domesticity. Women should have the right to choose domesticity over military service or any other profession. Or they can choose both. Women who serve as soldiers use coverture to escape ground combat training assignments: Pregnancy affords removal from military training for which the women legally obligated themselves. Bringing up a legal anachronism about women's control over their bodies in a discussion about women's roles in the military is a coded, highly charged appeal to feminists' fear that women will lose the right to control their sexuality.

Seventh, Dr. Fenner mischaracterizes one of my articles in the *Air Force Times*. Her synopsis suggests that I argue that women and men should not serve together—which is not the case. I wrote about a specific situation in which Air Force personnel are being bunked together as mixed-gender dyads for 48-hour work shifts. Her critique of my assessment of the social and economic costs of each sexual misconduct case that is handled by the military suggests a lack of direct involvement in such situations—which is understandable, given her many years in Washington and the Air Force Academy staff. My article was published in four military papers, yet there has been no public lambasting of my position by soldiers in the field. None of us who serve in operational units are exempt from the problems and opportunity costs I cite. Those who serve in schools and staff positions are removed from the harsh reality that bad policies create. I advocate that all policies should be based not on abstract theories but on pragmatic assessment and reassessment of the results obtained. Lives depend on close scrutiny of the effects of particular policies; hence, creating policy that is devoid of the experiences of professionals like myself who have had structural assignments in the field will never do. I hope that as a feminist, Dr. Fenner would not use masculinist abstractions to invalidate the implications of the reported experiences of other feminists.

In conclusion, I am grateful for the opportunity to read Dr. Fenner's manuscript, as well as for her critique of my own work. I believe that there is much work to be done before the issue of women's participation in the military is resolved in just, wholesome ways. Ultimately, the issue will be decided by Congress and the American public. I hope our work will inspire others to consider this issue with a sincere commitment to the well-being of women and our nation at heart.

Index